Close to the Surface

A Family Journey at Sea

Bethany Lee

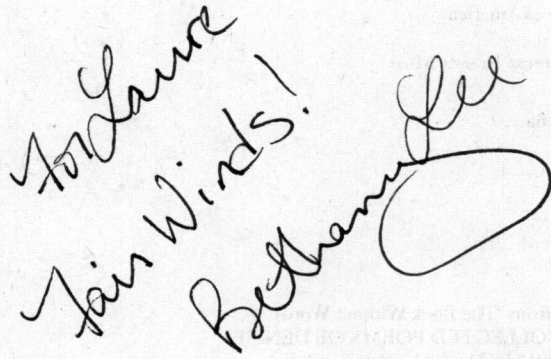

Fernwood
PRESS

Close to the Surface
A Family Journey at Sea

©2024 by Bethany Lee

Fernwood Press
Newberg, Oregon
www.fernwoodpress.com

All rights reserved. No part may be reproduced for any commercial purpose by any method without permission in writing from the copyright holder.

Printed in the United States of America

Cover and page design: Mareesa Fawver Moss
Cover photo: Bryan Lee
Author photo: Bee Joy España
Illustrations: Brett Rawalt

ISBN 978-1-59498-132-6

Epigraph from Chapter 16 from "The Book Without Words" By Denise Levertov, from COLLECTED POEMS OF DENISE LEVERTOV, copyright ©2013 by Denise Levertov and the Estate of Denise Levertov. Reprinted by permission of New Directions Publishing Corp.

For *LiLo*
and for Hannah and Meira, her intrepid crew
I'm proud to be finding my way with you still
And for Bryan
who always brings me home again

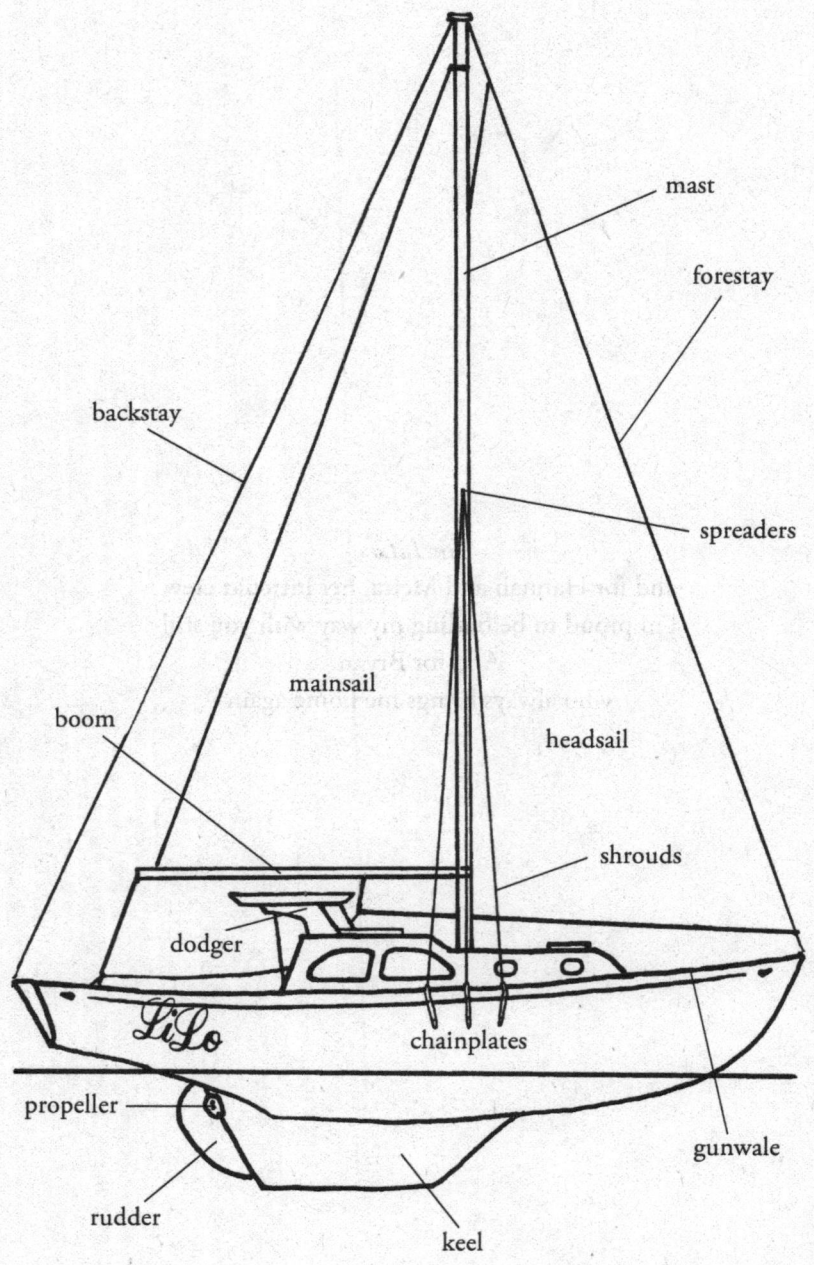

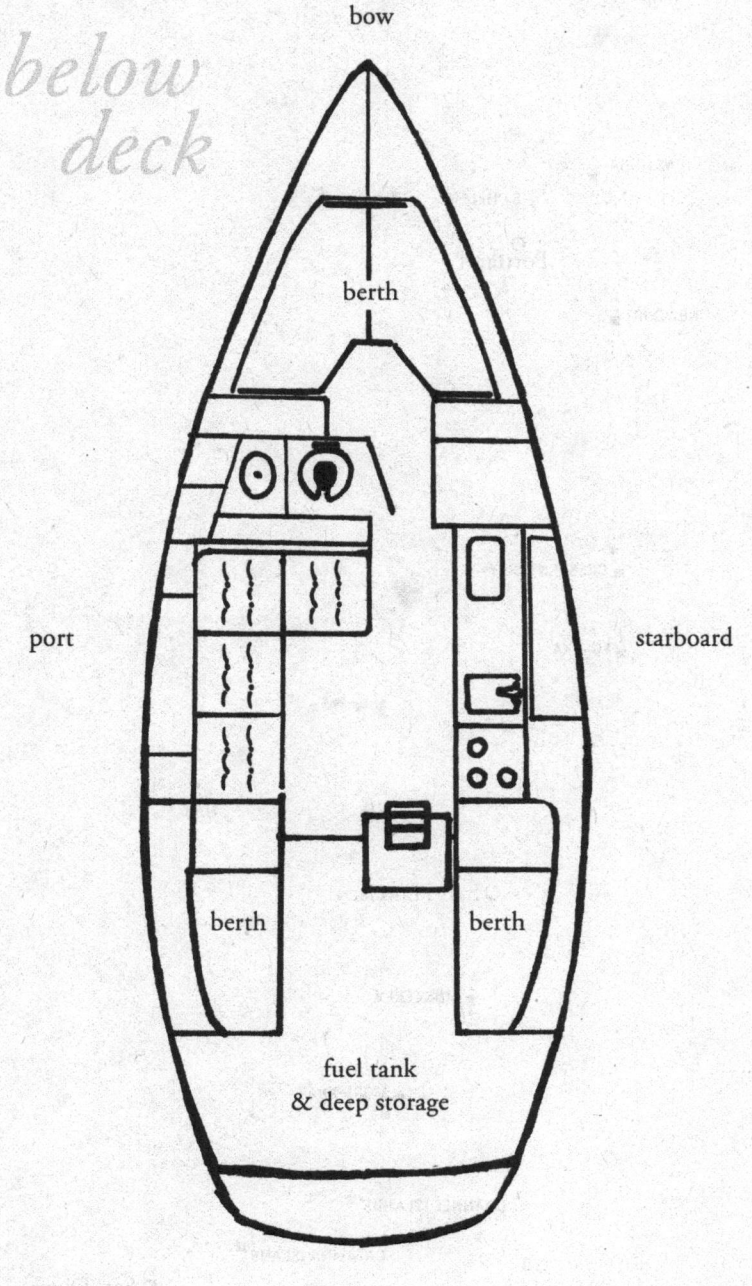

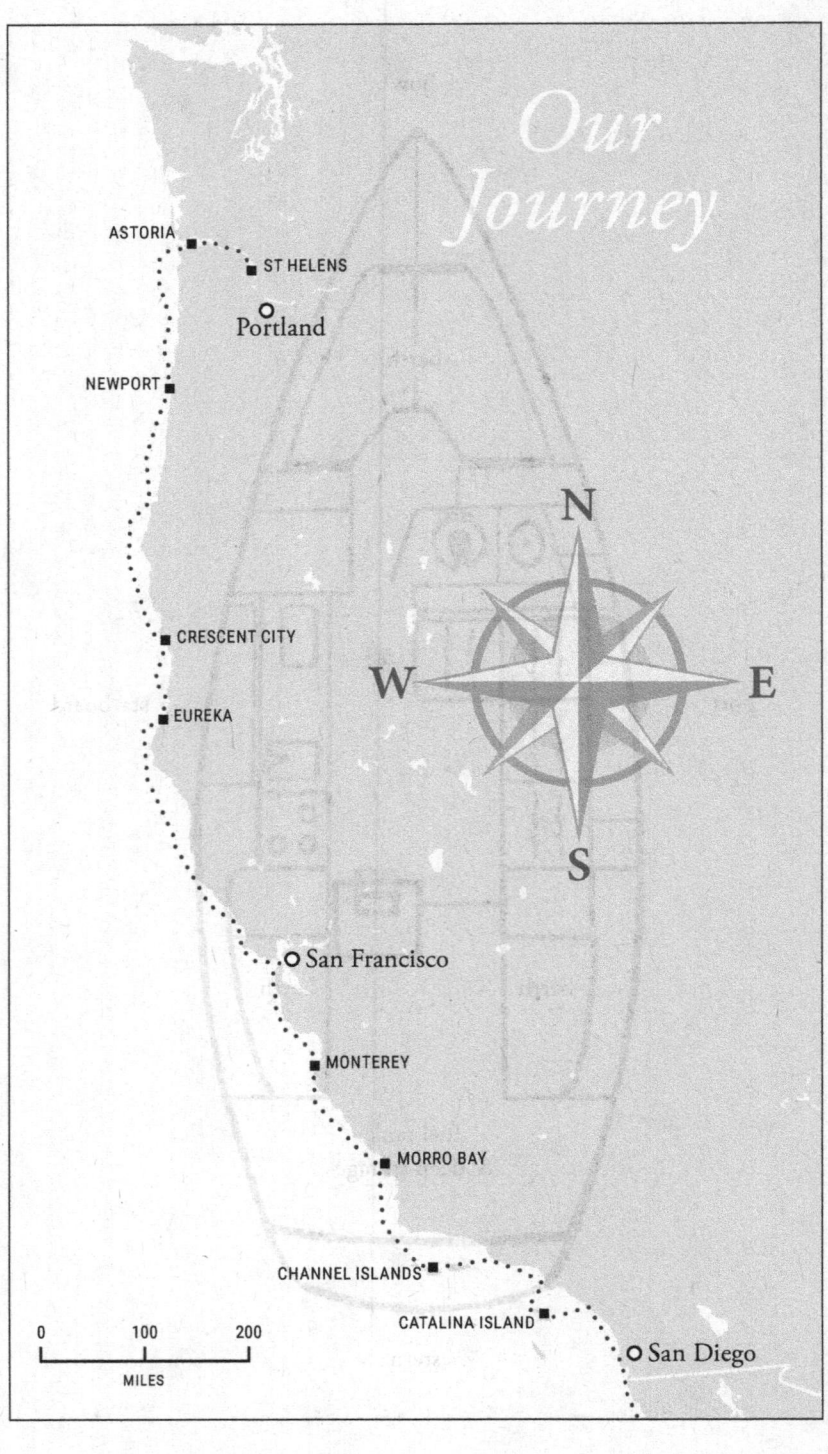

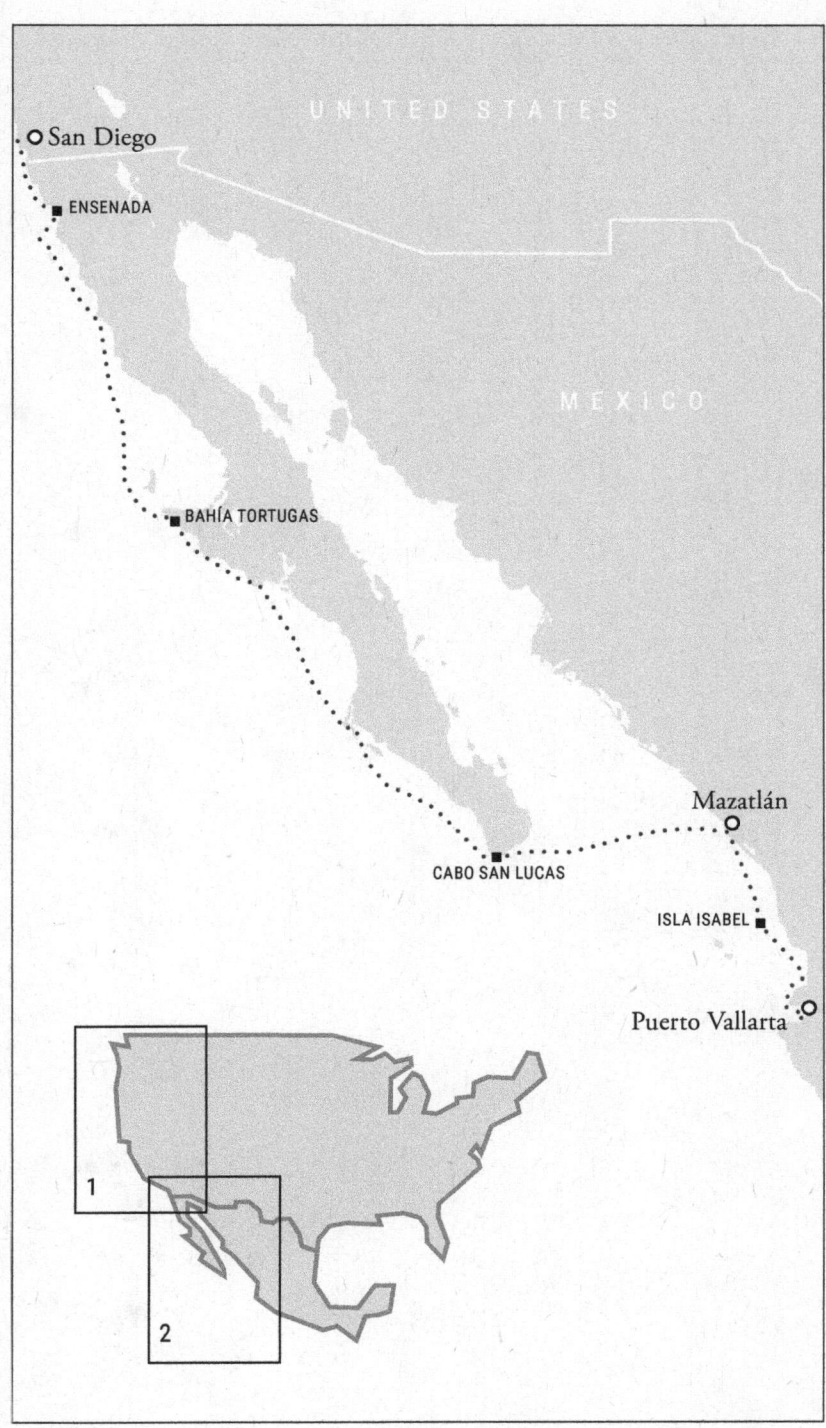

Contents

11	*Author's Note*
13	*Prologue*
15	Source and Way
25	Untying the Lines
33	Beyond the Oregon Trail
47	Light for the Way
57	The Currency of the Sea
69	Golden Gate and Evening Prayers
79	Life at Walking Speed
95	The Shape of Life Left Behind
109	How Much is Enough?
119	Breath at the Surface
129	All is Shaking Loose
139	That's when the sea will get you
147	This is Going to be a Story
161	To the Bottom of the Sea
171	If it Doesn't get any Worse
177	To the End of the Earth
185	When We're Done, She'll Float

193	Nothing is Going to Look Quite Like the Plan
201	Buoyed Once Again
209	All is Calm; All is Bright
219	Into the Luminous
231	Grandma's Dishes
241	No Boring Stories
253	We'd Come to Love
261	Cold Water, Sweet Bread
271	Courage Expanding
279	Abundance Leading the Way
289	Before the Sea Changed Her Mood
297	The World is Round
309	All the Water in the Sky
317	Caught in the Current
329	When There Isn't a Path to Follow
339	This Is How it Ends
345	Homesick Ever After
355	What We Could Not Do Alone
365	Epilogue
369	*Acknowledgments*
371	*Glossary*

Author's Note

A few things you might want to know:

The events in this book are true to the best of my memory and verified, as far as possible, with other resources including contemporaneous journals, and the memories of the rest of the crew. Any errors in this book are mine alone. You're welcome to feel clever if you spot a mistake.

Some names and pronouns may not reflect the individual's current usage. And speaking of names—we pronounce *LiLo* as Lie-Low unless in Mexico, where folks say Lee-Low. She answers happily to either one.

All uncredited epigraphs are my own work. Many of these lines are excerpts from poems published in my poetry collections, *The Breath Between*, *Etude for Belonging*, and *The Coracle and the Copper Bell*, all from Fernwood Press.

Prologue

"If you ever go skydiving," Mom once said, "jump first and tell me after."

She wanted me to take risks. She just didn't want to hear about them until I came through them alive.

So even though we'd been talking for years about going to sea, when we finally told my parents we'd given our notice and rented our house, it seemed to come as a shock. Questions gathered on their faces but they smothered their worries and offered their support. They didn't want their fears to hold us back.

I could have told them I, too, was choking back fear. Whatever they were imagining, my mind had conjured all the same dreadful scenarios and worse.

If taking a leap doesn't scare you, you might be irrational, reckless, or naive. I am plenty afraid of falling. But nothing scares me more than the thought of *not* jumping. Taking off the parachute and riding the plane down. Never learning what it feels like to soar.

"We love you," we said. "We'll see you when we get back."

Then we moved to the open door of our tidy lives, took each other's hands, and flew.

Chapter One

SOURCE AND WAY

Resurrection Bay, Alaska: September 1999: Waning Crescent
St. Helens, Oregon: September 2013: Waning Crescent, New Moon

*If you don't live the only life you have, you won't live some other life,
you won't live any life at all.*

—*James Baldwin*

I didn't expect becoming myself would involve so much water. Maybe I shouldn't have been surprised. My husband, Bryan, and I both grew up in Oregon, in the river valley between the Coast Range and the Cascades at the junction of the Molalla and the Pudding just south of where they flow into the Willamette River. Though neither of us spent much time on the water as children, this watershed defined the landscape of our youth. For years, Bryan's drive to school and back took him across the Willamette on a six-car ferry. I have no idea how many bridges my family crossed as we moved through the ordinary days of my childhood. I just knew the winding rivers felt like home.

A year after we got married, we moved to Alaska, surprising everyone who knew me and my homebody ways. Two years later, in September of 1999, Bryan's parents flew up for a visit.

We were eager to show them around our new state. We suggested that they might enjoy taking a boat tour out of Resurrection Bay, about two hours south of our Anchorage home. We couldn't afford the ticket price but they offered to foot the bill and we gladly went along.

I was seven months pregnant with our oldest child, Hannah, and my memories of the day are mixed. I remember dashing through several shops just prior to boarding time, looking for milk, the only drink that didn't nauseate me; I remember the fishy smell of the docks and the fried fish lunch that sent me sprinting out onto the deck, close to the rail, just in case.

But I also remember the wonder. Even the tour captain couldn't believe all the wildlife we spotted—the tufted puffins, the irresistible sea otters, the sleek curve of the humpback's flukes, the dancing Dall's porpoises—and I cannot begin to describe the sight of the glacier's terminus, the enormity of that leading edge and the cold, blue wash of ice and sea. The growl and bark of calving icebergs demanded our attention. I stood on the deck until we turned to go, unable to look away.

At the mouth of the bay the captain came on the loudspeaker and announced, as I'm sure he did every day at nine, noon, and three, "You're now looking over the longest expanse of open ocean in the world. If you headed due south from here, you wouldn't hit anything until Antarctica."

All those years ago Bryan saw the possibilities first. In that moment, the water on the map in his mind stood out in sharp relief against the earth around. Mountain ranges and borders split the continents, but oceans ebbed and flowed together, the sea both source and way.

"If we learn how to sail," he thought, "we could go almost anywhere." It wasn't long before I caught the vision too.

A little over a year after this visit Bryan's dad died suddenly. We grieved and began to learn to live with the loss, which throbbed within us like a heartbeat, a steady reminder of our limited time.

Over the next few years we read all we could find about sailing. Bryan bought a dictionary of sailing terms and I kept it by my side while I devoured sea stories and reference guides, stopping often to look up the unfamiliar words. In 2001 we moved from Alaska back to Oregon, where our families still lived, and, just a few weeks later, I gave birth to our second child, Meira. We settled into a routine of work and community and family time and we worked to keep our dreams of grand adventure from wearing away in the grind of everyday life.

One night, after our kids were in bed, Bryan put my thoughts into words. "My dad didn't even make it to sixty. Let's not put off our life until retirement. If we really want to go to sea, we should start making that happen."

The spring Meira and Hannah were three and five, we scrounged up the money for a down payment on a used twenty-one-foot sailboat. She lived up to the name we gave her: *Nissa*, which means "Friendly Elf." She was shorter than some of the kayaks we met out on the water and barely had space for us to sleep down below in her tiny cabin. Getting to the porta-potty meant taking the main bunk apart, and standing to pull my pants up required sticking my torso through the forward hatch like a bachelorette in a limousine sunroof. Despite all the inconveniences, we spent several summers on the Columbia River and the South Puget Sound transforming ourselves into a sailing family.

Hannah and Meira learned to color inside the lines on a table leaning fifteen degrees to starboard. I learned to read charts and tide tables, the barometer and the clouds. We developed hand signals to keep from yelling at each other in tight quarters and practiced man-overboard drills we hoped we'd never need to use.

When it became clear that Bryan was best at the tiller in an crisis, we designated him the captain. "It doesn't mean I'm more important than you or your mom," he said to the kids, "just that if something goes wrong, we know who is going to make the quick decisions. But we'll all keep practicing all the jobs. Who wants to help put up the sail today?"

By the end of our third summer, we started looking for a bigger boat. We didn't know if we would ever be able to achieve our dream of an extended trip but even the shorter journeys we'd taken had unified our family and deepened our relationships with each other and with nature.

After a few months of searching, we found *LiLo*, a thirty-two-foot Islander sloop. She was built in 1964, back when the first fiberglass vessels were being produced. Her sturdy hull and bluewater design had carried her through almost fifty years of ocean-going and her simple systems and small size kept her in our price range. She had separate bunks for each of the kids, decent storage, and a serviceable galley with a propane stove, icebox, and pump faucets. She didn't have radar, a chart plotter, an autopilot, or a heater, but we decided we could add what we needed and do without the rest.

The sellers were retiring from sailing and they passed along every bit of gear they had: life jackets, tools, books, dishes, even four castoff engines they'd been storing in their shed. We rebuilt the best of the bunch and loaded up on spare parts from the others, replaced the ancient rigging and sails on the boat, and, over the course of the next few years, challenged our sailing skills through the weather off the west coast of Washington and Vancouver Island, the currents of the San Juans and Gulf Islands, and the wild tides of the Columbia River Bar.

Only later did we find out this area is known as "The Graveyard of the Pacific."

The Columbia River has no delta to diffuse the current's power and the tidal flow extends far upstream. Near St. Helens, Oregon, where we moored *LiLo*, the force of the ocean from more than eighty miles away turns small tributaries completely around. If you time your passage wrong, the river becomes a treadmill beneath you; it can take all your power just to keep from being swept backward. When the breeze picks up opposite the flow, the resulting chop is sharp and brutal. Fun for the windsurfers in Hood River, miserable for the sailors of St. Helens.

The mouth of the Columbia River is especially deadly, with more than 2,000 large ships lost there over the last 200 years. Some of the most specialized mariners in the world, the Columbia River Bar Pilots, are trained to navigate cargo ships across the bar through the shoals and reefs at the ocean's edge. The Coast Guard station stands ready to send out rescue boats as conditions can quickly disintegrate. Though we have passed through these waters on glassy-calm seas, we have also navigated them for hours in waves that rattled both our teeth and our courage. Any voyage we attempted would begin with crossing this bar.

Early in 2007, we decided to take the leap. We started getting our house ready to sell and spent long evenings talking over all the necessary steps to extricate ourselves from our complex lives. We thought we could probably use our home equity to fund a year or more of travel as long as we lived very simply at sea.

Then the housing market crashed.

Selling our home was no longer a viable option but over the next months and years, we began making our way back to our dream. We simplified our expenses as much as possible, canceled our newspaper subscription, even cut back on our ice cream consumption. We drove our old cars until they broke down, fixed them in the driveway, and kept on driving.

We pasted a laminated world map to our dining room table and kept a set of dry erase markers handy for after-dinner voyage planning. Summer vacations found us out on the water, testing our equipment and our skills in more and more demanding conditions.

As the kids grew, we worked to find a dinghy that would carry the four of us—along with our food, fuel, and water—and still fit on *LiLo*'s deck. *Li'l Lo*, the fiberglass rowboat that had come with *LiLo*, was too heavy to lift easily and shorter than our family needed. We didn't want to have to pump up an inflatable every time we needed to go to shore and we couldn't afford the powerful outboard motor required to push its rounded hull through the surf. Most rowing dinghies were either too large for our boat or too small for our crew.

After a lot of research into alternative designs, we spent a winter building *Splitpea*, an eleven-foot nesting dinghy just right for our needs. She had a pointed bow and stable design, carried a heavy load, rowed easily through choppy water, and broke down into two stackable halves which fit on the cabin top between the mast and the foredeck.

Though Meira and Hannah were only seven and nine that year, they were involved with almost every step of the building process. I watched them stand taller and grow more confident as they mixed epoxy, wielded paintbrushes and sandpaper, and finally helped carry the finished boat down to the water for the first time.

The next summer, while on vacation aboard, we anchored near a tiny, isolated island and gave the kids permission to row to shore for their first solo expedition.

I gave them safety instructions. "Take the radio and row in. Tie *Splitpea* up. Tie her up again. Both of you, tie her up twice. Then turn left to the trail. Take every left you come to until you're half tired. Turn around and take every right all the way back. It's a round island so you can't get lost. Call us on the radio if you need something. Have fun!"

We sat in the cockpit and listened to their cheerful chatter as they made their way to shore and hiked partway around the island and back again. At the dock, Hannah and Meira met another couple heading in for a walk and struck up a conversation.

"Did your dad build this dinghy?" the woman asked.

Their voices rang out across the water as they answered proudly, "No, *we* built this dinghy!"

In January 2010, Bryan's company was bought out. We weathered another uncertain financial time as he made a career transition and began working in software consulting. The Big Trip seemed further away than ever.

Every year or so, we evaluated our plans. "Are we letting our dreams for the future overshadow our lives today? Are we just living for the possibilities of tomorrow?"

Each time we reconsidered, I couldn't think of a better way to raise my kids, couldn't imagine a better way to spend my days. Our hopes had focused our priorities and clarified our values. With our big goals in mind, we practiced small particulars, not just seafaring skills but traveling skills, the practice of saying yes to the unexpected, of becoming more open to our own lives.

One afternoon, in December 2012, I got a call from Bryan. "They want to renew my contract for eighteen months. If I sign, we'll be stuck here until Hannah's in high school. I may have just told my boss we're leaving this summer. Are we really ready to do this?"

The timing of any sea voyage is governed by the winds and weather. If you're heading south from the West Coast of North America, you have to leave sometime in late summer. You don't want to head into Mexico until hurricane season is over in early November, but you need to get out of the North Pacific before the fall and winter storms arrive. Somewhere we'd heard the advice: "You'll never feel ready. Pick a date and go. You'll become ready along the way." We circled Bryan's birthday on the calendar. September 3, 2013.

The last few months were full. Not Thanksgiving dinner full. Overflowing dumpster full.

We wrapped up the school year and made plans for boat-schooling in the fall. We were going to be away for Meira's seventh grade year and Hannah's eighth, and I hoped my curriculum choices would keep them on track for whatever came next for them academically. We found a family to rent our house and a friend to keep our cat. Since we were downsizing to move aboard, we took the opportunity to simplify our lives. We gave away half of what we owned, packed most of the rest into our garage and boarded it off. Gradually our piles grew smaller and smaller and I went through the "to take" boxes again and again, purging ruthlessly and hoping I wouldn't miss what I chose to leave behind. One by one, we untangled the threads that tied us to our life and, one by one, cut them loose.

Bryan's last consulting contract ran right up until the week before we planned to leave. Some days he went straight to *LiLo* after work, worked into the night on trip preparations, and drove right back to the office the next morning. On weekends, his mother joined him at the boat and painted every surface she could reach, twisting like a contortionist to get into the narrow quarter berths, emerging with speckles on her hair and arms. I double checked bank accounts and bill-pay settings, sewed custom sheets and gear bags, bought equipment and groceries and e-books.

We worked our way through the days of lasts—the last car repair, the last Monday at work, the last family dinner. Finally—and somehow suddenly—we were down to the last week. We took all but a few things to the boat, stashed and stowed for hours. I made lists and lists of lists, not trusting my memory about which lockers held what. Each time I felt certain we'd never find a place for one more thing, and each time a few more necessities found a home.

I said to Bryan, "I wish I could filter out all the exhausted and the freaked out and just leave the excited for a little while."

We were almost too tired to celebrate Bryan's last day at work. We marked the occasion by moving aboard. We made up the bunks and tucked our clothes into the pockets I'd stitched to line the berth walls. In the late summer heat, we took turns moving around below and came out into the cockpit to sit in the sun and wish for wind.

Monday morning, September 2, we pulled away from our slip and moved upriver to the St. Helens city dock. As the morning went on, well-wishers arrived. First came family, to help set up tables and chairs in the park, then friends, curious to see the boat, reluctant to see us off.

Two or three at a time stepped across from the dock to peek below at our living space. I welcomed the brave ones through the companionway. "Don't look too closely or you'll see all the things we hid at the last minute."

Some found reassurance in the well-laid-out space. "It's small, but you do have everything you need!"

Others were frankly horrified at the thought of living in such close quarters for so long—all four of us working, eating, studying, and sleeping in about 150 square feet.

One guest asked a very reasonable question, "What's your itinerary?"

"South," I said.

"That's not an itinerary," she said. "That's just a direction!"

I explained that we didn't know how fast we'd end up traveling or how long our savings would last. We had no idea which ports we'd stop at or where we'd want to spend extra time exploring.

"Schedules kill sailors," I said, echoing wise advice we'd been given from more experienced mariners. "If we set a firm itinerary, we'll risk making bad decisions to follow it. We can't just go out in any weather. We have to adjust to conditions as they arise."

She shook her head, "I couldn't handle leaving without a plan."

"We're not unprepared," I said. "We have charts stashed in the V-berth for the coastline from here to Panama, although we don't think we'll make it that far. And we're not sure what the return journey will look like. Maybe we'll leave the boat somewhere and go back for more adventures later. Maybe we'll sell it and fly home. A lot of people sail with the wind over to Hawaii and come back to the west coast by way of Alaska. Some get delivery captains to bring their boats back from Mexico. Whatever we end up doing, we'll have to figure it out on the way."

All afternoon, we chatted and smiled and posed for photos and tried not to think about all we had left to do.

And then we said, "Goodbye." One after another, friends peeled off to head for home. Family lingered as long as they could and we found quiet corners in which to say teary farewells. We handed our keys to Bryan's mom and she drove our car away.

After everyone was gone, we motored back to our slip at the St. Helens marina. I held the lines and jumped down to tie up, home here for the last time.

Chapter Two

UNTYING THE LINES

St. Helens to Astoria, Oregon
September 2013: Waxing Crescent

Make voyages! Attempt them ... there's nothing else.
—*Tennessee Williams*

Our departure day arrived. But instead of leaving the dock, we spent all day replacing our chain plates, the thick bronze attachment points for the shrouds that steady the mast. Our friends Herb and An Der came to wish us farewell and ended up helping with the project. Bryan had finished all but the last bolthole, but his drill bits kept snapping instead of cutting through. We strapped Herb's heavy duty drill to the side deck and tore up bit after bit trying to bore the hole through the hull. I drove to the hardware store and bought every spare bit they had while Bryan and Herb took turns operating the equipment. Back on the dock, I eyed the repairs. Six cables stretched from the top of the mast. Five of the six were already secured to the shiny bars bolted through the hull amidships. The last one hung swinging over the deck.

"I think we must be hitting a weld on the old plates inside the hull," Bryan said. "That's the only thing that makes sense. The rest of the holes went right through but this last one seems determined to keep us here for good." With no option but to keep drilling, he and Herb got back to work, sharpening the dull bits and discarding the broken ones until we were down to our last option.

"If this bit breaks we're stuck," Bryan said, "At least until we can hitch a ride to Scapoose for some more."

Herb reached across to take over the drill. "I'll baby it for sure. But don't worry. We'll help you get whatever you need."

I sat on the dock with An Der, willing the drill through the hull with my mind. Every minute or so, the men retracted the bit and brushed away the particles they'd managed to dislodge from the stubborn hole. Finally, the drill gave a lurch as it punched through the weld.

"That's it!" Bryan said, "We made it through." Herb held the chain plate against the boat as Bryan twisted the bolts into place and attached the final turnbuckle to pull the last shroud taut.

The dock shifted under our feet as we danced and embraced.

"I know you were trying to leave today, since it's Bryan's birthday," Herb said, "but it's too late to take off tonight. Let's clean up this mess and take you out to dinner."

The next morning, as Bryan upended himself in the stern locker, trying to organize equipment in the gaping space, I glanced up to see Herb and An Der walking toward us on the dock.

They handed cold drinks to the crew and said, "We're here to say farewell. It's time for you to go!"

Bryan tossed the last of the gear down the hatch and we prepped the nylon headsail. We'd given ourselves permission to start small, with only the hundred-yard hop across to Sand Island, and the wind was just right to sail away from the dock. We idled the engine in neutral as a backup. No need to be foolish just to make a fancy exit.

One last round of hugs and well wishes and we untied the dock lines and raised the sail. Slipping into their roles as crew, the kids took their places at possible problem points—near the neighbor boat at our bow, down the side deck. We raised our arms in victory and farewell and slowly eased out into the river.

The Columbia was low after the dry summer, but the current still swift enough to knock us off course in the light air. We boosted our power with a hit from the engine and eased up to the dock on Sand Island.

Hannah dutifully recorded our voyage in the log book. Departure: 4:07pm. Arrival: 4:15pm. A small journey, yes. But meaningful just the same. We'd untied the lines from our old lives and crossed the river into our new one.

We celebrated by cutting open a dragonfruit we'd been given at Monday's party. We sat in the cockpit and scooped out the flesh with a spoon, passing the halves around until only the colorful shells remained. Bryan leaned down and set them afloat in the current and we watched the little boats drift downriver.

The next morning, it was our turn to follow. We'd set our expectations low again, planning to stop at another favorite local anchorage after only a few miles. The buildup to our departure had been every bit as exhausting as we'd expected and we wanted a few quiet days to rest and acclimate.

By midafternoon, we dropped our anchor in the bight off Martin Slough, just in time to tuck down below out of a summer thunderstorm. I made dinner and went to bed early, falling asleep to the sound of rain on the deck.

We spent the next day motoring the forty miles to Cathlamet, about halfway to the Columbia River Bar. Bryan and I switched off at the tiller, easing into our new watch patterns. At one point, I ducked below for a few minutes to make some lunch and opened the cupboard under the sink. Water pooled on the lip of the shelves and overflowed onto the carpet at my feet. The thunderstorm had found every crevice in the sealant of our new deck hardware and invaded my orderly domain.

Lunch forgotten, I sat down on the floor to survey the damage. Labels hung askew on cans next to soggy rolls of spare paper towels. Not much was ruined but everything was sopping wet.

Hannah and Meira curled up in their quarter berths while I fumed and grumbled my way through the cleanup, wiping and drying and reorganizing, rehoming anything that wasn't water resistant. I took small comfort in the minimal loss, torn between pulling myself back together or giving into self-pity. I slapped together a snack, wiped my eyes, and headed out for a turn at the helm.

Bryan stepped below, relieved to get a break, and immediately stormed back out on deck. A valve in the head had cracked and the holding tank had leaked blackwater all over the floor of the V-berth. After a few deep breaths in the fresh air, he waded into the mess with paper towels and cleaner and soon had the floor mopped up. Suddenly, now that we couldn't use the head, everyone needed to go.

Finally through the channel into the Cathlamet harbor, we pulled straight into the pump-out dock. When well offshore, we could pump overboard; inland, we relied on pump-out stations in various states of disrepair.

Bryan emptied the holding tank and then did a more thorough inspection. The cracked valve wasn't our only problem. The bronze through-hull—the seacock that allowed us to discharge the holding tank at sea—had frozen closed.

I think it's time I told you about our toilet. On a ship, a toilet is called a head and it is inside a room also referred to as the head. Picture a small wooden outhouse.

No, smaller.

It has to be tiny so you can wedge yourself in during a storm and not go anywhere while you're going. There's a door, the only one on our boat, and on the inside of the door, velcroed down so it doesn't jump around, hangs a mesh shoe bag where we keep our small toiletries—toothpaste and nail clippers, which begin to rust the instant they come aboard. Sunscreen too, and a hairbrush that leaps out regularly but there's no better place to put it.

The only mirror on the boat is on the wall across from the toilet. You have to sit down to check your teeth. There's a tiny counter with a sink that doesn't work. It used to have a pump faucet but that corroded solid long ago and no one really wants to brush their teeth in the head anyway so we've never bothered to fix it. There's an old tennis ball plugging the sink drain because the previous owner's wife didn't like the way the ocean sometimes groaned and splashed up the drain hose in wild seas.

The cupboards under the sink are the rankest sort, never clean and often stinky. We keep holding tank chemicals there and a toilet brush in a half-open ziploc bag and all the packages of menstrual products a boat with three women needs. There is also a small bin of wooden cones in various sizes. These need to be handy in case something pokes a hole in the boat, but will only help if the hole is small and relatively round. I've dug frantically for them just once.

The toilet sits up on a wooden box, like the euphemistic throne it is, and there are rough-cut holes in the box to access the various important valves and hoses. One is there to let sea water in for flushing, one to let flush water out. No matter how clean these are, I want to wash my hands every time I touch them. The head is a little undersized so you have to aim carefully and advance planning is helpful. If you think a little extra lubrication in the bowl will be necessary, you can pump sea water in before you go. Mostly this water is clear but sometimes it's brackish and dark. Every once in a while, if you are going at night in the ocean, it's filled with a thousand tiny sparkles of bioluminescence—like peeing into a bowl of starlight.

I don't need to explain what happens next—relieving yourself is pretty much the same everywhere—but I will say that once, in a lumpy sea, I wrestled myself out of my layers—the rain pants, the yoga pants, the long underwear, the short underwear—hiked up my foul weather jacket and perched on the head for a quick pee. I must not have been bracing myself well enough because when the boat lurched off the crest of a wave I flew into the air, the toilet seat followed, detaching from the toilet and splitting in two, and we all came down in a heap.

So after you're done doing what you came to do, you need to flush. This is a multi-step process and, along with the fire extinguishers and the Mayday procedures, is one of the three stops on the visitor tour. There's a knob on one side of the head, about the size of a cabinet pull, positioned just right to cut into your hips when you're seated. This needs to be raised and lowered forcibly to pump the bowl dry. Then you flip a little lever and pump again. This brings in raw water to rinse the bowl. Sometimes what got pumped out comes back into the bowl and has to be pumped back out again. Then flip the lever once more and pump out the raw water to rinse the hoses so they don't absorb the smell. The microorganisms from the sea decompose in the hoses and produce their own special scent so it's not really odor-free but it helps.

If we're in port, we pump our blackwater into a holding tank so we have to ration how much flush water we can use. We go on shore every chance we get or pee serially, mornings and evenings, and then flush all at once to save holding tank space.

While you're pumping, you have to leave the toilet open so you can see if the bowl pumps dry but make sure you close your mouth. Sometimes there's splash back.

A toilet this convoluted is nearly impossible to unplug so we do everything we can to keep it from ever clogging. There is a sign affixed to the wall with the ominous warning, "Notice to landlubbers: A marine toilet is a complicated mechanism. If you toss even the smallest thing into it—even a paper matchstick or a hank of hair—it will probably choke."

To keep the head clear, all the toilet paper gets folded in on itself and tossed in the garbage can that lives on the counter because there's no room on the floor. Sometimes we remember to bungee it down before we go out to sea but sometimes we forget and it crashes down scattering debris everywhere.

Under the sink there is a quart jug of antibacterial hand sanitizer.

We pulled into the Port of Astoria weary as if we'd been gone weeks instead of days. I checked the weather right away. Winds from the south for seventy-two hours. We had plenty to do to fill the time.

More than once, we walked over to Englund Marine for parts and Bryan inspected *LiLo*'s systems again. I wedged my rolling grocery cart onto the tourist trolley and rode it uptown to the store for fresh fruit and ice As the good weather approached on the forecast, we started running out of excuses to stay. Only the through-hull to replace.

If all went well, it would be an easy fix. Unscrew the old fitting; screw in the new one. But if the seacock didn't unscrew smoothly or the casing around the valve cracked getting the old one out, we could end up underwater. Hauling out the boat for such an easy fix seemed extravagant and unnecessary. Still, we made sure to attempt the repair during business hours, when we could get an emergency lift from the boatyard if needed.

Bryan cleared space in the tiny head and sprayed the old fitting with lubricant. The fumes blew out the porthole straight onto the clean towels I'd hung on the lifeline to dry. He tentatively loosened the fitting and finger-tightened it back into place then came out into the cabin.

"Hannah, how brave are you?"

"Brave enough."

"Okay, come in here and get down. Do you see this valve in the middle of this hole? When I say, 'Go,' unscrew the old one and screw in this new one. But be quick. We don't want the ocean coming into the boat."

I stood in the cockpit with the boatyard on speed dial. Meira stood on the toilet lid and relayed messages between Hannah, on the floor of the head, and Bryan, out on the dock. Bryan laid down on the boards and reached under the water, suctioned his palm over the through-hull and hollered, "Okay, go!"

"Dad says, 'Go!'"

I held my breath for a moment until I heard Hannah's muffled voice.

"I got it out!"

"Great! Get the new one in!" Bryan hollered.

"Dad says, 'Get…'"

"I know! I heard him! I'm hurrying. Okay…it's in!"

Bryan pulled his hand away from the hull and shook it dry.

"How does it look?" he asked, peering in the porthole. "Do you see a leak?"

Meira had moved to perch on the counter and she stuck her face up to her dad's through the window. Hannah poked hers deep into the bottom locker.

"Nope. It looks good!"

No more excuses, I thought. *Tomorrow, we cross the bar.*

Chapter Three

BEYOND THE OREGON TRAIL

Astoria, Oregon to Crescent City, California
September 2013: Waxing Crescent, First Quarter, Waxing Gibbous

*When setting out on a journey do not seek advice
from those who have never left home.*
—Rumi

I turned on the radio to hear the bar report and stood on the steps watching Astoria's landmark bridge solidify and fade in the drifting fog. The tide had turned a couple of hours earlier and the twice daily battle between river and sea had almost been decided. The coast guard still reported dangerous conditions out at red buoy ten, but we knew the chop was likely to settle down any minute. I fought my own internal battle—eagerness and anxiety forging a reluctant truce of alertness.

We coiled up our power cord, stowed the dishes, started the engine, and loosed the dock lines. The prop-wash shoved us out of our slip at an angle and I gunned the throttle to reestablish steering. I turned the tiller over to Bryan, slipped up to the bow, and blew a long blast on the air horn as we nosed through the tight corner at the marina's entrance. Safely out in the Columbia, we turned toward the ocean, picking up where my ancestors left off, blazing a watery extension of the Oregon Trail.

Wisps of morning fog thickened before our eyes as we neared the jetties and shoals at the river's mouth. Bryan and I called for "all hands on deck" and Hannah and Meira hauled themselves out of their cozy bunks to stand watch. Bow watch, port watch, starboard watch, stern watch—eight eyes squinted into the fog for danger. Fog horns resonated eerily in the air—one long blast every two minutes from each ship in the channel. Eight ears strained over the water for any meaningful sound—the rumble of an engine, shouts from a fisherman, the distinctive crash of waves on rocks.

From almost directly ahead, a white light loomed out of the mist, high above our bow and bright in the dim morning. The bulk of the ship it preceded emerged more gradually, sharp steel blue lines on a tall white prow. We blew our air horn and the vessel responded as we turned to avoid a collision. We exchanged signals again and again until their stern vanished behind us, an antiphonal chorus singing the way to safety.

The radio squawked in the sudden silence and I stepped below to hear the latest conditions, though our senses told us what we needed to know. The chop had receded into a gentle roll.

"All restrictions lifted," the coast guard reported, and we slid past another buoy on our way to deeper water.

Our years of preparation had come to this and now we couldn't even see where we were going. We hugged the southern side of the channel, passing close to each navigation marker—buoy eight, buoy six, buoy four—and finally, at buoy two, we swung to port. South.

I looked back in the fading mist at the fog clinging to the river bar. Dangers once hidden took shape around us—the breakers on Clatsop and Peacock Spits, the colossal cargo carriers, colorful floats marking underwater crab traps. Beauty emerged from the clouds as well—the rising sunlight on the shore, pelicans in fleet formation, the wide expanse to the west.

A morning breeze prompted a few hectic minutes. I took the helm while Bryan raised the drifter—our light-air headsail—and Meira fried breakfast in the cabin below. We'd timed our departure to avoid the high winds so common on the northwest coast, but the swells rarely settle in this part of the ocean. Even when the wind dies down, the waves take another few days to calm and usually, by that point, the winds are back. Across the wide open fetch of the North Pacific, these swells build for miles. Even in the light winds, seas can combine to form towering waves that rise high above the cabin deck, higher than a house and at least as heavy.

We struggled to steer through the seas and our sail flapped in the fluky winds. To hold the drifter full, Bryan lifted a long aluminum whisker pole, set the base into place at the mast, then threaded the tip into the eyelet at the clew of the sail. He angled the pole over the water and I pointed the bow west-southwest to get clear of the land.

We ate a late breakfast in shifts and traded positions around the boat as we settled into our new rhythm. Every move required careful coordination to avoid hitting the boom or tripping over the tethers we each wore for safety. Eventually, the kids moved to their bunks to read and I kept Bryan company in the cockpit while he took the first official watch.

In a pattern that was soon to become as familiar as a morning coffee break, the afternoon breeze freshened into a brisk wind and we decided to replace the oversized sail with our smaller working jib. Before we could begin, a gust caught the drifter, which pulled taut, bucked against the wind, and snapped the whisker pole in two. I swung my gaze to the flogging nylon and the broken spar at its foot. The inner section of the pole hung disjointedly from the mast and the outer piece dangled over the water, held by only the friction of the tip in the eyelet. I slid into place at the tiller and Bryan rushed forward to retrieve both pieces of the pole, first reaching out for the thinner section before it fell in the water, then unlatching the thick end and tucking them both onto the side deck for later inspection.

He loosened the drifter's halyard at the mast, then pulled his tether along the jacklines—the safety line running the length of the side decks—to move to the bow as the sail came down. He fought to corral the billowing cloth into the sail bag and as the steadying effect of the sail gave way to an unpredictable roll, I glanced up at the rigging—a delicate balance of cables and spars. Halfway up the mast, wooden spreaders bisect the cables, their outer tips friction fit against the upper shrouds. But not this day. The spreaders drooped at an unruly angle and the once rigid cables slopped in the wind, threatening to end our infant voyage with a dismasting. Images of limping back with a shattered boat or injured crew flashed through my mind and I drew in a deep breath and called to Bryan. "We've lost our spreaders!"

Hannah and Meira grabbed their life jackets and popped out to see if we needed help. Bryan glanced up at the damage and nodded his understanding. While he secured the sail I reached for the ignition, turned on the engine, and angled our bow to cut through the seas. In these swells, a knockdown was a real possibility. If a wave hit from the wrong direction, or I faltered at the helm, *LiLo* could skitter sideways and capsize or somersault end over end—a nightmare possibility that might end our voyage, wreck our boat, maybe take our lives. Even a steep tilt had the potential to do major damage, turning unsecured items into missiles or felling our under-supported mast.

Once Bryan was back in the cockpit, we sent the kids below and took a minute to assess our options. Nothing moves very quickly aboard a sailboat; even a crisis typically unfolds in slow motion.

In the past we'd adjusted the spreaders in port or a quiet anchorage, standing on the cabin top, holding the whisker pole that now lay in pieces on the side deck. I glanced over at our telescoping boat hook and eyed the distance to the spreaders. No way would it be long enough. We'd installed mast steps to use for maintenance, but a climb up the unstable mast in the increasing swell was unthinkable.

Despite all the care we'd taken with our last-minute chain plate relocation and upgrade, we'd underestimated the impact to the rigging higher up, and the heavy load and wider angle of the cables had allowed the spreaders to fall out of place. We needed to get them into the correct position, and quickly.

Taking care around the sharp, broken edges of the whisker pole we lashed the two halves together, working to save every inch of length without compromising strength and always leaving one hand free to steer. Then, in the rapidly rising wind and chop, I adjusted the tiller to take each swell directly, reducing the side-to-side motion while Bryan crept up the cabin and climbed to the highest point, on top of the upturned dinghy. He wrapped his arms around the mast and tied a line between it and his waist to free his hands for the work ahead. I watched his feet grip the slippery surface and resisted looking up as he stretched both arms to lift the mended pole toward the spreaders. I knew I had to keep my eyes on the ocean, to guide the boat in the shifting seas. If I misjudged the swell the boat might drop off a crest sideways, jerking Bryan to the deck or over the side. Fear drew my eyes to his, as if I could will him to stay upright with my gaze. I forced my focus back to the helm and chanted aloud to calm the panic.

"Do your job. Do your job. Do your job. Do your job."

Finally, he lowered the pole and called back for me to check his work. We didn't want the spreaders to fall again, especially not with the approaching dusk but too much force would snap them past the correct angle and out of place, up out of reach. I braced my feet against the cockpit walls and craned up, working to keep the mast steady in my field of vision.

"That looks good enough, I think," I called and I stepped back in relief as Bryan reentered the cockpit and took over the helm.

Our next port lay seventy-five miles or so to the south, but a southerly weather system had moved in earlier than predicted and we could make no headway in that direction. We turned almost due west to keep the boat moving as smoothly as possible, still concerned about jarring our spreaders loose before we'd had a chance to inspect them in the harbor. I pulled out some granola bars for dinner and grabbed a handful of dried fruit.

As the sun set, I added a couple of extra layers and took over the watch. I huddled under the dodger to get out of the wind but the cold penetrated my layers and turned my fingers numb. Every ten minutes I stepped away from the shelter to scan the horizon for obstacles or dangers. I watched the clock almost as closely as the compass.

I'd spent the last few years preparing for this journey but I had been on an interior journey as well. Early in my thirties, I committed to taking this decade to grow into myself, to learning my true shape all the way down at the core. I didn't want to add another accomplishment or title. I'd seen enough to know these ebb and flow like the tide and I wanted to learn to live from my essence.

I asked myself, "When everything else is carried away, will I recognize the person I have become?" This trip seemed like a good opportunity to let the sea carry away anything that didn't belong.

Several times in the months leading up to our departure, people had responded to our plans, saying, "You're so adventurous!"

I always argued with them. "I'm not, really! I hate the feeling of adrenaline. The sea is a scary place."

"Then why are you going?"

I never felt like I had a satisfactory answer. I just said, "That's what I'm going to find out."

Now here I was, discovering just how uncomfortable finding out could be. Without a sail to stabilize us, I steadied myself, tired muscles contracting to adjust to the swell and the chop. Like riding a unicycle through a earthquake. The darkness trapped me firmly in my body, no space for connecting to my spirit. What little room I had for thoughts was consumed with a list of ways we could die.

I squinted into the dark, searching for a glimpse of danger.

Unlit vessels? Fishing gear? Whales on a collision course?

Drifting cargo containers are always a possibility, though unlikely as a lightning strike. Oh, and lightning. We could get hit by lightning.

If we could make it into Newport in time, my parents and my brother's family planned to meet us for one last visit before we sailed out of range. How was I going to talk with them about this? I didn't want to scare them, though there was plenty to be scared about. I felt myself withdrawing, filtering what I was going to say. I wanted to tell them the truth without worrying them about the possibilities I didn't want to speak aloud.

About the time I had worked myself into a complete panic, I heard Bryan moving around down below. Time to check the horizon and hand over the watch.

"They're here!" The lookout in the cockpit called to those of us frantically tidying down below. We'd made it safely into the Yaquina Bay harbor and after we had a chance to check our rigging, my family drove down to see us. We poked our heads up to see my brother and sister-in-law heading down the ramp with their kids, my parents, and the dog. Grateful for the dry skies, we found places for all ten of us aboard.

We chattered over each other about all the difficulties and excitement in our first few days and our hopes for the next leg of our journey while underneath the chatter hummed the awareness of our imminent separation.

Mom pulled out a pile of greeting cards, each one labeled in her familiar hand. We opened the congratulatory ones right away and stashed the birthday and holiday cards in a plastic bag for a taste of home on milestone days. We piled into vehicles, which already felt like a luxury, and drove to a nearby beach. The kids and the other adults walked down to the tideline with the dog but I figured I would have plenty of opportunities for sandy feet on this trip so I sat in the van with my mom saying nothing in particular aloud, saying everything important with our presence.

Before anyone got too weary, we brushed off the sand, loaded back into the vehicles, and headed to Newport's historic waterfront for chowder and cheesy bread. We took over the long table in the center of the restaurant and drank in each other's faces, trying to tuck away enough memories to tide us over until our return. We strung together all the family holiday traditions we could think of, sending

Thanksgiving and Easter greetings around the table, pinching anyone who wasn't wearing green, and later, outside on the street, we harmonized our favorite Christmas carols, our voices cracking on the familiar words.

Back at the marina, we circled up for a series of hugs, pretending we couldn't remember who we'd already embraced and going back for more. As we pulled ourselves away, the magnitude of our isolation began to sink in.

We'd intentionally crafted a life near our family and friends. We loved seeing our parents every few weeks and running into siblings and cousins on a regular basis. But now, our community contracted to just the four of us. Hannah and Meira slipped ahead under the streetlights and Bryan and I lingered behind, instinctively drawing a little closer to each other, the one constant who remained.

After another day or two, the weather, the boat, and our attitudes were all ready for another passage. We filled our gas tank on our way out of the bay, stopping to chat with the sailors on the fuel dock.

One shared tales from his own experience of sailing south. "It's the cold up here that makes it feel dangerous. Once the ocean and the air are eighty degrees, even the storms don't feel scary anymore."

A few minutes later, we passed along encouragement to Mike, another sailor dreaming about his own Mexican sailing adventure. Though we'd only been out a few days ourselves, we offered all the positivity we could muster.

"We didn't grow up sailing but here we are," Bryan said. "And a sturdy, simple boat is more important than lots of fancy equipment."

I chimed in. "If we can do it so can you. The good moments are totally worth the tough days."

I'm pretty sure I needed the reminder more than he did.

Mike helped shove us off the dock and we motored out past the jetties and headed south again. Low winds kept the waves down but a leftover typhoon swell still had us bobbing. When we dropped into a trough, the high seas blocked the wind and our sails drooped limp, opening with a bang when we rose on a crest. The noise set our nerves on edge and the gear couldn't take the strain. Reluctantly, Bryan flipped on the engine to steady our passage. The hum filled my awareness with worry—the expense, the strain on the motor, the diminishing fuel supply—and accusing voices added to the uproar in my head. *You aren't a real sailor if you motor this much. If you were better, stronger, hardier, you'd wouldn't have to compromise.* I couldn't seem to quell the disquiet and the hours crept by.

We came into Coos Bay on Sunday morning, pulled into the Charleston marina's fuel dock and waited. When no one came to meet us, we walked up to the shop. The sign on the door read, "Closed." We pulled into a slip across the fairway and took a quick walk to shore.

There were no gas stations in sight; not much of anything around, actually. Bryan finally took our jerry cans to the parking lot and stood around until someone offered him a ride. The crew and I stayed aboard. All the restaurants on shore were boarded up. I don't think it was just the Sunday lull that had things looking so tired and worn. Bryan got back, we filled the main tank, and took off right away.

The next morning, I woke to Bryan's cheerful words, "Welcome to California!" I poked my head above and he gestured toward land.

"See the cloud bank, there to the north?"

"Yes."

"And see the line there where the clouds end and the blue sky begins?"

"Yes."

I started to laugh as it dawned on me. "That's the California-Oregon border, isn't it?"

"Just about exactly, yep."

All along the northern coast, we'd stayed in deep harbors with tight entrances. Navigating the bars was tricky, but once inside we could be assured of calm waters and easy rest. Here in Crescent City the ocean swell sneaked around the point, through the wide breakwaters, and curled in small wavelets on the sandy beach.

The marina was still being repaired from the tsunami three years before so we'd anchored in the bay. More of a bight than a bay really, protected from the small, northern waves but open to the biggest swell. We'd stopped to avoid a weather front blowing through and we weren't quite certain of our ground tackle yet so we waited out the morning winds, bucking around on our anchor and checking the set every few minutes. The anchor held and the gale quickly blew itself out so we packed some snacks, dropped the dinghy, and rowed to shore.

We all preferred a long, quiet row to a quick, noisy trip with an outboard engine but since Bryan did most of the rowing and maintenance, he'd had the final say about our choice for the year.

"Given the kind of outboard we can afford, I'd spend all the time I saved on small engine repair. I'd rather just row."

We timed our approach just right, riding the waves and the adrenaline of our first surf landing.

While Bryan pulled the dinghy up above the tideline and tied it off to a boulder, the kids took turns running across a grassy ditch—down and up again, down and up again—their seafarers' bodies reverting to the joy of early childhood, running for the sake of running.

Hannah's cry of alarm brought playtime to a halt. She'd tucked her orthodontic retainer into her pocket for safekeeping but somewhere in the shuffle of the landing it had disappeared. We searched the shoreline and the grass, moving quickly through hope and despair to acceptance. I was sure this wouldn't be the last thing we'd lose on the trip, nor the most precious.

Finally, we gave up and moved inland. The tide was too high to walk across the rocky spit to greet the lighthouse that had kept us safe the night before. (As sailors, we're only comfortable getting close to a lighthouse from on land.) So we turned north past the city park, toward the city center, eyes out, as always, for the necessities—a grocery store, a laundromat, a chandlery.

We found art instead, a necessity of its own sort. Meira spotted it first—the delicate, life-sized sculpture of a horse fashioned from curves of bare driftwood, prancing in the gallery window.

"Can we go in, Mom?"

Once we'd made the big decision—taken the plunge, crossed the bar—we were left with only these little choices. So although I'd had other ideas for the day Bryan and I exchanged a glance and shrugged. *Why not?*

We stepped across the threshold to the jangle of the bells on the door. We took one glance around the artist's cooperative, at the fragile displays of ceramics and glass, and stripped off our backpacks and jackets, holding them awkwardly in our arms. The shopkeeper came out of her office to greet us. She was elegantly dressed, understated, perfect for the job of engaging rich connoisseurs. But she didn't blink at our ragtag crew. I suppose seaside store owners grow accustomed to grungy customers.

"Come on in! Feel free to leave your things there by the door." I'd already spotted the grand piano at the center of the shop. Bryan caught the direction of my gaze and asked on my behalf.

"Would it be all right if she played a bit?"

"Yes, of course. Yes, please, in fact. I'd love to have some music in here."

Before we went to sea, I'd resolved to play all the pianos I came across. The honky-tonks, the concert grands. Seeing this one was like meeting an old friend in an unexpected place. I moved to the bench and played a few arpeggios to get acquainted before launching into a favorite piece. Out of the corner of my eye, I could see Bryan and the kids wandering quietly, calling across to each other to admire the art together.

After a few minutes at the keys, I stood up to join them. Hannah and Meira dragged me from corner to corner, pointing out what had caught their eye. Bryan stood along one wall, entranced by the work of a local photographer, the rich seascapes printed not on paper but on glass.

The keeper hovered graciously. "Let me know if you have any questions." And then, a question of her own. "Are you visiting here?"

I started with the short version. "We're traveling aboard a small sailboat together. You might be able to see it in the bay." And when she clearly wanted more, I launched into the longer story. "We've been sailing as a family since the kids were three and four and dreaming of a trip like this for a long time. We've got a year off and we're heading south. We'll see how far we get."

We spent another couple of days in the area, waiting for the swell to die down at sea. We timed a trip to the lighthouse with the tide, making sure we wouldn't get stranded when the seaside knoll turned into an island.

One morning, Bryan rowed the gas cans to the eastern shore of the bay, schlepped them to the gas station on the edge of town, and returned to fill our main tank. We didn't like leaving a harbor without topping off our fuel but if there wasn't a fuel dock available, this often meant a long row and a long walk with the heavy cans.

Our last afternoon in town found us in the park again. The kids swung on the jungle gym and climbed through the wooden fort, stopping to mug for the camera when we called up to them. Bryan seemed to have something on his mind.

"What are you thinking?"

"I can't get those photographs out of my head. I know it's a little early in the trip for souvenirs but I think I might want to buy one."

We headed inland a few blocks, retracing our wandering steps to the gallery. The keeper was just closing up for the night but she gladly helped us make a selection, promising to pack it up and send it back to my parents for safekeeping.

We gave her a boat card with our contact information and a link to my blog. She sent us off with hearty blessings. "Stay safe! I hope you come again."

I nodded politely but knew our journey home would be unlikely to bring us back. Instead of beating against the weather up the coastline, many sailors heading to the Northwest from Central America tack all the way across to Hawaii and ride the sweeping current of the North Pacific Gyre home by way of the Gulf of Alaska, doubling their distance for the sake of an easier journey.

Perhaps we treasured our encounter more for its singularity, this moment a gift from a life of small choices. It's hard to miss the importance of the big events, the fruit or folly of major life decisions. Each course correction is a matter of degrees, after all. But who's to say which change alters a life more completely?

A small one can take you far out to sea.

Another might just bring you home.

Chapter Four

Light for the Way

Trinidad Head to Eureka, California
September 2013: Full Moon, Waning Gibbous

*More than once I saw things in darkness
I would never have seen in daylight*

On land, I watched the moon with wonder as she swelled and faded in and out of the sky to some mysterious rhythm. Sailors through the centuries turned to the moon for inspiration and orientation, for tidal intelligence and direction, but in the often cloudy Pacific Northwest I'd never really learned to read this cosmic timepiece, never tuned my being to its tempo.

Now at sea with a view only obstructed by a slender mast, I hoped to make the moon my teacher, to befriend her, and learn her phases to my bones. Out beyond the reach of clocks and calendars, the timing of the moon began to rule my days and nights, becoming a drumbeat, a steady companion, light for the way.

After the overnight passages down the coast of Oregon, we enjoyed the luxury of a simple day-sail from Crescent City to Trinidad Head. We'd heard there was good anchorage available there, but pulled in just after sunset to a cove crowded with mooring balls for the seasonal fishermen. We couldn't anchor between them without risking tangled or damaged ground tackle. Most of the fishing boats were already done for the year so, after much discussion, we picked an official-looking mooring, tied up, and went to bed, hoping no one came to kick us off in the night.

In the morning, we woke to the sound of a work crew hauling moorings up out of the bay. We rowed to shore and asked around. No one seemed to know for sure whether we were okay to stay on our mooring but, as one local said, "If you weren't supposed to be there, someone would have said so already."

After a nice loop around the head—named Trinidad by a Spanish explorer who stumbled across this beautiful point on Trinity Sunday—and a few minutes on the beach, we split some fish and chips at the seaside restaurant and rowed back out to the boat where we discovered a swarm of flies were setting up housekeeping. We quickly decided to head on down to Eureka for the night.

We battled the flies all the way from Trinidad Head to Humboldt Bay, slapping the curtains against the windows to smash them on the glass. Only the cockpit was free from the scourge, so we all took turns at the tiller. Calm seas, sunny skies. Such a rarity so far. Today's fifteen miles would only take us about three hours and we thought we'd make it across the bar before dark, before the tide turned, before the next storm hit. So many calculations occupied my mind, and none of them were certain.

But, of course, we were met with the one hazard I hadn't counted on. As we approached the entrance to Humboldt Bay, the sun was just starting to set out to sea, a few filmy clouds turning gold, then orange. I came up on deck and looked south where a thick cloud had begun to accumulate.

"Do you think that's blocking the entrance to the bay?"

"I don't know, Beth."

"Well, I know you don't *know*, but what do you *think*? Will we still have visibility to make it through the entrance? You know the storm is headed our way."

"I know. Let's just wait and see, okay?"

Bryan stayed irritatingly calm while I went up on the bow, hoping for a better view, willing myself farther south. Another few minutes brought the answer I'd been dreading. The clouds were low, dipping all the way down to the sea and visibility soon dropped too. We throttled down, though we hated to lose speed. I pulled up both our electronic charts and tracked our position as we inched toward the breakwater.

"I can't believe we don't see it yet. We should be within half a mile."

The sky was blank—flat gray against the flat gray sea. I cocked my ears in all directions, trying to pick out another engine against the steady hum of our own. We blasted our air horn but heard no reply. This high stakes version of Marco Polo depended on the commitment of all to play fair. I hoped anyone out there would be just as interested in avoiding us as we were in avoiding them.

"We're only a quarter mile away. Don't you see *anything*?"

I swept the horizon frantically, looking, listening. The fog dampened any sound the quiet sea might be making against the rocks. Finally, Bryan called out.

"I see a green!"

"Where? Where?" Green meant we hadn't overshot our target. Green for go. This green should be on the end of the northern breakwater. I squinted across the horizon for the marker. Nothing. Bryan caught my eye and pointed.

"Not over there. Look up." I lifted my chin and scanned up, up.

"Oh! Way up there!" We were so close to the breakwater, the dim light was even with the top of our wobbling mast. I'd been eager to see a navigation light but now it seemed far too close. We stayed our course a few more yards and began a wide swing into the main channel. Any chop across the bar would be difficult to spot but the calm continued and I began to relax.

A few more yards in and the fog bank dissipated as fast as it had appeared, the last of my anxiety dissolving with it. We turned north to drive up the bay to the marina, made the dogleg toward the east. I called back to Bryan.

"It gets shallow up in here. Watch the depth sounder!"

"Will do."

I was glad he was watching. I couldn't take my eyes off the moon, rising full in the east in the reflection of the pink sunset. Pelicans flew in formation just above the surface and a raft of kayaks floated aimlessly, revelers lit up with glow sticks and dive lights.

We found our way to Bonnie Gool Docks, the overflow marina, tied up on the shore side and stepped out. Three other sailboats lined the finger, all with the telltale solar panels and jerry cans of long-distance cruisers. I cleared the galley, started dinner, and mentally crossed my fingers at the possibility of meeting another sailing woman.

The next morning we woke to the tail end of Typhoon Odette. The fog from the night before had lifted just enough to make room for the rain. I'd been watching the approaching storm and hoping we could wait it out in a protected bay. We'd made it, but barely. For fun, I pulled up the West Coast bar reports. Quillayute River, Gray's Harbor, Cape Disappointment, Tillamook Bay, Depoe Bay, Yaquina Bay, Siuslaw, Umpqua, Coos Bay, Chetco, Humboldt Bay—each familiar name blinked bright red, "Bar closed."

Out on the open ocean, high seas can be treacherous enough but as storm swells near the harbor entrances the shallowing sea floor tosses them into wild crests, intensifying the waves into giant breakers capable of capsizing even the rescue boats kept at the ready in these danger zones. When conditions deteriorate and the Coast Guard makes the call to close the bar, any seafarer unfortunate enough to get caught outside has to ride out the storm at sea, where no matter the conditions, it's almost certainly safer than the harbor mouth.

I offered a prayer for our unknown comrades, grinned at our own good fortune, and started a batch of chocolate chip cookies. A few hours later, Bryan and I bundled up in our rain gear and walked down the dock to deliver some goodies and meet the other sailors.

One boat was shut up tight, the occupants away. In another, a sturdy Hans Christian double-ender, we found a singlehander, a Canadian man named Cameron, and his eyes lit up at the gooey treats. He was in the middle of some rainy-day engine repair so we exchanged quick introductions and moved on.

On the third boat, we met Will. He invited us below into the immaculate interior of his thirty-foot Hunter, *Thallasea*. Originally from Germany, he'd left his home in Canada about the time we'd left Oregon. Both he and Cameron were sailing alone in boats about the size of *LiLo*. They were shocked we could fit all four of us in such a small space. We couldn't imagine tackling the long, punishing passages without a crew to share the watches. After a nice visit and a glass of rum, we scurried back to our own boat. The cabin was full of cheerful crew members and much messier and noisier than our new friend's but, thanks to the wonders of shore power and a space heater, just as warm and dry.

The next morning dawned clear but a quick weather check predicted harsh sea conditions continuing throughout the weekend and most of the next week. We started making plans to enjoy our stay. I found information online about a nearby library and a farmers market. We spent Saturday exploring the library and the downtown shops. I followed Hannah through a used bookstore and made mental notes every time she exclaimed over a title, then sneaked back to pick up a few to tuck away for her upcoming birthday.

When it became clear we'd be in Eureka over a Sunday, I started tossing around the idea of trying to make it to a church somewhere. Back home, we attended a Quaker meeting, part of the Religious Society of Friends who believe that there is a divine light in each human being. We hoped to find opportunities to occasionally gather with others who were intentionally nurturing that same light.

I searched for churches within walking distance of our dock and found myself intrigued by the website for Catalyst. From the description online, it seemed like a laid-back, loving community that would welcome a sailing Quaker quartet.

I discovered they'd recently moved locations from Eureka to nearby Arcata. The congregation met in the evening. Riding public transit there would be easy, but the weekend buses didn't run late enough to get us home. I sent a note to the contact link on the church's website, hoping there would be some parishioners from Eureka willing to get us back at the end of the evening. One of the co-pastors, another woman named Bethany, responded right away with the assurance that she could make something work and suggested that we show up early for a community festival.

So Sunday afternoon, we hopped a bus to Arcata. We matched the stops to the intersections on our map and when we neared the town square, we pulled the bell cord and filed off. The crew waited a moment as I stood on the curb to get my bearings and then followed me a few blocks toward the busy Arcata Plaza. We smelled the fair before we saw it. The deep fryers worked overtime on crispy fair food. Vendors sold leather goods and flowing skirts, handmade glass work and jewelry. In the center of the plaza, a pair of acrobats tumbled and arched, holding impossible positions and then springing apart like nimble cats.

We split up. I criss-crossed the square and then wandered the perimeter watching for the crew. After a few small purchases, we cut back through the plaza on a search for cold drinks. The acrobats had returned to human form and sprawled, smiling, in the shade.

We picked up iced coffee at a nearby cafe and loitered in the quiet shop until a few minutes to five. We walked the last two blocks up the street to the century-old building and found our way into the cool interior. The bags on our backs and our wind-blown faces revealed our visitor status in the small community. Hannah and Meira hung back while Bryan and I shook hands and navigated introductions with every curious congregant.

A visiting musician led the gathering that evening. His songs and stories spoke to our need for community along this isolated journey. Afterward, we waited in line to meet the artist and his wife and found common ground with them in the intersections between our stories.

By the time the co-pastors, Bethany and her husband, Jason, dropped us back at the marina, we'd already made plans to join them and their family for dinner on Monday.

The next evening, we scrubbed up and found clothes clean enough to wear out. We walked up to the parking lot and waited for our ride. Soon, a van pulled up, the back door opened and we jumped in. A traveler wouldn't get far without breaking all the childhood stranger-danger rules, but we still laughed at the picture we made, disappearing into a van on the side of the road.

Our trust was not misplaced. We arrived to find Bethany bustling around the kitchen to get dinner out to the wide plank table. A friend or two had been added to the guest list and we introduced ourselves as our kids disappeared into the playroom with the other children. The piano against the wall, the warm hospitality, even many of the books on the shelves mirrored our own life back home and drew us in.

Dinner was simple perfection. Bethany ladled soup into pottery bowls and Jason passed around slices of fresh, homemade bread. The conversation was its own sort of sustenance. We told a bit of our story and heard a bit of theirs. After we'd eaten all we wanted, a platter of flaky turnovers appeared in the center of the table and we reached together, hands brushing hands.

After dinner, I found a place near the kitchen sink. I dried dishes and followed instructions to find a home for plates and bowls.

"It doesn't really matter where you put things," Bethany said. "We're moving this weekend anyway."

"What?" I looked around the room. No boxes anywhere. No sign of the impending chaos.

Bethany read my glance.

"It's okay. We have lots of friends who will help."

Bethany and Jason lived with such generosity, I was not surprised to see that it circled back to envelop them as well.

It was hard to believe from inside protected Humboldt Bay that the ocean outside was all worked up about something, but day after day the buoy reports from outside the bar warned us against heading out. Monday, our dock mate, Will, decided he'd waited long enough.

"Are you really going to let those little maps tell you when to go?" he said.

I glanced down at the weather forecast on my cell phone and back to him.

"Um, yes. It still seems pretty bad out there."

"Well, *I'm* leaving this afternoon!"

We helped him away from the dock and wished him fair winds, but a few minutes later he was back with stories to tell.

"I motored down the bay just fine and was about to turn to run out to sea when the Coast Guard called my radio. They said, 'Captain, what are your intentions.'" His voice dropped to mimic the universal seriousness of the Coast Guard's radio broadcast.

"I told them, 'I'm heading out to sea, obviously,' and they just said, 'You might want to reconsider.' Sure enough, I turned the corner to head out and there, right in front of me, the bar was full of breaking waves halfway up my mast!" We laughed at the good-natured chagrin on his face.

"I'm glad you turned around!" I said.

"Me, too!"

Tuesday was market day and we walked up to Eureka's old town on a hunt for fresh produce and sunshine. In the afternoon, we picked up Cameron, the other sailor we'd met at our dock, and rowed over to the Eureka NOAA weather station for a first-hand look at the forecasters and the facility. We'd heard they were open to visitors and had called to request a tour. The station was miles away by road, but just a few feet across the bay by dinghy.

A cheerful intern met us at the gate and walked us around the outside instrument stations, answering our flurry of novice questions. We moved inside and she introduced us to the day crew. They explained their process and we stared at the rows of monitors and radio equipment—the ingredients of the weather products we consumed every day.

I cornered the senior meteorologist and tossed all my questions his way.

"Is this all NOAA information or do you gather stats from commercial planes?"

"How does upper level hydration inform your marine forecast?"

"What's the difference between this red monitor and that green one?"

We'd come during a lull between the every-six-hour forecast deadlines, so he had time to answer all my general questions and confer about our specific situation.

"No, I don't think you should leave until the weekend at the earliest. The wind hasn't died down yet and the swell is going to take another day or two to settle after it does. The cape is going to be nasty for quite a while. But it looks like there's going to be a shift in the weather pattern after another few days. Keep checking in; call me directly if you want to talk it over. We want to keep you safe out there!"

We rowed back to the dock and gathered up dirty clothes. In our conversation the night before, Bethany and Jason had picked up on some of the awkwardness of our current lifestyle and offered to have us back again for showers and laundry.

"It won't be a fancy dinner," Bethany said, "just a pick-up family dinner. But if you'd like, you're welcome to our laundry room and shower ... and our piano."

Back we went, feeling like family this time. We kept the washer humming and transferred load after load of smelly clothes, damp towels, and dirty sheets. The kids played together again and I spent a few minutes noodling around on the piano in the corner.

The dryer buzzer cut me off. I pulled open the door and bent to pull out the warm, fresh clothes. There, on top of the dryer vent, still in one piece and very clean, was Hannah's missing retainer.

"You'll never believe this!" I hollered. "Hannah, guess what I just found!"

We stumbled over each other to tell our new friends the whole surprising story and celebrated over heaping plates of taco salad. The deepening connections in the room restored our spirits.

Sometimes what you think was lost is found.

Sometimes you find something you didn't even know you were looking for.

Chapter Five

The Currency of the Sea

Eureka to San Francisco, California
September 2013: Third Quarter, Waning Crescent

*The exhaustion of being beat to death by the sea
was nothing compared to the draining fatigue of constant fear.*
—Marie De Santis

We left Eureka at sunrise and headed out across Humboldt Bay Bar. The swell had died down considerably but was still confused and rough around the entrance. My stomach felt as unsettled as the sea and I lost my breakfast over the side just beyond the seawall. The galley drawer must have felt the same; it took a dive and spilled silverware all over the floor.

I worried about the possibility of worsening conditions around Cape Mendocino, just ten miles to the south. Anywhere land meets sea is potentially dangerous but the water around capes, where points protrude and confuse the flow of air and swell, can be especially messy.

Not today, though. Before we even rounded the cape, the sea had sorted itself out into a steadier rhythm. The wind was too light to sail and we flipped on the engine—the tradeoff for waiting out the gale.

I'd already done the math. "We don't have enough gas to motor all the way to Bodega Bay and I *really* don't want to have to stop in Noyo River. The entrance looks small and sketchy."

"Good thing we're a sailboat, then," Bryan responded. "I'm sure we'll find enough wind at some point."

I was frustrated with the weather patterns that had us harbor hopping. Sailors with far more ocean experience than us spoke of these waters as the most dangerous of their long careers at sea. When low pressure systems rolled through, I was glad to be close enough to duck in out of the tempest. But sticking close to land meant less predictable wind, more motoring through the swell, more stopping for fuel. We didn't have enough tankage to drive straight through and stopping every couple of days wasted a lot of time turning toward shore, finding our way across the bar at the entrance, chasing fuel docks instead of whitecaps. We needed to make it south as quickly and safely as possible to escape the reach of the North Pacific winter.

Toward afternoon the wind started to pick up and we put up the headsail and a reefed mainsail. Not too long after, the wind rose further and we took the headsail back down and shortened the mainsail again. By evening, even the double-reefed main was overpowered. The afternoon breeze, which normally died down a few minutes after sunset, had instead steadily increased at our back and wind waves piled up on the swell, rolling under us from stern to bow. Unless the wind dropped soon, we'd need to take down our sails completely and run downwind in the following seas.

I flipped on the VHF to channel 1, NOAA weather radio, and listened to the mechanical voices announce my reality.

"Thursday night, northwest winds, 20-25 knots, rising to 25-30. Gusts to 35. Swell from the north 8 feet at 14 seconds. Wind waves 3-6 feet. Friday, northwest winds 10-15 knots…"

I stopped listening and let the voices drone on. No change from the 6 p.m. forecast. Not a gale but high winds all night. Big choppy waves over a mid-sized swell. Not too bad for a downwind run.

We worked together to drop the main and, after a final check around the decks, Bryan went to bed. Even sailing under bare poles, we were making good time and things seemed reasonably stable. The autopilot was on strike, first steering wildly to starboard, then back through our rhumb line and off to port. I added an extra layer and sat down by the tiller, hunching my back against the wind. The backlight on the cockpit compass had shorted out, so I strapped the elastic band from a headlamp around a mug and duct-taped it all to the cabin top. I flipped on the red-light feature, pointed it toward the compass face, and slowly settled into alignment.

I leaned back and spotted a bright star above the shrouds, glanced at the compass, and pulled the tiller against the swell to hold us steady. The wind blew on the back of my neck and loose hairs floated forward to brush both sides of my face. A downwind course. I flipped off the compass light and put my trust in the wind and the star.

Someone is always on watch at sea. It seems obvious that this would be necessary on a big boat with a large crew—a cruise ship or a commercial fishing vessel. But even, no, *especially* on a boat as small as ours any risk of collision is too great to ignore so on *LiLo* someone is always on watch.

From my position at the helm, I can see less than four miles before the earth curves away at the horizon. A ship traveling at twenty knots can close that distance in twelve minutes. So on our boat, the watch person is charged with a horizon sweep every ten minutes, more often if it's foggy. We each developed our own system for a watch check. It might go something like this.

When your timer rings, restart it and step to the center of the cockpit. If you've been sheltering below, this means tethering in and moving carefully with the waves up the stairs to the companionway. If you've been sitting out in the cockpit, sync yourself with the rhythm and stand on an upswell. Once you're upright, reach with your right hand to grasp the dodger amidships and scan slowly, slowly out to port. If we're heading south, this is the land side.

Careful, now. On a clear night, the lights of another boat might blend in with the lights of a city or land-based navigation markers. Turn counter-clockwise and scan across the port stern quarter, across the stern and over to the starboard stern quarter. About here, switch to holding on with your left hand and stare back a little longer, making sure nothing has been obscured by the gear on the stern or camouflaged by the scatter of light from the aft navigation signal. It matters just as much to watch where you've been as where you're going.

Turn to starboard, out to sea. We travel out beyond the near-shore fishermen and in from the cargo vessels and cruise ships. At night, we move far enough out that if the watch person somehow turns directly toward land, they'd have two full hours to notice the mistake before running aground. The dark makes it easier to spot ships out to sea, though more than once, I've mistaken the setting moon for a cruise liner just below the horizon. If the waves are high, a quick glance might not be enough. From the depths of a trough, it's easy to miss another ship hiding in a deep trough of its own.

Make sure you've spotted the new positions of any boats you spotted ten minutes ago. Take note of their current location and direction to rule out the possibility of a collision course.

Scan across the bow. It's hard to see well through the salt-crusted dodger so grab the stainless support to the right and lean far out to starboard. Sway in time with the roll of the hull and scan on through every compass degree all the way to and just past the mast. Check the foredeck for the water jugs and jerry cans. Make sure the dinghy is still tied down and hasn't started shimmying loose in her chocks. Reach across to the support on the left, arms spread wide. Never let go with one hand before you're holding on with the other. Peer back across the bow. Take extra care to scan the obstructed area beyond the mast and sweep all the way back to where you started. Turn around again, passing hand over hand, spinning clockwise this time to untangle your legs from the tether.

Check the compass course, check the speed over ground on the GPS, check the set of the sail or the rumble of the engine. Listen for anything that sounds out of place—that hiccup that means we're almost out of gas, the creak of the sheet in the block on the traveler, the shake of the sheave at the head of the sail. Plot a fix on the chart if it's time for that—once an hour in good conditions, more often in bad. Check the watch timer and try to find a comfortable seat. Eight and a half minutes to go.

The wind died after midnight, so we motored the rest of the night and all the next day toward Bodega Bay. During my afternoon watch, I alternated between gratitude at the more comfortable seas and the guilt and worry of using up so much fuel instead of sailing.

A splash in the water drew my attention and I looked up to see a pod of dolphins racing toward our bow. I hollered down below. "Come up on deck. There are dolphins!"

I cut the throttle as the pod approached and we watched them frolic in the waves.

After dark the second day, we turned off the engine to check the fuel. *LiLo* rocked gently on the passing swells. Bryan opened the fill cap, picked up the bamboo stick we used as a gas gauge, and lowered it in until the tip landed with a thunk on the bottom of the tank. He held it up near the stern light to spot the glistening streak before it evaporated and estimated the depth between the lines we'd drawn marking empty and full.

"I think we'll have enough to make it in," Bryan said. "We should probably put in another five gallons, though."

He moved his tether shackle to the jackline and pulled it up the safety line to the foredeck, where he untied one of the full gas cans we'd stored along the rail. The tiller shifted with each wave and I held it loosely, though we didn't have enough momentum to steer. Bryan walked—heel-toe, heel-toe—on the narrow side deck, balancing his heavy load with an outstretched arm. Back in the cockpit, he opened the gas can and screwed in the pour spout.

Just as he tipped the tank, *LiLo* listed hard on a surprising swell. The nozzle sloshed gas onto the cockpit floor and I grabbed for the fuel rags.

"I'll clean up. You just keep the can steady," I said.

"The floor might be a little slippery for a bit, so watch yourself. And your shoes are going to need a good airing out."

"Maybe this will be an improvement," I laughed. "They couldn't smell much worse."

After we got back underway, I sat down out of the chill on the top step, pulled up the chart for the entrance to the bay, and held it where Bryan could see it while steering.

"I know we don't usually make entrances after dark and I don't want to be reckless just to get a good night's sleep but I've been looking at this for a while now. The entrance looks well-marked and well-lit. There are range lights for the dog leg at the outside and then it's a straight shot between the markers all the way in. What do you think?"

"That looks easy enough, even in the dark. Let's be prepared to turn away if we need but I think we should be okay."

I pulled up a second chart on the tablet. "This one has some information my phone doesn't have." I glanced into the quarter berths where the kids were resting.

"Meira, you up for helping out?"

"Sure, what do you need?"

Meira got out of bed and put on a jacket.

"Here, take this chart and sit between my legs. We can both feed information about the light patterns up to your dad so he can steer us in. Sound good?"

"Got it."

The moon had not yet risen, but the night was clear and bright with stars and the glow from the city. Meira and I tracked our progress and took turns hollering up directions. At one point, Bryan leaned forward, squinting.

"Bethany, come up here for a second. See that blinking red light?"

I followed his pointing finger. "That one? Yeah."

"Is that a navigation marker or a stoplight?"

After sorting out the confusion and winding through the entrance, we eased our way into the inner harbor, tied up to the fuel dock, and walked over to the marina to investigate. It was 10:30 p.m. and the docks were quiet. We finally found a fisherman who encouraged us to pull into the slip next to him. It was obviously a private slip, with permanent fenders tied to the dock but we figured it was unlikely anyone would kick us off in the next few hours and we pulled in and went to bed.

First thing the next morning, I heard the fisherman and his crew get up and on the way. We crawled out of bed and started to get underway ourselves but before we had pulled over to the fuel dock, they were back, trailing silently at the end of a tow line.

After they drifted into place and secured their lines, Bryan hollered over. "You okay? Have a breakdown?"

The captain stepped down onto the dock, shaking his head. "Yeah, We've got a crack in the engine mount and you can't fix *that* at sea. We'll have to wait until the shop opens to get some replacement steel. Hey—" His face brightened a little under his cap brim. "All our ice will melt before we head out again. Do you need any for your cooler?"

"Oh, yes, please! The water is getting warmer down here and ice melts so fast, we can't always keep the food cold."

A deckhand had already scooped a bucket of ice from the hold and he passed it over the lifelines. Bryan poured it into the icebox and passed up the empty bucket. I handed it back across the lifelines. This time it returned with another load of crushed ice, sodas and apples nestled at the top.

"We figured you might like some cold drinks and fresh fruit too."

Bryan poked his head up from where he'd been rummaging in a locker and held up a length of metal flat bar. "Is this what you need for the mount repair? I happen to have a little to spare."

"That will be perfect!" the captain said. "Now we don't have to wait out the weekend to get started."

"I hope you don't want your ice back," I said.

"Or this," Meira held up her soda, already half gone.

"No worries. We have plenty to share."

Sometimes, in the strange and beautiful currency of the sea, we received more than we gave. Today we were givers and receivers both.

Running the channel in reverse held none of the complications of the night before. Day shone bright on the navigation markers and seals sunned themselves on the sandbars just beyond the dredged channel. We headed offshore a few miles and ran down the coast, taking turns at watch throughout the day. After the last few disorienting passages, where day and night blurred together, this six hour run flew by. By late afternoon, we closed in on Point Reyes, curved up into Drakes Bay, and dropped anchor as the cliffs turned golden in the setting sunlight.

In the morning, fog had settled in, thick and deep, and we turned around and around in the cockpit like a broken compass, trying to sort the land from the open ocean. We'd seen another boat in the bay but if it was still there, we couldn't tell where.

We put our plans for a hike on hold. We might end up anywhere, rowing around in this mist. Later in the day, the fog lifted a few feet and we leaned down over the lifelines to squint across the surface. We still couldn't see the other boat but we noticed ripples in the water. In another minute, aluminum paddles came into view. Finally, I spotted the figure of a man, leaning back in his gray rubber boat.

We called out to him as he ghosted across toward shore

"Hey, boat neighbor! If you don't have anything else to do tonight, why don't you come join us for dinner?"

"I'm headed in for a hike to the point," he answered. "That sounds great, though. I'll be back in a couple of hours." He returned as promised just in time for a big egg scramble—all our wilting veggies and most of our aging eggs tossed in the cast iron skillet and revived into nourishment.

He asked where we were from, where we were headed. The obvious questions. And we asked the same. He, Al, was from Half Moon Bay, a community just south of San Francisco, but he kept his boat,

Jubilee, in the harbor on Treasure Island. We nodded like we knew what he was talking about and I'm sure he saw right through us.

Al and his family had spent years sailing in the area and had been to Mexico many times. He seemed elated to share some local knowledge but did so respectfully, seafarer to seafarer. I'd already grown weary of the patronizing type, who assumed, based on age or gender, finances, or our lack of polished brightwork, that we didn't know what we were doing and it was their job to instruct us.

Al brought out a tablet and pulled up his electronic charts, pointed out some places to avoid on the way into San Francisco Bay, and then whisked south, fingers skimming along the shoreline, to share stories of some favorite Mexican destinations. I made a cryptic note in my journal—"Island in Mexico, south of Mazatlán,"—and hoped I'd remember what it meant when the time came. It seemed like years away at this rate.

"If you stop into Half Moon Bay after you're done in San Francisco," Al said, "give me a call. I've got some charts and guide books I'd love to pass along."

By the time he was ready to go, the wind had picked up a bit and blown the clouds away. We exchanged thanks and sent him back to his boat before the dark replaced the fog. We watched him row back in the chop, only now noticing how rough the bay was becoming.

Al had said that sometimes the area at the foot of the eastern cliffs was more protected in a gale and sure enough, soon after we saw him climb back aboard, we heard his anchor chain rising, watched him motor away and reset in the lee of the bluffs. We followed suit but the calm we sought was not to be found. The wind rose throughout the night and by morning, we were pitching about at the end of our anchor.

The needle of my anxiety swung to weather, a frequent fear.

"Small craft advisory," announced the weather radio robots and I paid close attention to what they said next. We already knew the wind was blowing. Drakes Bay offered little shelter and we were getting jerked around by the waves and pummeled by the gusts racing down the cliffs where we'd anchored for protection. *Jubilee* had already taken off for home and we figured if Al thought it was safe to be out in these conditions, it probably was. But I was still anxious. Would the entrance to the bay intensify the wind? What if things got hairy trying to pass Potato Patch Shoal?

We talked it over for a few more minutes. But the anchorage was getting more and more uncomfortable and we knew that if we waited much longer, we'd miss the flood tide and be stuck out for the night.

"We can always come back if it's bad out there," Bryan said, as he headed forward to haul up the anchor.

We can always come back. Reassuring words unless going back means that you just got your ass kicked so bad you'd rather lose miles and use fuel to return to a crappy anchorage than keep going.

We hugged the shoreline pretty tight and I kept an eye on the depth sounder. I checked the chart again and again, always rehearsing the direction to deeper water so I could steer without hesitation should my worries prove true.

How do you distinguish between fear and self-preservation? Tell the difference between anxiety and awareness? The ruling is issued only after the fact. If nothing bad happens, you were just neurotic, a worrywart. But if it all falls apart and you go down screaming, at least you have the satisfaction of knowing you were prepared for catastrophe. You can tie your Boy Scout knots all the way down.

Even in this wind, high but manageable, and these boisterous seas we still didn't clock more than six or seven knots. The twenty-five miles to the bay took forever and then, all at once, we were there.

First we spotted the lighthouse on Point Bonita. I focused my gaze at sea level, too distracted by my search for the buoys marking the safe passage around the shoal to notice the tips of the bridge towers floating above the clouds. From the west, the Golden Gate looked nothing like the postcards, like my vague childhood memories. Before long we'd cleared the northern approach, and shot out into the shipping channel. The bridge glowed in the afternoon sun and the city spread out beyond. We had sailed ourselves to San Francisco.

We called the whole crew out on deck, everyone bundled up against the wind, clumsy as astronauts in our thick layers and tight life jackets. We each took turns at the helm. The double-reefed main pivoted to starboard and held steady as we made the turn to run the channel.

Now time cannot move slowly enough. This moment of approach begs to be savored. See the way the light plays with the water. Notice how *LiLo* is leaping over the waves and watch your heart leap too with every lift of the bow. Just for this moment, no one is seasick or cranky. The concerns about tanker traffic and tonight's destination fade behind the brilliant swell of relief and accomplishment.

Too quickly, we passed under the glorious bridge, then once again under her shadow. Cars thundered above our heads, racing across toward solid ground. Kite surfers played in the lively chop and waved a generous welcome. The captain left the tiller to the crew and leaned in for a kiss. I leaned too, up toward the high side and tasted him, tasted it all—fresh air and the sea, salt, sun, and victory.

Chapter Six

Golden Gate and Evening Prayers

San Francisco, Sausalito, and Angel Island, California
October, 2013: New Moon, Waxing Crescent

People usually consider walking on water or in thin air a miracle. But I think the real miracle is not to walk either on water or in thin air, but to walk on earth.
—Thich Nhat Hanh

We'd been traveling along California's Lost Coast for several days with no internet access or phone service so we'd missed the news that the US Congress had failed to pass crucial funding legislation and had shut down the government.

We'd heard we needed a permit to anchor in Aquatic Park, our intended destination near San Francisco, and when we called the anchorage on our way into the bay, we got a recording that informed us of the shutdown and offered us the option to leave a message, implying wryly that it might be a while before we heard back. We took a chance and headed in anyway.

Aquatic Park is a unique anchorage. Just steps from the famous Ghirardelli Square, its waters are only open to sailboats, human-powered vessels, and swimmers. As we approached, we spotted a walkway atop a series of pilings. These define the area of the bay, but allow the current to flow through swiftly. We eased through the entrance and dropped our anchor.

"Should we worry that we don't have a permit?" I asked.

"I can't imagine so," said Bryan. "You said the government had shut down, right? Well then, there shouldn't be anyone around to notice that we don't have a permit. Besides, we're the only boat in the bay. There's plenty of room left."

I looked around. Bryan was right. We had the place to ourselves so I gave my worries a few minutes off. We rowed into shore for a celebration dinner and rowed back illuminated by the city lights.

The next morning, I woke to the sound of Bryan grinding coffee and a voice off our stern.

"*LiLo,* huh? Where are you from?" Bryan took his coffee to the cockpit and made small talk with the swimmer treading water near our hull.

"We're from Oregon, headed south for a year. What about you? Do you swim here often?"

"Every day!" The man's face was red from the cold water and a shiny black cap covered his head. "I've been swimming here for twenty years," he added, proudly. "Rain or shine, it does a body good! I even did the Escape from Alcatraz." He pulled a dripping hand from the water and gestured at the notorious island. "I swam all the way from there to here!"

His head bobbed up and down as he pumped his legs in the chilly bay, stirring up the energy to move on.

"Well, it was good to meet you. Good luck on your adventure!"

Bryan ducked under the dodger and stuck his head down below.

"This is great! It's like drinking my coffee while the seals swim by. Only these seals stop to chat."

Hannah and Meira had taken the opportunity to get dressed while Bryan was on deck. I threw on several layers and we took turns at the galley sink to brush our teeth. I pulled Hannah's hair back into a ponytail and combed the salty tangles smooth. Eventually, we were ready to go. Bryan dropped the dinghy into the water, one piece at a time, and stepped into the stern to hook the boat together. He hauled *Splitpea* back to the cockpit hand over hand along the lifelines and lowered the cable gate.

"Okay, who's first!"

Meira popped up out of the cabin, life jacket already secured. She handed her backpack down and moved across to her spot at the bow. Hannah was next and she stepped down, found her footing, and then took her seat in the stern. I finished filling my water bag and slipped it into my backpack along with my sandals and some snacks. I could hear *Splitpea* bumping against *LiLo*'s hull.

"I'll be right there!"

I swung my pack up onto the cockpit seat and climbed the companionway steps. After one more glance below and a quick mental checklist, I loaded the dropboards into their slot and snapped the lock through the hasp. I handed my bag down to Bryan who added it to the pile at his feet. I stepped over the toe rail and the oar locks and dropped, all in one motion, to my seat on the starboard stern. Bryan stood to secure the lifeline gate and gently shoved us clear. I tensed my core as the dinghy rocked beneath us and relaxed as Bryan sat again and dipped the oars, sending us smoothly toward shore.

When we were a few feet from land, Meira picked up the painter—the floating rope hooked to *Splitpea*'s bow—and twisted to face forward. She waited for the scrape of the sand on the hull and sprang from her seat to land beyond the water. She spun back toward us and hauled hard on the line to add to our shoreward momentum. Bryan stepped up to his knees in the surf and heaved on the bow until it was clear of the tide.

Hannah waited in her seat while I stood and stepped—thwart seat to bow seat to sand. She followed me to the ground and we all went to work. We shucked our life jackets and handed them to Bryan, who tucked them into the compartment under the center seat. While I grabbed the dinghy towel and headed toward the road, he tied *Splitpea*'s painter to the nearest piling and hefted her beyond the high tide line so she wouldn't bash into the dock in the swell. Once at the road, we found a curb and perched, passed the towel down the line. Each crew member dried and dusted sandy feet and balanced stork-like to put on shoes without getting too much grit in the soles.

I spotted a uniformed park ranger picking up trash down the beach.

"Hey, Bryan, I'm going to go check in with that ranger. Maybe the government is open again."

I walked down the way and caught his attention.

"Is the shutdown over already?" I said.

"No, I just came down this morning to check on things. I'm not really supposed to be here, but I didn't have anywhere else to go." He looked a little sheepish, as if I'd caught him cheating at Chutes and Ladders.

"So can we get a permit to stay in the bay?" I pointed out to *LiLo*, who swung gently on her anchor. "We're hoping to be here a few days and want to make sure we get the right permissions."

"Well, there's no one around to give you a permit," he said, "but that means there's also no one around to ticket you. I can't *officially* give you permission to stay, but then, I'm not *officially* here."

I reported back to Bryan, who was just lacing up his shoes.

"That's good enough for me. Let's take off, then!"

We'd heard that we should lock up our dinghy in this public area, so the first stop was at a nearby chandlery for a length of stainless cable. They had just what we needed and even offered to crimp a couple of eyelets into the ends for us. We followed them into the workshop and watched as the craftsman bent and pressed the cable. The kids and I hung out near the book shelves while Bryan ran the cable back to *Splitpea* and locked her to the pier.

After following our noses—and online directions—to a European bakery, we walked the three miles up to the Golden Gate Bridge. Only a mile or so into the walk, I started having pain in my hip. Bryan carried my bag for me for a while to see if that might help. The stiff muscle didn't loosen up, but it didn't seem to be getting any worse either, so we kept moving. We walked through Presidio National Park, closed due to the shutdown, and on up to Golden Gate Park at the foot of the famous bridge. The city of San Francisco operates the museums and public spaces in that beautiful location, so we were glad to finally find interpretive centers and public restrooms open for business.

We continued on across the bridge to the first arch and stopped for a family conference. Our energy was beginning to flag, but we checked the bus schedules and decided to walk the rest of the way across the bridge and catch the bus back to the city. We'd worked so hard to sail under the bridge; walking over it felt easy by comparison.

We stopped at the top of the span to spot *LiLo* at anchor in the bay. It seemed unlikely she'd have dragged through the tight sea wall opening, but I was still relieved to see her safe.

We finally made it to the north side of the bridge, found the bus stop, and settled down in some nearby shade for a break. I pulled out a book and read a couple of chapters aloud while we waited, but soon the bus pulled up to whisk us back across the water. We must have looked completely bewildered; the bus driver asked us twice if we were lost.

"We're not lost, exactly," I said. "We just don't know where we're going."

We decided to get off near Lombard street and walk the four blocks up to the famous strip and down the hairpin curves. At the bottom of the hill were more hills. We turned to head back down to the waterfront and rewarded ourselves with fish and chips and hot fudge sundaes before rowing back to the boat for the night.

We'd expected to wake up sore and weary from our long day, but we had plenty of energy for new adventures. We rowed back in and walked up to the cable car station. There wasn't room for very many splurges in our tight budget, but we couldn't resist a ride on the rails. As we stood in the ticket line, a passerby approached.

"Any chance you could use these two extra tickets? We accidentally bought too many and just want to give them away to another family."

We carried our good fortune with us onto the cars and found a place to stand for the trip through the city. We rode to the end of the line and ducked into the cable car museum on top of Nob Hill. We read the informative signs and moved to the observation balcony to watch the cables turning around gigantic sheaves. I pointed these out to the crew.

"Look! On top of *LiLo*'s mast she's got sheaves just like that for the halyards. Only way smaller, of course."

I'd read about cable car maintenance and how all scheduled repairs were done at night. So I was surprised to see one of the turning cables stop. The monitors must have spotted the beginnings of a frayed line. We watched as men began to move into place and prepare for a splice. They cut the cable, loosened several strands on each side and, working as a team, unwound them back almost fifty feet. They overlapped the loosened ends of the cable and began to wind them back together along the whole ninety-foot length of the splice. They propped the cable up on sawhorses and several men held it taut while one hammered the strands into place. Each movement was swift and efficient. He swung two sledge hammers in wide matching arcs, arms fully extended and stretching with the force. *Bam.* The hammers hit the cable precisely in the center. He rocked them back, moved forward a turn, and swung them in again. *Bam.*

It takes a team of these skilled workers several hours to complete a splice, so we didn't stay to watch the whole thing. But I stood for long minutes witnessing the strength and accuracy of the men below. They worked together as a magnificent mechanism. Not a single one failed to twist the cable in time. And every hammer blow was perfect.

We finally turned away and headed down the road to Chinatown. The scents from the tea shops and eateries reminded us how long it had been since breakfast. We found our way to a dim sum shop and sat down on the balcony overlooking a busy alley where paper lanterns and laundry swung on cords across the narrow street. After so much walking, we enjoyed the slow-paced meal, savoring each new dish that came our way. But by the time we'd tucked away the green tea ice cream, we were ready to be on the move again.

There are so many sacred spaces carved out in this beautiful city but I'd read about the labyrinth in the Grace Cathedral sanctuary and always wanted to see it for myself. I convinced the crew to walk the mile back up Nob Hill to the church. The main entrance was closed for construction, so we headed in a side door and found our way up a narrow back staircase to the sanctuary. As we reached the top, we heard voices singing.

"Are they really piping in music to this hallway?" I asked. "That seems strange."

We bustled out of the stairway into the back of the sanctuary and immediately stilled our voices. In the chancel at the far end of the colossal space, a boys choir stood singing. Their clear soprano voices soared out over the resonant organ. We tiptoed past the baptismal font and across the labyrinth to find seats in the middle of the small crowd. We later learned that though the cathedral holds an evening prayer service every day, we'd happened along on the one day of the week they offer evensong.

I closed my eyes and soaked in the music, opened them up to take in the beauty of the room. Brightly colored ribbons hung illuminated from the high ceiling, trailing down like fireworks over our heads. Evening light poured in through the stained glass, and the glow touched each face. Through the tears in my eyes, I saw Hannah wipe her cheek. After the last "amen" we sat in silence. Slowly, one by one, we shouldered our bags and walked away, a little bit lighter for the moment.

Sailing away from an anchorage is ancient magic. We practice this ritual whenever we can. The morning we left Aquatic Bay was a perfect opportunity. Wind and current aligned to give us easy conditions for the tricky maneuver.

Bryan raised the jib and I steered us slowly west as he hauled in the anchor. As soon as the heavy chain was up off the bottom and the anchor flukes free, he called back to me from the bow, "Fall off the wind!"

I pulled the tiller toward me and the bow shifted slowly—northwest, north-northwest, due north, north-northeast. The ebb current set us toward the west so I steered to starboard a little more while Bryan hurried back and raised the main. The extra sail gave us just enough speed and steerage to slip through the break in the seawall and we glided on out into the bay. We had a few minutes of glorious sailing but soon the current strengthened and the west wind faded. Instead of firing up the engine to motor into our intended destination at Angel Island, we decided to adjust our plans and sailed up into Richardson Bay for the night. The bay shallowed quickly but the bottom leveled out at twelve to fifteen feet across the whole harbor. Perfect depth for anchoring with a nice muddy holding ground.

On the San Francisco side of the bay, industry and expensive moorages consume most of the available anchorages. So here, near glossy Sausalito, cruising boats and local liveaboards vied for space in the attractive bay. Some boats looked as if they hadn't moved in years. Green slime draped over rope anchor rodes and coated the listing waterlines. Piles of tarp-covered junk lined the side decks and jerry cans hung willy-nilly from sooty hooks. We motored slowly among the vessels, looking for decent swing room. I calculated the tides and depths.

"We're about halfway through the ebb so we shouldn't drop more than about three feet or gain more than the same."

Bryan did his own calculations for the scope we needed in this protected cove. "If we drop the anchor at ten feet, we'll need our chain and, let's see ... " His voice trailed off as he ticked numbers on his fingers.

Finally, we found a spot. Not too shallow, not too deep; not too close to the other boats or too far away from land for us to row in. I glanced through the binoculars at the shoreline and found a potential landing spot in a public park. As evidenced by all the boats anchoring out for free, the water belongs to all of us. The tideline is legally public as well, but the shore is usually privately owned and we didn't want to trespass. Once we found a spot, it didn't take long to get our anchor down. We settled in for a warm meal and a peaceful evening.

The next morning, Bryan and I rowed in together, then split up for independent errands. I'd located a local yoga studio online and found my way there to stretch and bend body and soul. Bryan walked along the waterfront a mile or so to the nearest marine store. We met after my class for a quick cup of coffee that stretched into a longer than expected brunch.

By the time we were back to the boat and ready to leave, the ebb current was running again, so we motored the few miles through Raccoon Strait to a secluded anchorage on Angel Island and took the dinghy to shore for an evening stroll.

We landed on a small beach, climbed a stone wall to the road, and walked up through an old military fort to the Angel Island Immigration Station. The buildings—former dormitories, prisons, and hospitals—stood empty around quiet meadows, the silence only broken by the footsteps of grazing deer. We didn't know if the historic site was closed because of the government shutdown or the lateness of the hour.

We read the words on the official markers and pieced together the tragic story of the events in this beautiful place. Hundreds of thousands of immigrants, primarily from East Asia, were processed at this site, known as the "Ellis Island of the West."

Unlike Ellis Island, however, where the vast majority of new arrivals were allowed to enter the United States, the facility at Angel Island was established in the wake of a series of racist immigration laws passed specifically to exclude Chinese immigrants.

At one point, the area had been a military reserve but in 1905 the War Department transferred 20 acres of the island to the Department of Labor and Commerce, who destroyed a Coast Miwok village site and burial grounds in order to build the immigration station and detention center.

From 1910 to 1940, when a fire prompted a move to a facility in San Francisco, immigrants, predominantly from China, were held here, often for weeks or months in unsafe and unsanitary conditions. They were mistreated, humiliated, harshly interrogated, and traumatized. Many were turned away.

Years later, the facility was converted into a state park and the buildings condemned. Before they could be demolished, a park ranger discovered Chinese poetry partially hidden under layers of paint. Detainees had used ink and pencil or carved their words into the walls to express their grief, rage, despair, and hope. Over 200 poems have since been recovered and restored and much work is still being done, especially by the Chinese American community, to preserve and publicize the stories of those who were held in this place.

We'd sailed 700 miles and entered this harbor, sure of our welcome. They came across thousands of miles of open ocean, only to be greeted with suspicion, rejection, and harm. By unspoken agreement, we joined the silence of the site, trying in our small way to honor the pain and perseverance of those who had come here before us.

Chapter Seven

LIFE AT WALKING SPEED

Half Moon Bay, Monterey Bay, and Morro Bay, California
October, 2013: First Quarter, Waxing Gibbous

*Care is renewed
for the one who must very often send
his weary spirit over the binding of the waves*
—Anonymous poem from Exeter Book

"Laundry time!" Meira said after dinner that night.

"But it's dark. It's almost bedtime," I said.

"I know," she whispered. "This way none of the other boats will see my underwear."

She dug around in the laundry bag by the V-berth and emerged clutching a small bundle under her T-shirt.

"The wash bucket is tied to the stern," Bryan said. "Here, take a headlamp so you can see what you're doing."

I called up after her. "Don't forget to rinse in fresh water or you'll be itchy from the salt."

"I *know*, Mom!"

The night was calm but morning brought wake after rolling wake as San Francisco Bay came to life. Tug boats darted out to assist incoming cargo barges. Container ships passed in the channel, their wake gentle and steady, a long slow swell. Sightseeing boats and shiny, white motor yachts zoomed close by and set us rocking wildly, once when their backwash passed the first time, again when its echo bounced back from the shore. Meira jumped out of her bunk to bring in her clothes and hung what was still damp all around the cabin.

I rowed Bryan in and dropped him off for a solitary hike up Mt. Livermore and then spent most of the morning catching and stowing our household goods as they flew across the boat. We'd gotten lax about keeping the boat shipshape in the few days off the ocean and now, as *LiLo* rolled wildly in the passing waves, every misplaced item (and a few we'd thought were secure) were demanding our attention.

"I've got the galley," I shouted during one particularly violent swell. "Hannah, can you grab the settee cushions and wedge those books back into place?"

The drying clothes hung straight while the boat revolved under them. The silverware drawer jumped in its track and I hip-checked it closed and clamped vise-grips to the stove's sea rail to hold the kettle in place.

"Ugh!" Hannah groaned. "I can't even sit still! I might as well stand by the window and let you know when another boat goes by."

"Well, I see your dad walking down the beach. I'll go pick him up and we can get out of here!"

We caught the end of the ebb tide and motored back out under the bridge and down the coast to Half Moon Bay, only a few miles south. We came in around Pillar Point just at sunset and it was all I could do to tear my eyes away from the view and help navigate into the protected anchorage. I kept looking up from the charts to take "just one more photo" as the sky deepened from pink to orange to red and faded into evening.

A little nervously, I called Al, who we'd met in Drakes Bay.

"Hi, Al. This is Bethany from *LiLo*. You said to call when we came into town. Well, we're here!"

"Yes! Welcome! I'm so glad you called. I'm betting you could use some showers and laundry facilities. I'm busy tomorrow, but Tuesday I'm all yours. How about I pick you up in the morning and bring you back to my place for the day?"

"Oh, goodness! That would be wonderful! We *do* really need showers. You can probably smell us from there."

We were glad for a quiet day aboard after the busy days in San Francisco. In the morning, while the crew slept only inches away, Bryan started water in the kettle, prepped his AeroPress, and ground some coffee.

He poked his head into the V-berth and whispered, "Are you ready for a cup of tea or are you still dozing?"

"Oh, I'll never turn down a cup of tea," I said, reaching for my glasses at the top of my hanging locker. I scooted up in bed, ducking to keep clear of the low ceiling, and wedged my pillow in for padding against the sharp corners of the locker. I pulled out my Kindle from where I kept it between the mattress and the hull and flipped through the free books I'd downloaded in Sausalito.

"You look cozy," Bryan said, leaning over for a kiss. "I'm putting your tea right here on the locker. No rush to get up. We're not going anywhere today."

I listened as he walked back across the cabin, lifted the drop boards, and stepped out into the cockpit. I reached over and loosened the latches on my porthole and lifted the window open. The air felt fresh but not cold. I glanced out Bryan's porthole to the west—clear skies all the way to the horizon.

I couldn't wait any longer to use the head. I pulled my legs free of the comforter and swung them over Bryan's side of the bunk, past his pillow, and down to the bag of laundry on the floor between our hanging lockers, pivoting my body to follow. I crouched to fit between lintel and threshold and tugged hard on the head door handle where the swollen wood always stuck. Once I was done peeing and pumping the head, I propped open the porthole and took an extra minute in front of the mirror to pull my hair back into a couple of braids.

I joined Bryan out in the warming sun. "Looks like it's going to be a great day. If you don't have any projects you need to do below, I think I'll see if the kids can get some math done."

"That sounds good. What if I get them going while you make breakfast?"

I shoved the dirty dishes aside and held the kettle under the faucet, pumping with my other hand and counting out of habit—twenty-five strokes filled the pot for another round of coffee and tea. I moved out of the way to let Hannah by and into the head, tucked myself tight against the galley when she came back through, and repeated the motion for Meira a few minutes later.

"How about pancakes?" I asked.

"That sounds good," Meira said, plopping down in the corner of the settee.

"Well, then you're going to have to move. I need to get into the corner cupboard for the mix."

"Oh, yeah. I forgot." Meira scooted down the bench and held the cushion back while I rummaged in the locker.

"Got it, thanks!"

Meira shoved the cushion back into place and pulled out its neighbor. "Want anything while I'm in here, Hannah?" she asked, rummaging around in the locker of craft and school supplies.

"Yes! Can you get my colored pencils and my green coloring book." Hannah glanced my way and added, reluctantly, "And you should probably pull out our school stuff while you're in there."

We had planned for the kids to keep up on math during sea passages but the curriculum we brought required computer access and with all our bouncing around in the North Pacific, the laptop's hard drive couldn't spin steadily enough to run the software. Today, though, in a protected anchorage with nowhere else to go, it was time for all the work we couldn't do at sea.

I flipped a pancake on the griddle and stuck my head up the hatch.

"After breakfast, I thought I'd write a bit. You good out here?"

"Yeah, I realized I need to change the oil at some point but I can sort out the stern lazarette first and tear into the engine later."

Friends frequently asked us what it was like to live the dream. "The simple life," they said. I looked around our compact cabin. We each had a bed to stretch out in, room for clothes and books and tools, water and food. We had enough space—as long as only one person wanted to move at a time. And on most days, our only tasks were life's simple necessities—cooking, cleaning, learning, resting. But in a home this small, with the pressures of constant movement and travel, the simple life was anything but easy.

I shoved the coffee press off the icebox cover, picked up my tea and the syrup bottle. "Here, hold these for me so they don't spill," I said to Hannah, then slid the icebox lid open just enough to reach in for a stick of butter. Last night's dirty dishes tilted against the wall and rattled back as I settled the cover flush with the rest of the counter.

Hannah took a sip of my tea and reached across the boat to set it down again.

"Anything else I can do to help?"

"Nope," I smiled at her to soften my words. "Just stay out of the way."

When Al called to say he was waiting at his yacht club, on the northern edge of the bay, we piled into *Splitpea* with our grocery bags and laundry and headed over. As we approached he waved us into a spot at a small dock a few yards from shore. Once on the float, I turned completely around, looking for the gangplank.

Al grinned at my confusion. "We have to take the ferry across," he said. "Come, look." Al stepped off the dock onto what looked like a tiny garden bridge jutting off the end of the float. I followed his lead and stepped onto the platform. Arched fences guarded each side; both ends were open and worn astroturf kept us from slipping. When the whole crew had squeezed aboard, Al flipped a switch and sent us across the water to the landing.

"We use this to get back and forth. It's attached to an underwater cable and runs on this little motor here." He pointed out the mechanism and the crew leaned carefully over to take a look.

Once on land, we walked through the club house and out the front door and crowded into his car for the ride to his home.

Al had already anticipated our needs. "I thought some of you could stay at the house and get showers and laundry going while Bethany came with me to the store."

"That sounds great to me," I said. "We could use a bit of internet access too, if that's okay. Hannah wants to download some new books and I'd like a few podcasts. And, hey—any chance you have a fax machine we can use? We're trying to sort out some issues with our mortgage."

"No problem. I'll give you the wireless code at the house and we'll get you all set up. I know it's tough to take care of business offline."

Once at his house, Al pulled out snacks and pointed the way to all the facilities. By the time he and I got back from a grand provisioning at the local grocery store, the laundry was drying and the crew was clean. I took my turn in the shower and came out into the living room where Al was showing Bryan pictures from his many sailing trips to Mexico.

"This is near La Paz, in the sea of Cortez. We loved the snorkeling there and up at Loreto as well. But the best is Isla Isabel."

He pulled out a chart and I leaned in to look, eager for more of his suggestions.

"Right here," he pointed at a speck off the mainland coast, "about halfway from Mazatlán to Puerto Vallarta is the most beautiful place anywhere. You're going to love it. They call it 'The Galapagos of Mexico' and there are iguanas and crabs and blue footed boobies. There's a bay on the south side, but the best place to anchor is off the eastern shore, just south of the rocks they call *Las Monas*. If there's a storm, you don't want to be there at all. But in calm weather, there's nothing like it. You can see thirty feet to the ocean floor, like you were floating on glass."

For almost six weeks, we'd been running from bad weather and chasing summer. For a moment, I stopped to remember all the wonder that still lay ahead.

"You know, my wife's health keeps us pretty close to home these days. I know we'll never sail *Jubilee* back there again. Let me see what charts I have around. You might as well get some use out of them."

Al dug into a drawer full of papers and books and plopped a stack of cruising guides into my lap.

"You're the navigator, right? Enjoy!"

We spent a day stowing all our food and clean clothes and waiting out a wicked swell. The same conditions that make Half Moon Bay a favorite for surfers make it tricky for sailors. I checked the data from the deep sea buoys and looked at the surf forecast for near shore predictions. Our next intended port, Monterey Bay, was about eighteen or twenty hours south, which either meant leaving midday for a dawn arrival or departing at midnight and coming in at dusk. We decided to leave as soon as the seas were calm. Never waste good traveling weather.

I flipped on NOAA weather a few times throughout the day and when it sounded like the swell was dying down, we made a plan to haul anchor around midnight. Right after dinner, Bryan and I went to bed and dozed to the companionable sounds of the crew doing the dishes. Meira was still awake a few hours later when Bryan got up, so she helped him navigate out the entrance and past a couple of shallow reefs before heading off to bed. The calm seas meant slow motoring but an easy ride. I got a few more hours of sleep and came on deck for a pre-dawn watch. The black sky faded to blue as the sun rose over the land. A breeze picked up from the south and ripples spread across the quiet swells. Our wake rolled out behind us in a "V," the tail of the autumn migration.

Further north, I'd spent every off-watch moment in bed, the safest place in rough conditions. Today was calmer, but the motion was too unpredictable to settle into a project like knitting or washing dishes. I was still adjusting to a life at walking speed, still adapting to this slow, floating pilgrimage.

Before we left, I wrote in my journal, "To what purpose, this fruit-basket-upset of my life? If it is change, I could join a gym. If it is novelty, I could just buy a new couch. No, this is incarnating the intention to live *wide awake*. Forcing myself into a condition where to fall asleep means to truly drift away."

When travel was an occasional part of my life, I coped by zoning out to the radio on a road trip or napping on the train, pressing pause on real life until the traveling day was over.

Now all my days had become travel days. I didn't need a motivational poster to remind me: "Life is a journey, not a destination." It was stitched into the fabric of my hours, but I wasn't sure I liked it.

When Bryan's brother and sister-in-law heard we'd be passing by Monterey, they contacted Stephanie, a friend of theirs who lived in the area. Stephanie immediately asked if there was any way she and her family could help. I jumped at the offer.

"Would you mind receiving a package for us? My parents want to ship us some things and without knowing where we'll be staying, we can't tell them where to send the box."

"We can do better than that. How about you let us know when you will be around and we'll skip work and take you sightseeing?"

We were all excited about the prospect of traveling inland faster than our feet could carry us. So in the morning, we rushed through breakfast and showers in the marina restroom and hid the clutter that always accumulates at sea—foulweather gear, life jackets, navigation equipment, dirty dishes.

When the phone call came that our ride had arrived, we walked up to the parking lot to meet them. They pulled out several gifts—the package from my parents and some treats from Bryan's family.

"Do you want to come down and see the boat before we go?" I asked.

"Could we?" Stephanie asked. "That would be great!"

Hannah welcomed our guests below. "Come down inside and look at my bunk. I have everything I need right here and the locker underneath is *full* of books!"

I showed off the compact galley. "And that's where we hang the table when we need a little more space in the cabin. Bryan designed it to slide together like that. Isn't it clever?"

A tour of a space as small as *LiLo* never takes long, so soon we were back at the van talking over plans for the day.

"I thought I'd take you on 17-Mile Drive down to the Carmel Mission. The drive is a toll road along the ocean with beautiful views of the sea." Stephanie laughed as she realized what she was saying. "Although, you probably get to look at the sea all the time."

"Yes, but not from the shore side," I said. "I'm sure we'll love it!"

As we drove along the winding coastline, I stared out past the rocks. The sea went by in a blur and I made mental notes of the hazards and landmarks we'd be passing on our next leg of the journey. We stopped for a few moments on Carmel Beach and dipped our toes in the sand.

"We can stay here longer if you want," Stephanie said. "But we can come here any time and you probably get plenty of time on beaches these days."

"Yeah, I think we've got enough sand in our shoes and the kids are probably getting hungry."

"I know just the place. Do you like Mediterranean food?"

"We like anything we don't have to cook!"

After lunch, we drove over to the Carmel Mission, where the cashier waved us in for free.

"There's a wedding going on in the chapel and by the time they're done, you'll only have another hour to look around. Enjoy!"

She pointed the way through the dim gift shop to the arched wooden door at the back. We ducked out into the sunny garden and began a meandering circuit of the grounds and the structures surrounding the central chapel. Old photographs, sketches, and tiny captions lined the walls of the buildings. We read the history piecemeal—a mishmash of facts about the mission founder, Junípero Serra, the artwork, and recent restoration.

The paths were empty and we wandered alone until we came out into a courtyard with a statue of Serra at the center. A docent stood near the statue sharing some of the stories of the place.

At the time, I didn't notice the stories that had been omitted—the violent acts of displacement, forced conversion, conscription, and genocide Serra and his company perpetrated against the people indigenous to this area.

I found out later that in 2015, despite the atrocities committed throughout the Spanish Missions in California, Pope Francis declared Junípero Serra a saint.

Today, the Ohlone Costanoan Esselen Nation, the Esselen Tribe of Monterey County, and the Costanoan Tumsen Carmel Tribe—descendants of those devastated by the Carmel Mission—are still working to recover and pass on their culture, language, and land.

The next morning a marching band startled me awake blasting "Yankee Doodle" over the water. I poked my head out into the cockpit just in time to hear a pianist on the wharf banging out "O Solo Mio." A few minutes later, the music was joined by the sharp crack of cannon fire and the echoes bounced back from the sea wall. Confused, but preoccupied, we dressed and started in on our to-do list.

Splitpea was looking a little bedraggled, so Bryan took advantage of our time at the dock to mend some worn places and touch up her paint. I kicked the crew out into the cockpit so I could get some work done down below. Hannah took her crocheting with her and promptly dropped her crochet hook overboard. We could just see it glinting on the bottom, six or eight feet down. She and Meira tied a retrieval magnet to a line and tried picking it up, but after a few attempts conceded defeat.

"I don't think it's magnetic," Hannah said. By this time, we were all crouched on the dock peering over the side.

"Maybe we could snag it with our fish net," Meira suggested.

"Can't hurt to give it a try," Hannah said.

She popped up to the stern, pulled the net out of the locker, and stepped back over to the dock.

"Here, Dad. You have the longest arms."

Bryan dipped the net all the way down and fished around.

"Don't scoop the sand over it, Dad!"

"I'll try," Bryan said, sweeping the net gently through the water.

"We might have to tape the net to the boat hook to make it a little longer," Meira suggested.

"Wait just a second. I think I got the hook caught in the mesh."

We held our breath until it reached the surface and Hannah plucked it out of the water.

"Yay! Thanks, Dad!"

The small victory bolstered us for the rest of our work. By dinnertime, we were ready to relax. We walked up to the wharf only to discover each restaurant serving clam chowder samples in honor of the town's Italian Festival. We went from door to door tasting and comparing. We weren't the only ones out for an evening stroll; several groups walked by in Civil War-era costumes. I glanced up toward town and saw a small encampment, pots hanging over fire pits and men strolling through in gray and blue uniforms. The confusion of the day lifted.

"Oh, that explains the marching band."

"And the cannons!"

"And the pianist must have been here for the Italian Festival. We picked a busy weekend to sail through!"

The next morning, the competing festivities wound up again. "Yankee Doodle" went to town, "O Solo Mio" answered, and the cannons kept time—"boom boom boom." A group of Zumba dancers added to the din, whooping over their amplified music on the plaza and the sea lions on the breakwater joined the chorus. I shook my head and got back to work.

"What is wrong with the stove? The pancakes keep spilling off the back of the griddle." I turned around in frustration and grabbed for a paper towel. "Now there's batter all over the place."

I checked the gimbal hardware to see if the oven was locked and leveled.

"It looks like the whole boat is listing. What's up with that?" I glanced out the window to get a stable reference point.

Bryan stood and squatted a bit, testing the slant with his knees.

"You know, I just emptied the water from the port tank into the main one. I'm betting that's throwing us off a little. Let me see what I can do."

He pulled out a tool bag and rummaged in the side pocket.

"Here!" He turned with a grin. "I knew I saved these chain plate ends for a reason." He tucked the nub of metal under the edge of the skillet. "That shouldn't burn or melt. Try another pancake."

I ladled another batch onto the pan and watched the circles form and hold steady.

"That did it!" I wagged my finger at the kids in their bunks. "Now everybody stay right where you are so breakfast doesn't run away again."

Later in the morning, I belayed Bryan while he climbed the mast to adjust the anchor light. Then, while we had easy access to water, we washed the salt spray off the dodger windows and filled the water tanks. I ran to the store and picked up a new electric heater. Ours had stopped working along the way and, though we couldn't run it without shore power, we loved having the option on cold days at the dock. We picked up a bit more fresh produce from a nearby market, took advantage of the free showers in the marina, and stopped to watch the otters drifting by our slip.

Anticipating the long watches ahead, we finished our work and took a few minutes to relax before heading out to sea. The crew hung out aboard soaking up every bit of available screen time and Bryan and I went out for a quick date at Starbucks. After all the novelty we'd been experiencing, it was nice to sit in such a familiar setting, recharging my phone and myself before the next passage.

Bryan's energy seemed limitless. "Ready to go back to sea, sailors?" he called as we stepped back aboard. "We'd better get going while we can."

We refilled our tanks at the fuel dock and motored slowly past the sea lions on the breakwater out into a setting sun and dying wind. We missed the quiet pleasure of sailing, but needed the calm weather for our trip around Point Conception.

Rounding the point at the dogleg of California is a little like crossing the Columbia River Bar—it can be calm and easy, or it can kill you. Northwest gales whip around the cape and the warring currents confuse the seas where the land turns the corner north of Santa Barbara Channel.

Before Cabrillo named the headland Cabo de Galera, before Vizcaíno dubbed it Punta de la Limpia Concepción, the Chumash people called it Humqaq, which means "The Raven Comes." They revered this area as the "Western Gate," a sacred space where spirits pass into the realm of the dead, and they work to care for it still. Many sailors consider it "The Cape Horn of the Pacific," and plan passages carefully to steer clear of this dangerous coastline.

I plotted a course from Monterey to San Miguel, the outermost island in the Santa Barbara Channel and hoped staying well offshore would keep us safe.

That night during a watch change I grumbled to Bryan over the drone of the engine. "Why isn't there a West Coast Intracoastal Waterway? We could travel by day and sleep at night and we wouldn't have to choose between sailing through a gale or motoring through a calm. At this rate, we're going to have to stop in Morro Bay for more gas before we round the point."

"It's okay, Beth. It's hard to be a sailing purist on the Northwest Coast but if this is what it takes to get south of the point before winter really socks us in, I'm good with that. If there's any wind at all, I'll put up the main and see if we can at least motor sail part of the way."

About two o'clock the next afternoon, we neared Morro Bay. The entrance was impressive, with a huge sea stack and breaking waves on the jetties. There was a disabled motor boat just outside the channel and we drove closer and called them on the radio to offer help. They'd already contacted the harbor patrol and a few minutes later we saw a little runabout splashing out to tow them in. We motored up and back the narrow channel looking for a fuel dock. All we could see was a tall commercial fuel pier, so we found a public dock with a three-hour limit and tied up.

We walked our gas cans down to the pier but the fuel attendant was busy fixing the plumbing for the live crab tank at the neighboring fish market. We waited around for a few minutes until the smells from the market overcame us and we ordered some fish and chips, leaning over as we ate to guard our meal from diving seagulls.

We finished eating about the time the employee was finished with the repairs, so we got some gas and hauled the heavy jugs back to the boat. We must have been quite the sight, Bryan carrying two tanks—"for balance"—the crew sharing the load, and me, bumping along with the last one strapped to the frame of our rolling shopping cart.

Just after we got back to the dock, the harbor patrol boat stopped by. I expected him to remind us about the three-hour limit and encourage us to move along, but he pulled alongside and asked if we needed anything.

"I've been trying to figure out how to get my propane tanks refilled," Bryan said. "Is there a spot in town within walking distance?"

"I can do you one better," the patrolman replied. "Let me just dock the boat and I'll drive you over myself." A few minutes later, he pulled up in the parking lot in his patrol truck and Bryan and I hopped in with our empty tank. He drove us to the fill station at the local U-Haul center and exchanged small town gossip with the attendant until we were ready to go.

Back at the boat, Bryan lifted the tank aboard and lashed it into place. I stayed behind on the dock to thank the patrolman.

"We really needed that, thank you. It means a lot that you would help."

"No problem," he said with a smile. "It's what we do. Stay safe out there!"

Chapter Eight

The Shape of Life Left Behind

Point Conception, Channel Islands, and Catalina Island, California
October 2013: Full Moon, Waning Gibbous,
Third Quarter, Waning Crescent

Only messy people have a heritage.
—Dr. David Brauner

The afternoon winds were still blowing hard by the time we left Morro Bay. The winds were predicted to die down before we reached Point Conception but we'd heard it could be rough regardless of the surrounding waters and I was skittish.

Soon after we crossed the bar the gusts began to fade into an evening calm. Bryan and I were starting to establish a more consistent watch pattern. I took the evening hours and he navigated through the night. By dawn, we were south of the cape, only a few hours away from our destination and reveling in the sudden summery warmth. We'd rounded the point in the still of the night, just as we planned, and by midmorning, we pulled into Cuyler Harbor on the northwest coastline of San Miguel, and dropped anchor.

We'd heard through the cruiser grapevine that the island was closed due to the government shutdown. But we'd also heard that, even on ordinary days, visitors weren't allowed to venture off the beach without a ranger escort. We spotted other boaters heading in and assumed it was safe to go for a walk on the sand. So after a few hours of rest, we launched *Splitpea* and rowed into shore. The evening air turned purple around us as we wandered. We stepped carefully to avoid shells in our path, stopping to turn over first this one, then that. We steered clear of the seal pup rookery, giggling quietly as they inchwormed their bulgy bodies across the soft sand.

A tall man in a ranger uniform appeared through a rift in the island's steep center. We paused in place as he approached.

"I'm so sorry," he began. "The island is closed because of the shutdown."

"Even the beach?" Bryan asked.

"Yes, even the beach. Technically, you're not even allowed to anchor in the bay unless you're here to fish or are taking refuge because of engine trouble. I'm assuming you're fishing, right?"

We grinned a silent response, united in the ridiculousness of the situation. The US government, which usually pays the solitary ranger to guide visitors around the island, was now paying him the same wage to keep them off. We could almost see his eyes rolling as he continued, "It sounds like the shutdown is winding up. If you have time to stick around, listen to the radio tomorrow, and if the closure ends, call me on your VHF the next morning. I'll be happy to show you around."

We spent the next day aboard, a welcome respite from our recent busyness. Every few hours, we flipped on the radio to listen to the news. The US Senate passed the spending bill and we, energized by the mild suspense, listened live to the House of Representatives as they too voted to end the crisis. From our floating home, miles from the mainland, a tiny cheer went up. We set an early alarm and went to bed.

The next morning, as promised, we called the ranger on our radio. A few other boaters in the bay listened in and contacted us after our conversation to ask if they could tag along on our hike. We all set off for shore together, but their powerful outboard quickly outpaced our little rowboat. Halfway in, they slowed down, tossed us a towline, and pulled us into the beach close to the gully trail. The surf was higher than where we had planned to land and in the scuffle between boat and shore I lost my balance and fell, drenching my pants. I squelched up the dune with the rest of the adventurers and we found our way to the Nidever Canyon Trail and from there, the mile or so to the ranger station.

Ranger Ian met us and gave us a brief introduction to the island. We huddled around a trail map and chose a hike to Harris Point, about six miles round trip. Hannah and Meira requested Junior Ranger booklets and immediately set about filling in the pages.

Ian got all of us moving in the right direction, letting the sailors from the other boat take the lead and joining our family at the rear. The kids walked haphazardly, one eye on their papers, one eye on the trail. Ian grinned and adjusted his pace to their steps. As we walked through the changing landscapes, he shared stories of San Miguel, speaking of the island as one would an old friend. He talked about Cabrillo, the first European explorer to land on the island, the sheep ranchers who homesteaded from 1850 to 1948, and about the filmmakers of *Mutiny on the Bounty* who planted the four palm trees on the sandy beach.

About halfway to the point, Ian said, "Let's pause here for a minute," and I looked around to see why we'd stopped.

Ian gestured to the ground under our feet. "You're standing in the middle of an important archaeological discovery. This is a shell midden, a garbage heap, basically. The first people on this island, the Chumash people, worked and ate near here starting over 10,000 years ago. The mussel shells and scraps of woven grass they discarded here are a treasure trove for modern archeologists. The differences in the shell layers tell us a lot about the changes to the civilization and climate over the centuries, almost like rings in a tree."

We stood in the path until our eyes saw what his did. White crescents of sea shells poked out of the soil and hid behind tufts of grass, evidence of the ancient community. With every step, we connected more firmly to the past. So much had changed, but the people who once lived here sat on this hill, worked together to feed their children, gossiped about their neighbors, laughed and grieved together just as we do. We fell silent for a moment. I could almost hear ghostly voices in the wind.

A bit farther up the path, Ian stopped us again, and this time he pointed to a collection of strange shapes jutting out of the soil. The chalky white formations lay twisted on the ground like broken statues in a Roman ruin.

"Welcome to the Caliche Forest," Ian said.

The chunks of curving stone were pale and pockmarked, like pumice. But they began life as ancient trees. Long ago, the native plants had drawn up mineral-rich water through roots into trunks and branches. Over time, while the water nourished the plants, the minerals stayed behind, clogging the lifeline, taking the form of the twisted limbs, eventually both destroying and preserving the trees, only the shape of life left behind.

As we climbed around the last bend in the trail to Harris Point, the ranger hung back, letting us discover the stunning view for ourselves—the wide horizon, the curve of the bay dotted with our bobbing boats. We found a spot to sit on the rocks and set out the lunch we'd packed. I spread chicken salad into tortillas and passed them around our circle, set a bag of carrots in the middle. We sipped from the water bags in our backpacks and admired the view. I checked *LiLo*'s position in the bay against the cliffs and the other boats, relieved to see our ground tackle appeared to be holding.

After lunch, the other sailors packed up and headed back. We lingered over our meal and took our time on the trail, pestering the ranger with questions the whole way.

"What is this plant?"
"What do you eat when you're here for a week?"
"What is it like living in two places?"
"How many people visit the island in an average year?"
"Why are these snails all dead?"
"What's your favorite island animal?"

He answered each inquiry patiently, smiling at the crew's enthusiasm.

At an unmarked ravine crossing, Ranger Ian stopped us and pointed south. "That clearing right there is the site of the first ranger station on the island. I lived in a little house there for several years before we built the station in the new location. This seems like a good place to swear in a couple of new Junior Rangers."

Hannah and Meira stood solemnly as he checked their booklets. After all the questions they'd asked on the hike, they'd gathered far more information than could fit in a few pages but he verified that they'd done their duty. They raised their right hands, as instructed, and promised to be good stewards of this natural treasure and to do what they could to leave it better than they found it.

Back in the chaparral forest near the ranger station, we came around a corner and ran into what looked like a man on stakeout, hat pulled low, listening equipment in hand.

Ian greeted him warmly and introduced us. "This is one of the fox researchers who work here on the island." He explained how his gear helped him home in on the radio-tagged foxes so he could keep track of a sample of the endemic population. We asked him a few questions about his job and he pounced on our interest, happily sharing stories of his solitary work.

"We like to keep track of the live foxes but when we see that one has been still for a day or so, we really pay attention. We like to find the dead ones right away, before the scavengers get to them, so we can figure out what is killing them. But we really love it when we get Jesus foxes."

"What?" I thought I'd heard him wrong. "Jesus foxes?"

"Yeah," he grinned. "Sometimes the signal has been still for more than a day so I go out expecting to find a dead fox but when I get right up close, the fox jumps up and runs away. Jesus foxes. They're the best."

By the time we got back to our dinghy, the afternoon wind had kicked up a swell. Sizable breakers crashed onto the beach. I was leery after our wet landing of the morning and the sailors who'd towed us in had long since returned to their boat. We decided to let Bryan row the dinghy alone, out through the surf and around some rocks, and meet us on the beach upwind where it seemed calmer for launching the dinghy with all of us aboard.

I watched from the shore as he rowed hard to keep *Splitpea* straight in the swell, timing his launch between the breaking waves. Then, as he started to row up the coastline, the kids and I followed on land. I'd accidentally left my shoes in the dinghy so I hiked barefoot over a couple of rockfalls and gave the lounging seals a wide berth. We reached the other side just in time to help pull the dinghy up to dry ground.

I stared past *Splitpea* at the rhythm of the waves. "Bryan, I don't know if the surf is any smaller over here."

"Maybe not but I think I can get us through."

He glanced over his shoulder to gauge the timing and rowed hard up and over the lowest breaker in the set. The crew sent up a cheer and Bryan settled into an easy cadence across the slow roll of the bay.

You're not supposed to stand up in a rowboat but when you live on a sailboat, there's no other way to get back on board. It's tricky to step from one heaving boat to another and there's always the potential for disaster. Here's how it's supposed to work.

When *Splitpea* comes alongside *LiLo*, reach across to grab the gunwales on the edge of the deck. If it's choppy, it might take two people to hold the boats together.

(Watch your fingers between the rub rails and the hull.)

If you were quick enough to call dibs on the head, grab the dinghy line and stand up.

Move to the center of the dinghy and step up onto the seat.

(Everyone else, lean away to counter balance.)

Wait for a wave to lift *Splitpea* and step up.

Hold on tight but don't brace yourself on anything breakable or unstable.

Don't trip over lifelines or winches.

Don't hit your head on the dodger.

Don't drop the line in the water or *Splitpea* will float away.

Don't—for heaven's sake, don't—drop your backpack in the ocean.

Step forward onto the side deck to tie up and get out of the way. It's someone else's turn.

Once everyone is aboard, there's a traffic jam in the cockpit so don't trip over each other while fumbling with the combination lock and opening up the boat.

(It's probably dark. You might have forgotten a flashlight.)

Don't clog up the companionway on your way into the cabin or break the sacred pact inherent in our "dibs on the head" system. You call it first, you pee first, no exceptions.

(Unless someone else can convince you that they are really, really desperate.)

Unload your pack without too much complaining and hang up anything that got wet in the journey. (There's always *something* that got wet.) The legs of soggy pants fit perfectly in the grab rails over the galley, but please make sure they're out of the way before you light the stove for cocoa.

After a few more days in the Channel Islands, we were running low on fresh water and clean clothes so we headed over toward the southern California mainland and pulled into Channel Islands Marina. The harbormaster sent us to a nice slip, just at the base of the ramp near the shower and laundry facilities. We'd been rationing our limited solar power but as soon as we plugged into shore power, we set Hannah and Meira up with some computer games and checked messages from our week off the grid.

A voicemail from my sister-in-law, Tamarah, asked if there was any chance we would be in the LA area over the weekend. She and our oldest niece, Kesia, were planning to be down on a college visit and they were hoping to see us while they were in the area. Our tentative itinerary had us in Redondo Beach over the weekend, plenty close for them to drive over. But that gave us just one day in the marina to get all of our boat chores done. We spent the morning cleaning the boat and running up and down the ramp to change the laundry and get everyone clean.

With only a few quarters on hand, the kids and I planned our shared shower with military precision.

"We only have six minutes to do this. First, you get in and get wet," I said to Hannah, "and then you, Meira, and then me. We can soap up away from the water and take turns rinsing off. If we have enough time, we'll get around to conditioner but you'll have to rinse off in the sink if you don't get all the shampoo out so make sure you hurry."

Everyone made it through before the water shut off and we dried off and dressed and brushed out our wet hair in front of the foggy mirror.

In the afternoon, we loaded everyone up with backpacks and walked to town for provisions. Hannah's shoes had become so worn, they made disturbing frog-like croaks with every step. We stopped at a Big Lots, hoping to find a new pair but instead found good deals on shelf-stable food. We took our haul out to the sidewalk and divided it among our backpacks, heaviest things at the bottom. We lugged them along on the rest of our errands—the hardware store and the local West Marine—then rewarded ourselves with Panda Express for dinner and, refortified, marched back to the boat singing silly songs all the way to lighten our heavy load.

We planned to leave early the next morning to make it to Redondo Beach before dark. I sneaked out before we cast off and walked to a nearby convenience store for cereal and a half gallon of milk. Our icebox extended down past the waterline, and this far south the water temperature kept it too warm for perishables so we'd given up on ice and started using it for canned goods. Milk was a luxury and anything fresh had to be consumed right away.

I showed up in the companionway and announced to the sleepy heads in the quarter berths, "I've got cereal for breakfast."

Meira propped her pillow against the oven at her head and sat up. Hannah flopped over onto her stomach.

"What kind of cereal?" she said.

"Does it matter? We have *real* milk!"

I pulled four bowls from behind the sliding doors of the cupboard above the oven, assembled breakfast for the crew, and washed a spoon for myself from the pile of dishes in the sink. When everyone had eaten all they wanted, I gave Meira the last of the cereal and the rest of the milk.

"Here, have the leftovers. Good thing you're always hungry."

Everyone came up on deck as we motored down the narrow fairway and out the harbor entrance. We soon settled into an easy flow, trading off at the helm. On one of my horizon checks, I noticed a distant pod of dolphins speeding across the surface of the water. It seemed they had spotted us, too, and I eased the throttle as they headed our way. They swam across the crests of the waves, bursting out the leading edge and skimming through the air over the troughs. As they closed the distance between us they dropped their speed to match ours. Dorsal fins flashed in the sun to port and starboard and dolphins took turns riding the wave at our bow, turning flips in the air while we squealed and laughed.

The pod approached and retreated throughout the day, finally speeding off as we turned toward the anchorage. Inside the seawall, the Redondo Beach Harbor Patrol and a colony of barking sea lions met us at the dock. We tied up and filled out the paperwork for our free anchoring permit. I had worried about spending so much on marina fees in northern California, assuming it would only get more expensive as we moved into the more populated areas south of Point Conception, but all along southern California we found free anchorages, even some, like this one, with officials who could keep an eye on our boat when we were away. We dropped our anchor in the quiet basin and went to bed.

When living in Oregon, we often went several months between visits with the Washington side of our family but the sea had somehow stretched the days between us, leaving me yearning for a connection from home.

I did the dishes with one eye on my phone and when the call finally came—"We're parked on the road by the marina!"—we grabbed our sunscreen and ran up the hill. Tamarah and Kesia burst out of their car at our approach. We stopped in the street for a round of hugs and greetings and then turned toward the pier and slipped into conversation.

Talking with Tamarah had always been a refuge for me; the power of our troubles dispersing as they flowed between us. We'd traveled through life in stride, sharing the joys and hardships of parenting newborns, then toddlers, now navigating the middle years, and looking ahead to an empty nest. But here, though we walked together along the boardwalk, our paths felt disconnected.

Hannah and Meira bounced along near their cousin, sharing carnival food, telling stories of funny moments and good days. I didn't know how to describe the depths of my watery life to those planted so firmly on solid ground. Fears I shared reflected back magnified, like a wave bouncing off a cliff. Words swelled up in my throat, stayed trapped behind my smile.

The hours flew by, light as cotton candy, but at the end of the day, when we said goodbye, Tamarah held me close, as if she'd been listening all along to everything I couldn't say.

The next day, the weather report announced a small-craft advisory. I noted the conditions and called up to Bryan, who was working on deck.

"There's a small-craft advisory out, but listening to the forecast I don't even know why. It sounds like great sailing across to Catalina."

"Sounds good to me. I'm just about done here and then we can head out."

We whisked along in the lively winds under our reefed main and the working jib, our medium-sized headsail, but the trip to Catalina Harbor, on the west side of the island, still took most of the day. We sailed into the harbor at dusk and discovered most of the anchorage was taken up with private mooring buoys. Any boats at anchor in the space remaining had set both bow and stern hooks to keep from swinging in the tight space. Weary from the day, from the weight of so many days of motion, I sighed at the thought of the work still ahead—setting first one anchor, then the other while staying safely away from cliffs, shoals, and other boats.

"Hannah," Bryan called down the hatch. "Your mom is tired and we're all getting hungry. How about you come help me set the anchors so she can get dinner going." By the time they had settled us in for the night, the clam chowder was simmering. Bryan and Hannah came below flushed from the evening chill and smiling at their success. We gathered around the table in the stillness, warmed with gratitude.

In the morning, Meira rowed us to shore for a walk over to the small town of Two Harbors. It was an easy row but rather long, so I brought a book. For years, I read aloud on family road trips or during long delays in waiting rooms, often books about sailing and adventure, though we usually chose autobiographical selections. We wanted to be sure our heroes made it back safely. This day, the family tradition continued with a selection from Arthur Ransome's *Swallows and Amazons* series titled, *We Didn't Mean to Go to Sea*.

The irony amused the crew every time I picked it up. "But we *did* mean to go to sea!" Hannah always exclaimed.

The kids split their attention between the chance voyage of the fictional *Goblin* and the diving pelicans and colorful sea life all around *Splitpea*. For all its frustrations, this slow speed was a gift. We traveled *through* each experience, inhabiting each discomfort and joy, instead of rushing *past* them. My legs, my eyes, my mind all seemed calibrated for this pace where nothing blurs around the edges, no moment moves too quickly to be lived.

Two Harbors is likely a bustling place during the busy summer season, but on this midweek, off-season afternoon, there wasn't a whole lot going on. Sun umbrellas stood furled over vacant tables. The swings in the playground hung empty over sandy soil. Shuttered shops stood watch along the peaceful street. We welcomed the quiet day, the leisurely walk, and the long row back. This time, Hannah took the oars and I read from the bow. Bryan and Meira rode together in the seats at the stern. If, as Annie Dillard wrote, "How we spend our days is, of course, how we spend our lives," we were spending our lives awake and together.

The next day, we motored on around the island to the main harbor of Avalon. In my time off watch, I stirred together a batch of bread dough, using a scoop of clean ocean in place of fresh water and salt. I covered it tightly and set it securely in the icebox to rise.

The harbor patrol met us at the outer edge of the bay, showed us to our assigned mooring buoy, and helped us get tied up. Before we could even head below, a man from a neighboring boat rowed over to greet us and pass along information about the island. He must have sized up our interests pretty quickly, because instead of suggesting fancy restaurants or shopping, he told us about a volunteer opportunity with the Catalina Island Conservancy. Every Thursday, a driver takes a van of volunteers up to Middle Ranch, an area in the interior of the island, to spend the morning working at the native plant nursery. We had planned to leave Avalon on Thursday but we were intrigued by the chance to exchange a little work for a tour of the island's interior. We rowed to shore, walked to the conservancy office, and added our names to the list.

On our way back to the beach Bryan had a suggestion. "How about we stop in at the store and pick up some salad and some meat for the grill. I can grill the bread too if you want to keep the cabin cool."

"That sounds great. I was so tempted to ask if we could eat out tonight but if you're up for cooking, that's even better."

We bought some ice cream and ate it before it had a chance to melt, then sat outside in the evening sun eating dinner in turns as it came off the grill, watching the sea lions chase schools of fish around the boat in the clear water.

We'd been warned several times that the conservancy van driver would leave promptly at 7:30 a.m., so we went to bed early and set several alarms. Everyone was out of bed before six and we bustled about, bumping into each other in the predawn light. Bryan fried bagels while I threw together a pasta salad for lunch. By seven, the sun was coming up and we, bundled against the morning chill, were in the dinghy, rowing for shore, and enjoying the last of the color in the eastern sky. We pulled *Splitpea* up to the crowded dinghy dock and hopped over the other boats to tie her up. We walked up the hill the few blocks to the conservancy parking lot and met up with the other volunteers.

The roads into the island's interior are closed to all but a few residents and tour guides, so the drive was a treat. We rode up the hills and down the canyons like little owls, swiveling our heads to take in each new vista, hollering out loud at the sight of one of the herd of non-native bison that roam the slopes.

At the worksite, the naturalist greeted us with a well-practiced speech.

"Welcome to the James H. Ackerman Native Plant Nursery. Here at Middle Ranch, we grow over eighty-five different native plants and store over 2,000 seed collections. We work all over the island to mitigate invasive species and ensure biodiversity in the wilderness and in local landscaping. Our botanical garden back in Avalon introduces visitors to the beauty of the ecosystems in our area, but the work starts here. Today we're going to be prepping soil and seeds and transplanting seedlings. Who wants to get their hands dirty?"

Bryan and Meira volunteered first and were put to work breaking up soil from the clumps of dirt packed in old pots. Hannah winnowed seeds and I transplanted seedlings to trays while Bob Marley blared in the background. The day started cold, but as we worked the sun came out and soon there was a pile of discarded jackets on a side table.

On our way into the interior we'd seen evidence of recent fires, but as we drove back out I looked more closely and spotted the native plants the conservancy had used to replant the damaged areas. Without the opportunity to touch the seedlings, I never would have noticed the blossoming.

"Okay, crew," I said, back in the parking lot, "Let's find a place to sit down and eat some lunch." I reached into my pack and frowned.

"Hey, did anyone else happen to remember to pack forks? Because I sure didn't."

"I don't think we want to eat pasta salad with our hands," Bryan said. "I'll row back and get some."

One of the volunteers was still standing by the van.

"Did I hear you say you don't have any forks? I'm living on the island for the winter and my place is just down the way. I could run over and get some for you."

"Oh, that would be great," I said. "Want to join us for lunch? We have plenty of everything ... except forks."

That evening after dinner, we rowed back in to join the town's Halloween celebration. Hannah and Meira wore outfits scrounged together from boat gear and their Dad's clothes locker and joined the trick-or-treaters parading from shop to shop on the waterfront streets. Bryan and I found seats at a sidewalk cafe and lingered over coffee and pastries, smiling at each group of costumed kids walking by.

"So this is what a Catalina Halloween looks like," he said.

"I guess so," I said. "It makes me wonder where we'll be by Thanksgiving."

Chapter Nine

How Much is Enough?

Dana Point to San Diego, California
November 2013: New Moon, Waxing Crescent

At sea, I learned how little a person needs, not how much.
—Robin Lee Graham

Bryan attached the tiller extension and sat against the cockpit wall, steering gently as the breeze blew us back toward the mainland. I curled up under the dodger with a notebook and pen and wrote "To Do Before Mexico" at the top of a blank page.

"We're definitely going to want to exchange our autopilot," Bryan said. "There's a big West Marine in San Diego that should have one in stock but when we get in, we should call ahead to check."

"I'll add it to the list," I said. "I've been trying to think of all the things we want to get before we head across the border. I know we'll find plenty to eat but it would be nice to have some familiar foods when we're exploring in new places."

As we edged south, the sailing had become easier and easier but many of our daily tasks were about to get a lot more difficult. Once across the border there would be no more NOAA weather radio or passage planning websites. No West Marine stores, Trader Joes, or Safeways. No more tucking close to shore to pick up cell service for a quick phone call to a marina. It had been hard enough navigating each new town with a smart phone and Google maps. Soon we'd be finding our way with phrase books and guesswork in a language I spoke like a toddler.

"When we can find a steady internet connection, I have a lot more research to do about customs requirements and paperwork. It looks like even if we only carry hooks in our emergency kit, we're required to buy Mexican fishing licenses for the whole crew. San Diego looks tricky, too. There's a cruiser's anchorage for people passing through but we'll have to get inspected first. They want to have a peek in our bilge and holding tanks, I guess."

Bryan responded more to my tension than my words.

"We've managed to get ourselves this far. I'm sure we'll just keep figuring it out."

Later that evening, after anchoring in Dana Cove, we sat down to look over our shopping lists together.

Bryan turned his phone screen my way. "We're going to have to get some of this stuff online. I'm sure we could locate most of it in San Diego *somewhere* but I'm not sure we'll be able to find it on foot."

"Is there an Amazon Locker someplace close to the water?" I asked.

"I already checked. The packages are too big for even the biggest lockers."

I pulled my phone off the charger and swiped at the screen.

"You know that women's sailing forum I'm on? I'm betting I could find someone to receive shipments for us."

"I don't know. I don't want to bother some strangers with our stuff."

"They're not strangers," I teased, "just friends we haven't met yet."

"You think the whole world is 'friends you haven't met yet.'" Bryan laughed.

"Just give me a couple of hours to see what I can do."

Sure enough, within minutes online, I'd raised three offers of help and several suggestions about the area from local sailors. When one woman said she lived within walking distance of the bay, I replied, "Okay, Helen ... you win!" She messaged me her address and phone number and we made arrangements to meet up in a few days.

I looked up from my computer and grinned at Bryan. "It worked! I got a shipping address, a loaner car, and a bunch of new friends."

After a few days in Dana Point, we pushed on toward San Diego. Fishing buoys and thick beds of kelp clogged the approach near Point Loma. Once in the entrance channel, we kept a sharp lookout as we motored in the busy traffic. Several small boats patrolled a perimeter around docked military vessels and a large warship slid past us on their way out to sea. We spotted a submarine in dry dock, helicopters, and airplanes, and we listened to the intimidatingly proper radio chatter as we came into the dock for our permit inspection.

Once cleared, we drove across the bay as directed. Bright yellow buoys marked the borders of the anchorage and inside, a bevy of boats packed the available space. These were obviously voyaging boats. Thick woven straps held fuel tanks in place on each side deck. Solar panels stuck up like cormorant wings. With her worn teak rails and sun-bleached water jugs, *LiLo* seemed right at home.

We motored through the fleet and edged close to the rocky sea wall, looking for enough room to anchor. I spotted a couple sitting aboard a boat with "Hood River, OR" painted on the stern. The blond woman in the cockpit smiled and waved. Her face was tan, serene, and so welcoming, I wanted to stop right then and row over for a chat. But there wasn't any room near their boat and by the time we found a spot to anchor, over on the other side of the anchorage, the opportunity had passed. All the boats around us were shut up tight, sailors down below or on shore for the evening.

As we headed to bed, I admitted my disappointment.

"I know it seems like a little thing but I was so hoping to finally get to meet a woman out here. I've loved getting to know everyone so far—the men and the people on shore—but it's been over two months with no one to talk to about what it's like to be a woman at sea. It would be so nice to find someone who really understood."

I didn't say how often I'd hidden the fear that I wasn't enough, that I was letting everyone down, that a crisis bigger than I could navigate might at any moment crash over me.

From my view on our floating home, it seemed everyone else was doing just fine. The men we'd met spoke of impossibly long hours at the tiller, shared stories of storms I could only imagine. I'd thrown up sailing to Catalina Island. The books on our sailing shelf listed recipes for cooking at sea, fell open to pictures of bikini-clad women smiling on the bow. I fed my family granola bars and almonds, had spent many hours neither bikini-clad or smiling.

I didn't think I was the only one struggling to find my footing on the water. I just wanted to tell my story and hear someone say, "It's hard for me too."

The next morning, I called Helen about our deliveries and made arrangements to rendezvous with her after work. We got ourselves together and rowed past the Coast Guard station to the dinghy dock. Bryan headed out on the folding bike in search of Mexican fishing licenses, a West Marine, and a haircut. I needed to do more research about current Mexican clearance requirements and make some copies of our documentation, so the crew and I set off on a walk to the San Diego Central Library, about three miles away.

"When you were a baby, Hannah, and I was pregnant with *you*," I poked Meira in the side and she slid away, giggling, "your Dad and I came down here for a conference. We were mostly in LA but we drove down to San Diego for one day and we must have walked this same street." I pointed to the *Star of India* moored at the Maritime Museum. "I remember seeing that tall ship last time I was here and wondering what it would be like to sail out into the bay or the ocean."

"And now you sailed yourself back!" Hannah said.

"And now, with your help, we sailed ourselves back."

By early evening, we'd finished our work and walked back to the dinghy dock where Bryan was waiting with a pile of purchases.

Hannah reached him first. "You got a new hat!" she said.

"I needed a new one anyway, but it turns out," he said, as he lifted the brim, "you shouldn't get your hair cut near the navy base unless you want a navy haircut."

The kids collapsed on the dock in laughter as Bryan replaced his hat on his almost-hairless scalp.

"It'll grow back. Plus, I got offered a military discount everywhere I went. Everyone was so confused when I turned them down."

By the time Helen arrived, Bryan and Hannah were back from delivering the day's acquisitions to *LiLo*. We introduced ourselves and piled into her car for the ride back to her house.

"I know your kids don't know us." She spoke in a gentle British accent. "And you might not be comfortable with this idea but if you want, they're welcome to stay with us for dinner while you run your errands."

Within minutes of our arrival, we'd opened all our packages and letters from home and the kids were shooing us out the door.

"We're good here," Hannah said, looking up from a game with her new friends. "You go get provisions."

The next few days were full of errands and boat projects. We took full advantage of Helen and Glyn's loaner car to pick up snorkel gear, clothes, medication, and lots and lots of food. Our busy schedule mirrored that of our last few days at home, a steady cycle of shopping and stowing, so by Thursday night we went to bed ready for a break.

"What is that?" I whispered urgently. Bryan lifted his head from the pillow and stilled, listening.

"It sounds like high-powered electrical lines. Or sizzling bacon." He swung out of bed and went up on deck, returned a moment later.

"You can't hear anything up there. It's something in the water echoing through the hull."

"If we had a wood hull, I'd be afraid something was eating it. But nothing would eat the fiberglass, right?"

"No. Electrolysis can eat away our propeller but I've never heard anyone say you can hear it."

"Well, I'll ask Helen and Glyn about it tomorrow. I'm sure they'll know."

I laid under the covers willing the crackle to fade into white noise so I could sleep.

From the other side of the bunk, I heard Bryan grumble, "Now I want bacon for breakfast."

Friday morning, at our friends' urging, we moved over to the La Playa anchorage, hoping to get a good spot before it filled up for the weekend. Helen and Glyn planned to bring their boat out to join the fun and we wanted to have our chores done in time to enjoy our last day in San Diego. Soon after we were settled, a fellow sailor rowed over to chat and we asked directions to a nearby laundromat and loaded up our washing for a trip to town, heaving three heavy bags at our feet in *Splitpea*.

We beached the dinghy at the edge of the cove and walked up a few blocks to the cleaners, holding the sail bags of laundry steady on our heads. We stuffed all our clothes into two huge washers and left the crew to watch it while Bryan and I walked down to the marine store.

As we wandered the bright aisles, I found myself growing increasingly apprehensive. Behind the familiar chore was the awareness of how soon it would no longer be simple to find these essentials and how our family's lives might very well depend on the choices we made. There was no way to buy enough equipment to ensure our safety. Too much gear would consume limited funds and weigh down the boat beyond its capacity. I eyed the canned air horns. *Do we have spare air horns? What if our spares rust and we get stuck in fog without one? Should we buy more?*

This pattern repeated itself in my mind down every aisle until I began to lose my nerve. The days ahead were going to require more from us than money, more than fancy equipment. I knew the most precious commodities in a crisis at sea are common sense, a calm mind, ingenuity, inner resilience. You can't buy those at a store; they are do-it-yourself projects. I wondered if I had enough.

On a small boat, how do you ever know how much is enough? Fuel is easy. We can calculate miles, gallons per mile, take into account what we know of the currents and the pressure of the wind. And we are a sailboat, after all. Even if we run out of fuel altogether, we won't drift forever. We might not get where we want to go but eventually, there will be some sort of wind we can use to get somewhere helpful.

Food? There is food tucked in almost every locker and cranny. Fruit in the fruit hammock, eggs in the icebox. In the main pantry storage, there are cans of beans and meat, packages of dry goods. There's the deep storage in the backs of cubbies with extra items—dried fruit and pancake mix.

The emergency food bin is always a mystery. Once every month or so we send someone spelunking through the quarter berth into the space beyond to retrieve the battered blue tote. They shimmy out backward, hauling it with them one tug at a time. I lift the lid with Christmas-morning expectation, with gratitude to my former self who packed it away weeks ago.

There's usually something good—a package of Oreos or a wilted chocolate bar—and something bad—an explosion of boxed milk or tinned pineapple, the packaging chafed through from the constant motion. We rinse the cans from the bottom and tally the contents. Two cans of black beans, three cans of green, two cans of chicken, and a jar of olives. We open the peaches right away and dig in, four forks stabbing simultaneously. At our next stop we'll rotate some of our fresh stores back for next month's hungry sailors, keep this out to eat before more of it spoils. For now, there's enough.

Water—there's just never enough fresh water. The worry is like a bad smell. It doesn't go away but we become accustomed. Even with topped off tanks and a short passage planned, there's just never enough for all eventualities. And there are so very many eventualities at sea.

I stood in the checkout line, hands full of emergency gear, mind full of doubt. *We've managed to get ourselves this far,* I remembered Bryan saying. *I'm sure we'll just keep figuring it out.* We picked up the kids and the laundry, and as we walked back to the dinghy, we could see fog blowing in over the water. The weather was shifting.

We'd promised Hannah that we'd try to leave in time to celebrate her birthday in Mexico and we still had to set up the devices we'd bought for off-grid communications. We spent most of Saturday afternoon at a local coffee shop downloading updates and testing equipment. Sunday we left the kids aboard, headed into shore again, and found a Home Depot for the last few things on our list.

We arrived back at the beach to see Helen and Glyn's 44-foot sailboat anchored near *LiLo*. *Splitpea* bobbed between the boats with all five kids aboard, Hannah at the oars. We waved and hollered and they waved back, their laughter drifting in on the surf. We waited on shore while Hannah dropped her passengers off at the larger boat and then headed in to pick us up. We crammed the three of us and all our purchases in the dinghy and dropped her off with her friends while we went back to stash the last of our gear.

We were planning to leave around three in the morning so we had to be ocean-ready before bed. I rushed around, hoping we could finish in time to spend a few more minutes with our new friends. When everything was wedged into place, we grabbed some appetizers to share, and rowed on over. The kids played down below while we sat in the cockpit and talked into the evening. We needed to get some sleep before our early departure but we put off our goodbyes as long as possible. I finally remembered to ask about the mysterious nightly bacon sounds.

"I know you're a glaciologist not a marine biologist," I said to Helen, "but maybe you know what makes that crackling noise under the boat. Tell me nothing is eating holes in my hull."

She laughed. "Yeah, the water further north has probably been too cold for Pistol Shrimp."

"Pistol Shrimp?"

"Pistol Shrimp. Snapping Shrimp. Yes, that's what you're hearing. They snap their claws so fast it sends a jet of water to stun their prey and makes a noise like a tiny sonic boom. Like underwater thunder."

"That explains a lot! What a strange world it is down there."

I went to bed that night and made several last-minute phone calls while I still had cell service. I talked to my mom last. Beyond her words, I savored her tone, rising and falling, her voice the primal music of my life.

I laid awake most of the night running through lists and plans in my head. The pressure of guiding our family through the culture and systems of an unfamiliar country weighed heavily. We'd prepared for everything we could imagine and bought all we thought we might need. The remaining minutes to our departure ticked rapidly away.

I reached for my phone and messaged a friend. "I'm not sure I can do this."

Her response came quickly despite the late hour.

"You are brave and strong even when you don't feel it. Especially then."

Chapter Ten

BREATH AT THE SURFACE

Ensenada, Mexico
November 2013: First Quarter, Waxing Gibbous

*I cannot remain in company
with wonders from beneath
caught as I am
in the air below the stars
But I want to be in attendance
when they rise*

When the alarm went off, Meira got up to make sure Bryan didn't go back to sleep, and then crawled into his warm spot in bed with me. I heard him make a cup of coffee, smelled his early morning fried-egg sandwich, and stayed awake through all the clanking above my head as he pulled up the anchor. I made sure he was back, safe in the cockpit and tethered in, then cuddled down into my pillow for a few more hours of rest.

I woke about seven o'clock to a sunny day. I called up, "Are we there yet?" Bryan left the autopilot steering and came to greet me. "Welcome to Mexico!"

He still had plenty of energy, so I took my time getting up. Somehow, most of my stress had evaporated overnight. I made a cup of tea and fried up an English muffin for breakfast.

I stepped up into the companionway for a look around. The Coronado Islands rose brown and bare to the west, and the buildings of Tijuana glittered underneath the morning sun. Behind the city, the mountains of Baja traced a row of minuscules on the sky in beginner's cursive. A fishing line trailed behind the boat, the silvery lure bounding in the wake. The slightest of breezes pockmarked the sea in patches, here a collection of ripples, there a glassy pond suspended in the blue.

"You still look a little sleepy," Bryan said.

"A little. You good up here?"

"Better than good. Go. Take it easy."

I crawled back in bed with Meira. Only a few minutes later an alarm went off and my heart jumped.

"What's that?" Meira asked. "Is it the oil pressure alarm?"

"No, that's louder and solid. It's not the high temp alarm either." I rolled over and looked past the bulkhead at the lights on the navigation station. "The propane sniffer is all green. Nothing there."

The sound ebbed and flowed, fading into silence then building to a piercing shriek, like feedback from cheap speakers.

I mentally scrolled through all the options. "Dad didn't set an anchor alarm, did he?"

"No, and even if he did, why would it be going off just now?"

Between the shrill notes, strange clicks and trills penetrated my confusion.

"It wouldn't. I'm beginning to think that's not actually ... "

Meira caught my eye and finished my thought. "That's not an alarm. That's dolphins."

We leapt out of bed in a tangle of feet and elbows. I made it to the cockpit first.

"Where are the dolphins?"

"What?" Bryan said. "There's no dolphins. What are you talking about?"

He glanced out to sea, whirled back to port at the sound of watery breath at the surface.

"Wait. How did you see them from down below? I didn't even see them up here."

We talked over each other trying to explain.

"We didn't see them. We *heard* them."

"We thought it was an alarm or something but it must have been their whistles through the hull."

Bryan reached to cut the motor and listened in the ensuing silence. "Even knowing they're here, I can't hear them. The hull must have just the right resonance to amplify their sound."

"Do you think they were talking to us or about us?" Meira asked.

"Maybe they were just talking *despite* us."

We arrived in Ensenada just before sunset. I'd emailed one of the marinas in the area in hopes of securing a reservation, but I hadn't heard back from them, so I didn't know if we had a spot to stay. The marina looked pretty full and we pulled into a long guest dock and prepared to go ashore for information. Before we could hop onto the dock, a uniformed official walked up to the boat. We ventured a few words in Spanish and a few more in English and set off for the marina office, pretty sure that's what we'd been told to do.

One of the office staff spoke excellent English and we got a slip assignment and instructions to be back at 9 a.m. for a ride to the customs and immigration center. We'd heard the check-in requirements had been much simplified in the past few years, with all the necessary offices in one location instead of scattered around town. But we were still grateful to have some help navigating the multistep process.

Our marina lay adjacent to the cruise ship dock and though there wasn't a cruise ship in at the moment, we saw several security checkpoints and yards of fences surrounding the area. We wove our way out and walked over a small bridge to the tourist district.

At certain moments we could almost believe we were just exploring the next new destination in the United States, but the next moment a sight, sound, or smell would remind us—we made it to Mexico! We took in our surroundings while negotiating uneven sidewalks and avoiding potholes. The streetlights blinked in patterns deceptively similar to those in the US, and more than once, we found ourselves rushing across the six-lane crosswalk as drivers patiently ceded their right-of-way.

Neon signs flashed in Spanish and English—"Churros! Tacos! Jewelry! Viagra!" We pinned the churro shop on our mental map and walked back down toward the bay, the whole crew on watch for a place to get some dinner.

Tucked between an open-air hat shop and a popcorn kiosk, Tacos El Chente was open to the street, only a half wall across the front dividing the restaurant from the sidewalk. We went in and sat down in red plastic chairs around a red plastic table with a red-and-white-checked plastic tablecloth. In the middle of the table were napkins, hot sauce, and a small pile of bottle caps. A server swooped in and scooped the caps into his hand, motioning us to the menu behind the counter. I collected orders from each person and stood in line reciting them to myself—three carne asada tacos for Bryan, two more for Meira, an al pastor and carne asada for Hannah, and two tacos with carnitas for me. I watched as the person in front of me paid for their meal, counting bottle caps to total up their running tab.

I turned back to Bryan at the table. "So it looks like we just get our drinks from the cooler and pay by the cap when we're done eating."

Hannah's face brightened. "We can have a soda?"

"Yep," Bryan said. "Sodas for everyone!"

Our food came and we ate and ordered a second round of tacos for Bryan and Meira.

Hannah pushed her chair back from the table. "When we got here, I wanted some popcorn from next door but now I'm too stuffed to think about it!"

"Maybe we'll have to get some for your birthday," I said.

"And churros, too?"
"Why not? Churros, too."

"Feliz cumpleaños a ti. Feliz cumpleaños a ti. Feliz cumpleaños a Hannaaaaaaaaaah. Feliz cumpleaños a ti." I woke up the crew with my raspy morning voice. We didn't have time for a full-scale celebration before our clearance appointment but Meira and I spent a few furtive moments tying up birthday gifts in colorful scarves and I pulled out a couple of cards from home. After setting up a heap of birthday surprises, we dug into our clothes lockers for the tidiest options, trying to look a little more presentable than usual for our important day. I gathered our documents and we walked up to the office to wait.

Enrique, our guide, arrived a few minutes after nine, and we hung out in the lobby with some other cruisers while he helped their captain arrange his paperwork. I picked up a brochure on the table and idly flipped through it.

"Oh, no!" I looked over at Bryan. "This says we need copies of our Mexican liability insurance and our engine serial number."

Bryan shifted into action. "I'll run back to the boat to find the engine number. You see if Enrique can help you get the insurance info printed out and I'll be back before we leave."

The door slammed behind him and Hannah peeked over my shoulder at the list. "I guess this is why you always say to read everything, 'just in case.'"

Enrique set me up on an office computer and I picked my way through the Spanish interface, clicking optimistically in likely looking places and typing tentatively on the unfamiliar keyboard. As the documents came out of the printer, Bryan arrived back in the office, out of breath but smiling.

"I had to tear apart the whole engine compartment to find the number and then I couldn't find a piece of paper." He held up his hand, displayed the inky digits scribbled across his palm. "Hopefully I'll be able to read this if we need it."

When all the sailors were ready, Enrique shuttled us over to the customs and immigration office. We pinballed around the building, bouncing between teller windows to pay all our fees and get our passports stamped. Each office had different rules: one required cash payments, another sent us around the corner to make copies of the travel visa we'd just been issued across the room. We held our breath at the last window, where a system of lights randomly chooses boats for inspection. Green—all clear.

Back on the boat, Hannah opened her cards and the books we'd bought for her. I'd wondered about finding ways to celebrate birthdays aboard, even considered packing wrapped gifts in advance. But she was more than satisfied with her presents and settled down to read her new Tolkien book right away.

Meira joined her on the settee with a book of her own and Bryan and I conferred about the next passage.

"I'd like to take off tomorrow if we can," I said. "What do we need to do to be ready?"

"I need to filter some water into the tanks," Bryan said, "and I didn't refill our propane in San Diego. I think I'd like to top off one tank here before we head down the coast. It could be a while before it's easy to find again and the sailors we met this morning said they could help me find the propane depot."

"Well, I thought I had everything we need but we're running low on oatmeal. How about you go with them and we'll head out for groceries and a birthday dinner when you get back."

"Don't forget churros," Hannah said, "and popcorn."

"Don't worry," I said. "We won't forget it's your birthday."

The next stretch south, almost 300 miles to Bahía Tortugas, would be the longest so far without a major harbor. There wasn't an easy place to pop in for fuel but there were plenty of small bays to tuck into if the weather picked up or if we got tired of waiting for wind. The forecast called for several days of easy travel and we wanted to take it slow and enjoy the calmer seas and warmer weather.

After the birthday celebration, Bryan stayed up most of the night before we left, pouring water through our filter into the tanks. It took almost an hour to filter each five-gallon jug and this process required regular attention to keep the cans from shifting as they lightened. By midafternoon the next day we were ready to leave and we decided to hop about ten miles to Islas Todos Santos for the night. We'd read there was an anchorage on the east side of the islands, but knew better than to assume reality would match the guidebooks.

About seven miles out, the engine stopped.

There are so many ways for an engine to die and by the sounds ours made this time, we were pretty sure we'd sucked something into the propeller. The air was dead still, the swell was small, and the water warm, but the sun was setting so we made some quick decisions. Bryan changed into tight-fitting long underwear, paying for a little warmth with the loss of a little buoyancy. He set up the swim ladder, strapped on a life jacket, and tied himself to a dock line. We weren't in any immediate danger; the current was carrying us only slightly to the south, and there was plenty of room for passing vessels to avoid us. Still, we all resisted panic as the captain lowered himself over the side. You may be able to drown in six inches of water but it sure feels more likely in sixty fathoms.

With one of us overboard, the small swell felt amplified. I was acutely aware of the rocking keel, picturing the damage if the hull crashed down on an unprotected skull. Bryan stood on the ladder, gulped in air, and dove.

He surfaced a few seconds later and shook the water from his eyes.

"Yep, we picked up a piece of tarp in the prop. I could see it but I couldn't get deep enough to grab it." His knuckles turned pale where he gripped the swim ladder.

"Can you get down far enough to reach it?" I asked.

"I'm going to have to."

The first few times he went under, the life jacket and line kept him from getting deep enough to tear the tarp free.

He paused for breath and Meira called out a suggestion. "What if you tied the life jacket to the line as a float?"

As scary as it was to loosen his only tether to *LiLo*, we could all see the wisdom in her idea. He would have more freedom of movement, both to dive and to escape if the boat rocked too close, but he'd still have a lifeline near. He climbed up the ladder a step, stripped off the life jacket and tied it to the dock line, inhaled deeply, and dove again.

I caught myself breathing for him—in, out, in, out—watching for him to surface, his dark head shiny as a sea lion's. I listened for his breath—that quiet spouting of exhale and inhale. If he were to lose hold, come undone, float away injured, how would I begin to rescue him? No wind, no engine, and the dinghy up on deck. I had little idea how to contact what help might exist. How do you hail the Mexican Coast Guard?

He kept diving. I kept watching. The sun kept setting. He worked, with hands and boat hook, finding an easier rhythm—a few breaths above, a few kicks below. Finally, he came up, elated, shredded tarp in one hand, the other arm slung over the makeshift float.

"Got it! Let's get in for the night."

Back aboard, Bryan ducked below to change and warm up and I motored the last miles across to the islands. As we started to nose into the bay marked on our charts, a panga, a small fishing skiff with a powerful outboard, turned and motored directly toward us. We paused in the water and waited until we could hear his instructions.

"You can't anchor here," he called over in English. "It's forbidden." Best we could tell from his words across the water, the bay had been converted to a fish farm and the nets and moorings didn't leave room for a visiting sailboat.

We turned away, all of us exhausted by the ebbing adrenaline but reluctant to head back into Ensenada in the dark and waste our good weather window. I offered to stand a long sunset watch to give Bryan some rest. We didn't want to use up fuel on such a calm night and putting up a sail in the dead air would just mean extra wear on the equipment as we bobbed around so I kept an easy hand on the tiller and let the current carry us.

Just about the time we cleared the southern end of Islas Todos Santos, the only navigation hazard for days, a cruise ship pulled out of Ensenada and motored smoothly past us. Not too close for comfort, the city-at-sea came near enough I could count staterooms, watch the well-dressed folks walk the side decks. I caught a glimpse of the enormous movie screen on the stern, imagined, just for a moment, what it would be like to be up there engrossed in someone else's story, a soft, warm, clean bed waiting for me.

I looked away, into the starry night, scanned the rest of the horizon and glanced down into the dark water. Just then, a silvery fin broke the surface. One at first, and then more and more. And I remembered why I was choosing a story so close to the ground, here on the surface of the water. There might be dolphins leaping in the moonlight around the cruise ship, too, but no one would ever know.

Chapter Eleven

All is Shaking Loose

Coastal Baja and Bahía Tortugas, Mexico
November 2013: Full moon, Waning Gibbous, Third Quarter

*Being hove to in a long gale is the most boring way
of being terrified I know.*
—Donald Hamilton

Our journey from Ensenada to Bahía Tortugas, about halfway down the coast of the Baja Peninsula, took us six days, some heading slowly south, some waiting out weather in the shelter of Bahía San Quintín. Not too far out of Ensenada we discovered all the water we'd stored was bad. We'd filtered it thoroughly so no one got sick. It just tasted terrible.

"How many other things do we have to drink," Bryan asked and I ran through my mental inventory.

"We have a case of root beer in the stern and six gallons of fresh water in individual jugs. We have four or five boxes of juice—maybe a gallon of juice in all. Are all the tanks bad?"

"Yeah, I filtered water into all three of them."

"I wonder if there's something off with the pH. Hey, kids, want to try an experiment?"

The seas were calm enough to stand at the counter without hanging onto anything. We pumped out two cups of water and mixed one with baking soda and one with vinegar to see if we could elicit a chemical reaction.

"My cup isn't bubbling or anything," Meira said.

"Mine either," said Hannah.

"It might be over-chlorinated," Bryan suggested.

"Chlorine evaporates," I thought out loud. "If I can find a place to set an open pitcher without spilling it, maybe it'll be more drinkable in a few hours. It tastes terrible but it probably won't hurt us. Still, let's drink the other things first and try to make them last until we get into port again."

The last night of the passage, our water supply became the least of our worries. We'd rationed well and were coming in with more than enough, but the weather had kicked up out to sea and the winds were whipping around the islands near our destination. We reduced sail, lowering our headsail and double-reefing the main but neither the autopilot nor I were strong enough to fight the tiller and keep us on course.

Bryan loaded up his pockets with snacks and went out to take over.

"You might as well get some rest," he said. "It's going to be a long night."

And it was. Every hour he lashed the tiller to port and came below for five minutes, leaving the boat hove to with the sail and rudder set to counteract each other and stall our movement. He came up to the bed to check in with me, got another cup of coffee or used the head, and then stepped out for another hour in the wind.

I laid in bed worrying. *Maybe I could take the tiller for an hour or two.* But I'd already tried and I knew I couldn't manage the pull. Overuse and the demands of our lifestyle had aggravated an old shoulder injury and I couldn't risk permanent damage.

I kept an eye on our progress on my phone's navigation app and dozed a bit but I was awake every time Bryan came below. Fifty-five minutes outside, five minutes in—for twelve hours. Each time he came inside, his face was a little more weary, his report more subdued.

"Are you going to make it?"

"What else is there to do?" he said, and pulled his hat down a little lower over his ears.

Dawn arrived but the wind didn't slow.

"We're making good time," I told him during his next break. "I think we'll make it in by lunchtime."

"I don't care how tired I am. As soon as we drop anchor, I'm rowing into town and finding fish tacos."

Living in the present may sound like a good idea on sunny days at the beach or at that late summer bonfire with comfortable friends and gentle air, but what good does it do to try to be here, now on a day like today?

The seas are short and sharp. Before we have fully risen on one, another hits us from abeam, tossing cans from shelves, knocking teeth in my skull. Suddenly there are no waves at all and we fall into the negative space. Weightless and then not. Everyone has gone to ground, only there is no ground to go to. Hannah, as always, takes refuge in her bunk, so stuffed with books and clothes she is somehow able to sleep in relative stillness. Meira is wedged in the prime spot, back to the corner cushions, feet on the galley wall, knees locked. She too is resting, or at least her eyes are closed.

The captain is out in the wind. His pose mimics Meira's below—feet braced athwart ships, back tucked against the combing. His face shows the strain of the work of stillness, the constant adjustments it takes to stay upright.

We slide sideways off the swell and smack into a new crest, proving again and again the fact of surface tension, the elementary laws of physics.

I bear my own sort of surface tension. My skin shakes, holding the rest of me together; muscles tremble as I fly and fall, fly and fall.

Staying grounded in my body feels like a joke. No ground. Too much body.

I find the floor and reach deep inside for stillness, past the whirling thoughts, underneath the clutching fear, deeper than the tumbling sea—presence, an elusive seed of peace that's gone in a moment.

I can't maintain a connection to anything—no thought, no sensation, no person. All is shaking loose, shaking free, falling away. What will be left when we make it through this storm? What will be left of me if I make it through this journey? Is there a center that will hold or will I need to start anew?

Are we talking transformation or complete annihilation?

A shift? A change? Or death and resurrection?

By midmorning, Bryan was reaching the last of his strength.

"I'm going to need your help getting in. I'm so tired I can hardly see straight."

"Got it. I've already been looking at the chart."

I bundled up, sat on the companionway steps, and fed him information about the reefs and rocks near the Bahía Tortugas harbor mouth. The wind diminished as we moved into the shelter of the point. He sat down on the cockpit seat and stretched his neck.

"You know," he said, in the quiet moments as we eased across the bay, "I spent the night picturing you down there worrying about me."

"Yeah, I *was* worried about you. I hated that I couldn't help."

"If we weren't together I would be here on my own, though. Last night wasn't fun, but I wanted to do this. I wanted to come. And even if you couldn't ever help at sea, it would be worth it just to have you with me on shore. Plus," he gestured to the chart in my lap, "there's no way I would have been sharp enough to navigate in after the night I had. If I wasn't worried about you worrying about me, I would have just done my thing. Next time, rest."

I stepped to the tiller as Bryan moved forward to drop our anchor. He bowed deeply over the chain, measured lengths of rode with an outstretched arm. A figure-eight to hold the line fast and a thumbs up to me for the anchor set. I kicked at the throttle with my foot and waited, watching his back tense as his whole body listened to the the feel of the rope. He raised an arm for the final okay and stepped back. I eased the engine into idle, turned the key, and straightened as he joined me in the cockpit again.

He leaned over for a kiss. "Never forget. It takes us both to do this together."

Just as we'd planned, we dropped the dinghy and rowed to shore right away. We beached *Splitpea* a little ways from the the main fishing operations, out of the way of all the tire tracks in the sand.

As we walked up toward town, we spotted a small concrete building with "Restaurant and Bar" painted on a wall. A man stood above us on the ledge of one of the open windows and he waved and called down.

"¡Pásale, pásale!" *Come in, come in!*

I wanted to see a little more of the town before we sat down to eat so I hollered back in broken Spanish.

"Thank you! We'll be back soon."

We walked a few blocks up and down the sandy streets. We didn't find any other options for lunch, so we headed back down to the restaurant and climbed the steps to the doorway. We walked over the gravel floor of the small outer room into the cement pad of the main patio area. There were no tables, no chairs, no furniture at all. My brain struggled to offer possible explanations as my mouth fought to shape appropriate greetings.

Carlos, our patient host, led the all-Spanish conversation and soon we understood the situation. He and his wife used to run a restaurant, but after she died, two years earlier, he retired and now enjoys spending time with his children and making friends with sailors who come through.

He pinpointed our priorities immediately. "Do you want to eat?"

"Well, yes. Are there any good restaurants in town?"

"I will tell you where to find one," said the former restaurateur slightly dismissively, "It's not as good as ours was, but it's okay."

I listened closely to Carlos's instructions, but considering my weak grasp of right and left in Spanish and what seemed like a total lack of street signs, I was pretty sure we might spend the afternoon following our noses around the small town without finding food.

Finally Carlos gave up and motioned for us to follow him. "Come. I will drive you there."

We didn't want to assume every interaction was transactional but we didn't want to put ourselves into Carlos's debt without an understanding of what he was expecting. After raising a few eloquent eyebrows in Bryan's direction, I finally fell back on our policy of saying yes whenever possible. We piled into Carlos's SUV, seat belts optional, and bounced through the town, minds rushing to keep up.

He came to a stop in the middle of the road and gestured to a building nearby. He didn't seem to be waiting for payment and we hoped we weren't offending him as we offered only profuse thanks.

Bells on the door jangled as we walked into the empty restaurant. A woman sat bent over some work at a table near the back.

"¿Abierto?" I ventured. *Open?* She nodded and gestured to us to pick a spot to sit. She brought us menus and I started to translate the options before realizing the facing page was written in English. We played spot the differences and noticed some traditional items were only offered in Spanish. Bryan ran his finger down the page.

"Fish tacos!" He slapped his menu closed. "That was easy."

On our way back to the boat, we passed Carlos's place again and he joined us for the walk down to the water's edge. Again he offered help.

"Do you need water? Gasoline?"

By now, I was so weary I couldn't make a plan. "Maybe tomorrow," I said, and we stepped into the dinghy and pushed off into the bay.

The next afternoon Bryan and I left the crew on board, took in our water jugs, and filled them at Carlos's spigot. He pulled out a chair and pressed drinks into our hands, beer for Bryan and soda for me. We took in the peaceful view and relaxed in the warm breeze as we worked to communicate a bit beyond the basics.

We learned about his history, his kids, where they live and work, a bit about his grandchildren, and his holiday plans. We shared about our own family tree and, prompted by a question about homeschooling, even delved into a discussion of the pros and cons of differing educational systems. Don't get the wrong idea about my Spanish skills from this; it's amazing what you can eke out from a few hundred words and supplemental hand gestures.

Carlos asked if we ate bread or tortillas.

"I bake our bread," I said, "but do you know where we can find some tortillas?"

He brightened immediately. "Don't go to the market. You must come with me to a woman I know who makes them. They are very good. Wait—I will fry you one!"

And before we could demur, he shot into his little kitchen. We sat expectantly, listening to the thumps and clangs of hospitality. In a moment, he was back, warm tortillas held in his outstretched hands—a priest with the sacraments.

"These," he said solemnly, "these are the good tortillas." And they were.

Carlos reiterated his willingness to help us get gas, so we made a plan to come in the next day. By this point, he'd made it more than clear that he wasn't doing this for money; he just likes making new friends. We still wanted to reciprocate somehow and decided to invite him out to the boat for dinner. I issued what I hoped was an intelligible invitation for the next day.

In the morning we were relaxing aboard when a sudden commotion drew us to the deck. We watched, fascinated, as fishermen put out sardine nets in the bay and pelicans came banking down in fighter-jet formation for a feast. One fisherman drove his panga around at high speed banging a stick on his hull. Later we found out this mimics the sound of the fish and leads the birds and sea lions away. It was not quite a fool-proof system. We watched the fishermen free a sea lion from their huge circular net and toss encroaching pelicans back into the sky.

That afternoon we rowed to shore with three gas cans and two water jugs. We filled the water jugs again, and Carlos drove us over to the gas station. He chatted with the attendants while we got the fuel we needed and then drove us over to the tienda for groceries and on to the tortilla house.

His friend, the cook, came to the door apologetically. "No tortillas today, sorry. Come back tomorrow."

Back at *Splitpea*, we loaded all our jugs and provisions. There wasn't enough room for Carlos, so he helped us launch the heavy dinghy through the surf and waited on shore. Bryan rowed us out, dropped me off, and soon returned with our dinner guest.

Carlos and Bryan sat in the cockpit chatting, mostly in gestures, while Bryan cooked our bread on the grill and I finished up dinner down below. Despite the language barrier, our conversation was wide-ranging. Carlos talked more about the different school systems in town and told us about the fishermen in the area and the system of collectives they created to manage the fishing industry.

At one point, he stopped and asked, very seriously, "Are you Catholic?" I knew this question had prompted much animosity throughout the centuries and I didn't have the vocabulary to talk about my Quaker faith. I shook my head, "No," and he followed up with, "What's the difference between Catholics and Protestants?"

I took a deep breath. Even in English, I'd be hard-pressed to find a brief, coherent response to this complicated question, but in Spanish, I was totally lost.

I condensed hundreds of years of messy church history into a few idealistic words. "I think we have different practices, but the same heart."

Carlos nodded and pointed out to sea with a casual air. "It might rain tomorrow," he said, and I squinted at the clear sky, trying to see what he could see, grateful the conversation had moved on from religion.

The next day we woke to the sound of rain on the roof. Carlos was right. It showed no signs of letting up and I couldn't imagine making our way through the muddy streets, even for the good tortillas. Without a way to contact him, we decided to trust that he'd understand our decision to stay aboard for the day.

By the next morning, the rain had blown through and we were starting to plan for another passage. Before we left, Bryan and I headed into town to track down the tortillas. The roads were muddy, but passable if you didn't care too much about the state of your shoes. Carlos had some friends over, so we passed by without stopping in. We wandered through the town for a bit and finally found our way back to the right house. The woman who answered the door recognized us right away.

"¿Quieren tortillas, sí?" she asked. "They aren't done yet but you should come back at four."

Now that the rain was gone, the sun was warm so we walked away in search of popsicles. We didn't know what time it was so we walked back to the tortilla house too soon.

"Come back in another hour," she said.

We walked around town for a little longer, not an hour, but long enough apparently. When we showed up again, a grandmother was waiting on the porch for tortillas too. We bought two large packages and the cook picked out the payment from the coins we held in our palms.

On our way back to the boat, Carlos caught us. "Come in! Come in!" By now our feet knew the way up the path to his house and across the gravel to the table by his kitchen. Carlos reached over for a hug, pulled back for a handshake, reached in again for a hug.

He was only mildly disapproving that we hadn't stopped in earlier. We told him we didn't want to interrupt his time with his friends. "You are my friends, too," he said.

I blinked back tears at the gift of being welcomed so generously into Carlos's circle of affection. My own words echoed in my mind, more true now than I could have ever known when I spoke them: *we have different practices but the same heart.*

Chapter Twelve

THAT'S WHEN THE SEA WILL GET YOU

Bahía Asuncion, Punta Abreojos, and Bahía Santa Maria, Mexico
December 2013: Waning Crescent, New Moon, Waxing Crescent

*There are three sorts of people; those who are alive,
those who are dead, and those who are at sea.*
—Old Capstan Chantey, attributed to Anacharsis, 6th century BCE

Wide, rolling swell rocked us gently up and down and an onshore flow carried us south on an easy reach from Bahía Tortugas. Our mainsail and jib bellied full in the steady breeze. This was the sort of sailing we'd read about in books, the sort we'd only dreamed about while getting knocked around in the North Pacific.

We moved easily about the boat while the miles streamed past. While on watch, Bryan heated water and washed dishes at the sink. He set them on a towel on the counter to dry and they stayed put. The good weather continued through the night and into the next day, and by late afternoon we pulled into Bahía Asuncion and dropped anchor.

We rowed into shore and walked the hot streets. An elderly chocolate lab lay across the sidewalk as if melted by the sun. In the soil by the road, a hose nozzle sat in a curved shell, sprinkling water over a thirsty garden. Under the church steeple, a man swung on a bell rope calling out the hours to the town—one, two, three, four, five.

"Five o'clock! We should get some dinner." I said.

We had some business to take care of that required internet access and we found a small internet cafe and paid for a few minutes of service. The connection was as slow as the snail on their logo, but eventually we managed to complete our work. I decided to ask for a restaurant recommendation.

"Anywhere good to eat around here?"

"Yes!" he answered in Spanish and I strained to keep up. "There's a place by the water with a window."

A window. Hmmm, maybe it's a walk-up stand?

I tried to clarify. "What color is the restaurant?"

He shook his head and spoke again. I listened, then turned to the waiting crew.

"I think he said it doesn't have a color. I'm not exactly sure what we're looking for, but I'm pretty sure we can find something."

We walked back toward the beach the way we'd been pointed, looking all around for any sign of an eatery. Finally we came across a beachside restaurant. The walls were thatched halfway up with open windows all around.

"Oh, I *did* hear him correctly! It's a place with windows and no color!"

"I don't care what it looks like." Bryan said, "I mostly care what it tastes like."

We'd decided: no matter how nice the weather, we wanted to spend Thanksgiving in port and not on a passage. This was our first major holiday without family and we knew it was going to be a bit hard to be so far away.

The night before, we planned a menu.

"I'll take the dinghy out in the morning and go fishing," Bryan said, "If we're lucky, we can have fish for the main dish. If not, well, we'll just have to have something else."

"I'll make mashed potatoes," Hannah said.

Meira chimed in, "I'll fry some sweet potatoes and heat up some green beans."

"I guess all that's left for me to make is pie," I said.

"Hmmmm," Meira said, "that's a lot of pots and pans. I don't know how we'll get all those things to come off at the same time."

"I can cook the fish on the grill," Bryan said.

"I need the big cast iron skillet for the pie."

"I need the pressure cooker for the mashed potatoes."

"Wait, wait!" Meira rummaged around for a piece of scratch paper. "I need to make a spreadsheet!"

She questioned each of us about our preferred crockery and timing and soon produced a schedule for the day.

"We should put you in charge of the watch schedule," I said. "You'll have us all organized in no time."

Thanksgiving morning, before anyone else was up, I sat at the table and wrote in my journal.

This living outside my comfort zone thing isn't comfortable. A lot of the unanswered questions are staying unanswered for longer than I'd like. For that matter, I'm not even sure I know exactly what questions I've come to seek answers for. And something in the cupboard at my back smells like mildew.

It doesn't feel like Thanksgiving—no family, not even another boat around. Ham from a can or fish if we catch some. No rolls baking. Pumpkin pie without a recipe. A hole in my heart where the home table is.

But the present is good too, this warm, blue, peaceful present. Today, another gifted day to be with the ones I was given, the ones I've chosen to journey with. Today is a day of thanksgiving. And maybe tracking down the mildew.

Before long, Bryan and the crew were awake and we took the time to send our families a greeting through the satellite tracking system. We didn't have a satellite phone or any other long-range communication instruments aboard, but we'd splurged on a tracker that had the ability to send brief texts. Email addresses took up much of the space we were allotted so we labored over the message, hoping to convey our well-being and our love in 160 characters.

Bryan took a fishing pole and rowed out in *Splitpea* while the kids and I prepped dinner in the cabin. We took turns at the sink, the counter, and the stove and followed Meira's chart to the letter. By the time Bryan returned with his line of fish we were almost ready to eat.

He cleaned and grilled the small bonito and brought them below. We often traveled with the table tucked away, but we'd pulled it out for the special occasion and set each place carefully. We slid in around the settee together and joined hands to circle the space.

"Are you grateful?" This simple question often served as our family's grace, bringing us fully present and offering us a chance to express our deep thankfulness.

The chorus around the table was heartfelt.

"Oh, yes."

Past the poignant distance of those we left behind, past our awareness of the unfilled chairs made by our own absence, there was deep gratitude.

"Oh, yes."

We'd made the meal the way we'd made this journey—all hands serving each other with love.

"Oh, yes."

Our next stop was Punta Abreojos. It means "Point Open-Your-Eyes." It only takes a glance at the chart to see why. Reefs and obstructions foul the approach to the shallow bay.

We'd come so far from the Pacific Northwest but were still a bit surprised at what passed for harbor here. No bars to cross, that was nice, but no calm refuge on the other side either. Just a hook, a bight, a little bay to tuck into—like playing hide and seek by ducking into a doorway.

Our charts of Mexico were originally drafted by hand. The x-marks-the-spot notations were once drawn thin as a pencil line, but now, zooming in on our electronic charts, the symbols cover half a mile of sea floor.

Though the rocks on our maps could be lurking anywhere in the area, they're not too worrisome. Most stick up above the water or rest far below our keel, and we've got plenty of time and space to swing wide, to go around. We can play better-safe-than-sorry all day long.

Reefs though, those long, shallow ribs of the earth rising to just below sea level. Those are the deadly ones. If you can see them, the way they churn up the flow to a ripple or heave the breakers back toward the sea, you're probably far too close. At night sometimes, with ears that detect direction better than distance, you can hear the waves wrecking themselves on the spiny backs. That comforting roar of the ocean we love on a trip to the seashore? From the other side it is anything but comforting.

I feel like I'm saying the same things over and over again. The sea is treacherous. This life is scary. There's always something that could kill you.

This is no trip to the beach for a year; this is a voyage. Still almost as perilous and harrowing as sea voyages have always been. And the day-after-day motion of it all—boat, body, and ocean--never shifted into a comforting rhythm.

So if it all sounds the same, that's because it was. Over and over, we sailed through whatever weather was out there to a new place, found our way through hazards that looked and felt like ones we'd conquered already but could end us just as easily.

Never let your guard down; that's when the sea will get you. Don't even think about the idea of being secure; that's when you tempt all the gods you don't believe in—Neptune, Poseidon, Triton, Davy Jones. Even feeling safe is dangerous.

We left Punta Abreojos as part of a small convoy—three boats all traveling the same direction. One, a much larger vessel named *Vales Valeo*, carried a midlife couple and their two daughters. I kept watch all night for the running lights across the water and the next morning, the four kids took over an open radio channel for an hours-long game of twenty questions that kept all the boats in earshot entertained while we finished the passage to Bahía Santa Maria.

We all anchored in the wide bay and rowed over for sundowners on *Vales Valeo*. There were several other boats in Bahía Santa Maria, but Paul and Susie had the biggest boat, ice for cold drinks, and a couple of daughters desperate for comrades.

We scrambled up the swim ladder onto the side decks and found places around the glossy cockpit table. Our kids disappeared into the cavernous interior and their young hosts found snacks and games to share, offered drinks from the magical, humming refrigerator.

Here I was, finally meeting another woman living the cruiser life, traveling with her family on a small boat in the big ocean. I sat holding my cold glass, holding back my misgivings. Susie seemed almost as overwhelmed as I was but we didn't know each other well enough to say so.

"How's boat-schooling going for you?" she asked and I, noncommittal, pulled out my stock answer.

"We homeschooled before we left so it hasn't been too much of a change." I wanted to imply an airy ease without casting judgment on the look on her face, that quirk around the lips that said things weren't quite proceeding according to plan.

I wasn't ready to say that we'd jettisoned science and our US history curriculum before we even left the dock, trusting a Kindle and a math book to supplement this life experience and hoping that would prove to be enough.

I really didn't want to admit even *that* plan went by the wayside most days. It's hard to count on your fingers when you're hanging on with both hands. We lobbed the crew boat algebra instead—no constants, all variables—speed, fuel, distance, time.

I couldn't escape my worries for our kids' future. We left believing that you can't fall behind on a path you don't take. But what if our decisions narrowed their choices? What if they wanted a more conventional life? What if they resented us for dragging them out to sea?

While Susie and I exchanged timid confidences in one corner of the cockpit, Paul's voice boomed out across the water. "Did you see that weather coming into Bahía Asuncion? Six foot swells! Biggest seas we've seen all trip!"

I glanced at Bryan and resisted a smile. If we hadn't started out on the Northwest Coast, those would have seemed like big seas to us as well. *Maybe diving into the deep end wasn't such a bad way to start.*

As evening gathered, we sat a little closer, talked a little more openly. I felt more at ease just knowing I wasn't alone in my fear.

By the time we pulled ourselves away the darkness was complete. We'd forgotten to turn on our anchor light and the head lamp we were using as a navigation signal shed just enough light to be seen, but not enough to see by. Even after all these weeks, we didn't have our system down.

Worst case scenario, I told myself, we could row back to *Vales Valeo* and ask for some help—a bigger light, a faster dinghy. It wasn't the worst case yet though, and I calmed my nervous breath by singing Christmas carols into the black night. Hannah and Meira joined me, belting out harmony over the splash of the oars as we slid across the water, squinting into the dark.

Finally Meira raised her arm and pointed. "There she is!" Bryan glanced over his shoulder to locate *LiLo* and angled us in the right direction. Once aboard, we blinked our anchor light across the water. The light on *Vales Valeo*'s tall mast flickered in response.

While the kids settled down to sleep, Bryan and I took a few more minutes in the cockpit. The warm evening breeze and the glow of new friendship lulled me into a contented calm.

Bryan ran his hand down my bare arm and I shivered and moved closer. "We've been running from winter since we left," he said, "worrying about storms and pushing to get south. I think it's safe to say, 'We made it.' I think we can finally relax."

Chapter Thirteen

This is Going to be a Story

Bahía Santa Maria, Mexico
December 2013: Waxing Crescent

You went expecting to return but
you are discovering
along with all who have left
there is no way back
only beyond

It was a beautiful morning. Pearly white clouds strung out across a sky blue sky. I reached down below for the camera and framed a shot. The sun had just begun to rise over the low dunes to the east but the clouds were already leafed with silver. No way to fit all this glory into a photograph.

Down in the cabin the crew had also begun to rise. I took coffee to Bryan and started thinking about breakfast. The kids popped out of their bunks full of Christmas energy. They pulled out craft supplies and started cutting paper snowflakes to decorate our tropical environment. I stepped back out to see how the light had changed, glanced over the side of the boat, and felt the morning peace shatter.

"Did you move *Splitpea*?" I called down, trying to find an alternate reason for the empty spot on the port side. The bright yellow painter hung loose on the stern and a panicked glance around confirmed my alarm. Our dinghy was missing.

Fear hit immediately, then a rush of questions: How could she have come loose? How are we ever going to find her? What are we going to do if we don't?

Bryan came out on deck to see for himself. He rushed up to the bow and back again, eyes tracing ever widening circles in the hopes that this was a mistake or that *Splitpea* had just slipped free and was floating an arm's reach away. I spoke gently to the wide-eyed kids, unable to hide my tears, and they started crying too. *Splitpea* had been more than just transportation. She was closer to a beloved pet, a creature of our own making, our responsibility, our survival.

Bryan knelt on the stern, inspecting the ends of the dinghy line. We'd never gotten around to melting the ends, so we couldn't tell if the cut was from our initial purchase or more recent. We looked around the anchorage at all the other boats, their far more valuable dinghies trailing behind the mother ships like obedient ducklings. This bay was so remote, so safe, some had even left expensive outboards on their tenders and they remained untouched. I went below again, cleared my voice, and put out a radio call to the other boats.

"Bahía Santa Maria, Bahía Santa Maria, Bahía Santa Maria. This is sailing vessel *LiLo*." I told our story and asked all the boaters to respond with any relevant information. Our friends on *Vales Valeo* reported hearing some bumps against their hull in the night and we wondered if it was related. No one admonished us for our foolishness or reminded us that we should have pulled our dinghy up or cable-locked her to the boat. It didn't matter; we were punishing ourselves enough.

As Bryan and I prepared to haul the anchor and search the bay, Meira dried her eyes and stepped to the stove. "You're going to need to eat something," she said, and went to work, frying tortillas for breakfast.

Will, our friend from our time in Eureka, had just pulled into the bay the night before. Now he called over on the VHF. "*LiLo, LiLo, LiLo.* This is *Thallasea.* Come in?" He offered us the loan of his inflatable dinghy, knowing we'd need a way to retrieve ours should we happen to spot it on shore. He rowed over and Bryan ferried him back to his boat.

We did our jobs in silence. Bryan hauled up the anchor and I kicked the engine into gear. I stood at the helm and kept the boat barely moving through the water. Bryan stood on the cabin top, arm around the mast, and scanned the shoreline through binoculars. Baja had been so brown, but the recent rains had greened the land and that made it difficult to differentiate our little green dinghy from the vegetation on shore. Hannah and Meira left their craft project to comfort me and we cried and pulled ourselves together and cried again during the long drive around the circumference of the bay. We made the conscious choice to stop using a gendered pronoun for *Splitpea*. It felt like a search and rescue exercise and I had to remind myself, "*Splitpea* is not a person or even a pet. It is wood and glue and paint."

Behind the sorrow of loss, fear lurked. Between waves of tears, I started tallying our resources. Limited cash—while in Ensenada, we'd projected our spending on Baja and pulled out a little extra for a cushion. But we'd spent a little more time on the peninsula than we'd expected, and now were down to only a couple hundred pesos, less than fifty dollars. Even if we had cash, we couldn't get to shore to spend it. Power might become an issue. Our batteries didn't seem to be charging correctly from the solar panels, though a recent string of gray days made it difficult to know if the problem was electrical or meteorological. We had plenty of food aboard, although dinners might get strange as we ate through our fresh food and dug into our canned reserves. Water—now that might become a problem. For now, though, we had enough.

No the real difficulty was long-term. Part of the reason *Splitpea* was so perfect for us, part of the reason we built her—no, *it*—in the first place was now much of what made its loss so devastating. With four of us aboard such a small boat, we needed a dinghy that would carry us and all of our gear without filling up the foredeck or requiring a large outboard for surf launchings. *Splitpea* was eleven feet long, but split at the double bulkhead in the middle. Each half floated independently and the stern nested neatly into the bow; the two halves only took up six feet on our cabin top, leaving the foredeck free for sail changes and anchoring maneuvers. We'd considered an inflatable option but ultimately decided the hard dinghy was right for us. The sharp bow cut through the surf under rowing power alone, saving us from buying or maintaining an expensive outboard. The lightweight design didn't require a lifting harness or dinghy wheels, both of which added weight and expense.

Now we faced the same problems that brought us to this decision in the first place, only without the wood shop or time we'd used to build a solution. An inflatable—even a used one—would be expensive and would require adding a much larger outboard to our arsenal, assuming we could even find one for sale without a vehicle or the internet. Another hard dinghy would have been difficult to come by in the US but it was almost beyond our imagination that we could find one here, the right size and buoyancy.

The day was turning warm and bright. I steered with my thigh and rubbed in some sunscreen. Before we left for the trip, we'd read so many stories of other sailors in similar predicaments. Often their runaway dinghy appeared just when they'd finally given it up for lost. We couldn't help but hope the same would happen to us. The thought crossed my mind more than once: *This is going to be a story. Maybe it will be a story about the kindness of strangers, the resilience of this crew, and how we made our way despite this loss. But right now, I'd love a story with an anticlimactic conclusion—"And then we found the dinghy. The end." I don't want an inspiring story; I just want my damn dinghy back.*

A couple of times Bryan called back for me to slow down or stop while he focused on something on the shoreline. Coolers, beach chairs, all sorts of flotsam washed up on the sand, but no sign of our dinghy. On the southern end of the bay, the last length to search, sand gave way to rocks and waves crashed high. If *Splitpea* had been blown this way in the night, it was likely smashed to pieces in the surf. I was ready to give up but Bryan pushed on, hopeful or stubborn, I couldn't tell. We drove all the way to the end of the rocky point guarding the entrance of the bay, searched every last crevice and tide pool. Finally, Bryan called, "Okay, that's it. Let's head back."

I throttled up the engine and turned north to head across the entrance of the bay. I didn't want to look to the left, out toward the horizon. Almost certainly, our dinghy was out there somewhere, and I shied away from the loneliness and loss in that thought.

As we approached the anchorage Bryan walked back to the cockpit and gave me a break at the helm while I started pulling together a script in Spanish to ask for help on the radio. In the middle of all our rushing around that morning, we'd spotted a new boat in the anchorage. Not another cruiser; this boat was gray and imposing, clearly an official vessel of some sort. We discussed trying to raise them on the radio, but thought it might be easier to make ourselves understood face to face.

In the US, the Navy sends gunships out to patrol a wide perimeter around any of their big ships. We were used to being warned away with a show of force. But here, as we came near, the seamen started waving us over, tossing down old tires to act as fenders, pulling out cameras and taking pictures of us. We eased up next to the ship, our fenders hanging uselessly between their huge ones, our gunwales low against their tall topsides.

I stepped up onto our cockpit seat and stumbled through some introductions. Eventually, the officers waved me aboard and I clambered up to their solid deck, conscious of my wrap skirt in the breeze. I'd looked up several terms for "dinghy" in my dictionaries and I trotted them out hopefully only to be met with blank stares and confused looks. Rowboat, dinghy, tender—there are multiple names for it in English too.

Finally, a young seaman stepped forward and spoke tentatively, "I speak a little English." Of course, his idea of "a little English" surpassed my spoken Spanish by far. I gratefully shifted languages and explained our predicament. My translator passed the story along in mellifluous Spanish. I caught a few words and tucked them away for future use. The captain responded graciously, asking to see a picture of *Splitpea* and promising to send out a radio call to the other Navy boats in the area. "We're a supply ship," he said, "and we support the patrol boats up and down the coast. When the patrol ship comes into the bay, we'll send them around to take a look for you, too. Oh, and do you need any water?"

I relayed his offer down to Bryan, still in *LiLo*'s cockpit, and he untied one of our jerry jugs and passed it up to me. The captain's eyebrows flew up. "You only want twenty liters? Do you know we have 150 *million* liters of water on this ship?"

I laughed and shook my head. "No, twenty will be fine. That's all the space we have in our tanks." I glanced around the deck, noticed the large-scale versions of familiar tools, puzzled over the free-standing washing machine on the side deck. *No wonder they need so much water.*

It seemed like we'd covered all the details but I wanted to give the Navy my contact information in case they ran across our boat or heard anything. "My name is Betania," I said, using the Spanish version of Bethany. The young translator brightened and turned to lead me into the cabin. We stepped over the raised thresholds and ducked low ceilings. I assumed we were headed into a navigation area, someplace with a desk, paper, and pen to take down our information. We came to a stop in a tiny bunk room and I glanced around, bewildered. "In here," he said, and gestured to an even smaller marine head.

Everything clicked into place. "I was telling you my name. You thought I was asking for a bathroom!"

We wove our way back out to the deck and he spoke again to the captain, who pulled out a clipboard and pen. I set them on the top of the washing machine and wrote our details in an elementary mix of Spanish and English. We smiled and spoke our thanks and I accepted a hand back down to my boat where I took over the helm.

Bryan worked with the crewmen to loosen our crossed dock lines and shove our boat free of their gear. I steered a wide circle away from their ship and glanced back to see crew members snapping more photos. Bryan grabbed our camera too and captured a few memories of our own. "If this wasn't such a sad day," I said, "this would be a really cool experience."

By the time we set our anchor back among the other sailboats in the bay it was late in the afternoon. We called over on the radio to our friend, Will, shared the news of our failed search, and offered to row his dinghy back over. "Just keep it for a bit," he said. "Some friends I met up the coast arrived last night too and I'm having them over for dinner. We only made enough for three, but give us an hour or so after you see them arrive, and come join us for after-dinner rum."

I didn't really feel like going out, but I felt even less like staying home. So we scrounged something for dinner and kept an eye out for movement in the bay. Pretty soon we noticed a young couple tossing a tiny blue inflatable dinghy off their bow. She climbed down easily and he followed, folding his long arms and legs to fit. They took a few strokes with their canoe paddles and then settled into a practiced unison, her dark hair bobbing on the port side, his bleached curls leaning off to starboard.

After a reasonable amount of time, we made ourselves company-presentable, set up a movie for the kids and paddled over ourselves. We hadn't seen Will since our time in Eureka, but we anticipated a repeat of the relaxing evening we'd spent there aboard his cozy boat. As we rowed over, tears kept gathering in my eyes. Just when I thought I was done, new tears spilled over. I wiped them off on my sleeves; a little more salt water wouldn't hurt.

Will had seen us coming, of course, and he came out on deck to greet us and help us aboard. We stripped off our life jackets and stepped below. My red eyes felt at odds with the warm smells and cheerful atmosphere, but Will put us at ease right away.

His friends introduced themselves: "He's David and I'm Carolyn, but Dave calls me Rosie. We're on the twenty-six-foot Contessa, *Crazy*

Love." They'd heard our sad news already, so we didn't dwell on it, instead sharing tales and comparing destinations.

By the end of the night, my tears had receded and we'd made two more new friends. We all intended to stay in the bay a little longer. We planned to exhaust every possible search option and they wanted to rest up from a few days of wearying travel.

The next morning we woke hopeful and determined. We'd done some calculations about wind and tide directions and figured our best shot at finding *Splitpea* was walking the sand dunes by the mangroves. If the wind had blown it in just the right direction and the tide and surf was just high enough, it was possible that our dinghy had been swept up and over the sand at the tideline to the mangroves beyond. There was no way to see this from our boat; we needed to get to shore.

We checked the tides—no point in going in at high tide when the land would be underwater or inaccessible—and started trying to flag down a ride. I wrote a script in Spanish and put out a call on the VHF radio, listening hard to the rapid-fire responses, hoping I was understanding correctly, setting aside my self-consciousness about being heard by everyone in the area.

We didn't always leave our radio on all day when anchored out; we didn't have the battery power for that. But most other boats kept theirs scanning all day and the fishermen and Navy vessels would be listening in as well. We sat in the cockpit watching the estuary entrance for any action. The entrance was shallow but swift and the pangas sped up to run the twisting channel on a plane, the only way to keep from running aground. At one point I thought I'd raised some sort of fishing dispatcher on the radio and spent an hour in agitated expectation, waiting for a return call or the arrival of a panga. We got everyone ready to go—water, snacks, life jackets, sunscreen—and sat, our tense anticipation seeping away like helium, the heaviness of our sadness filling in the gaps.

Several times a panga came shooting out of the estuary entrance and sped along the shoreline to the west. Bryan and I stood high on the boat and waved bright towels and life preservers, hoping to catch their attention.

Finally a boat diverted our way. But by now the tide was flooding; we'd missed our chance. As they approached, we called greetings and they pulled up alongside and cut their engine. We attempted to explain what we wanted. "We need to search for our lost dinghy, but have to wait for the low tide. Is there any way you could come back in a few hours to take us to shore?" Either we weren't clear or, more likely, they were busy working and couldn't make any offers of future help. Instead they offered what they could—a portion of their fresh catch of lobster. We waved it away, turned them down more than once. "We really just need a ride into shore." But they wouldn't be deterred. Finally one spoke firmly, "Give me a bucket." We passed over our blue bucket and they dug into the seat compartments for their gift. "You are sad. This is for your family." They passed the bucket back and sped away while we counted, "One, two, three ... seven lobsters! What are we going to do with seven lobsters?"

We didn't feel like we could go anywhere until we'd searched in all the ways that seemed possible. But this day had run away from us and we'd missed the tide. With nothing better to do and morale at a low, we called Will and our new friends, David and Carolyn. "How about a lobster dinner?"

I'd started a batch of bread dough earlier, when I still had energy, and the idea of fresh-baked bread was more than enough to lure our oven-less friends. Will sheepishly admitted to a lobster aversion, so he volunteered to come by after we ate for the post-dinner fun. The wind had really started blowing by the time Dave and Carolyn were ready to row over. We called them to see if they were still up for coming and laughed at Dave's reply, "We'd row through a hurricane for fresh bread!"

We took turns poking our heads up to check on their progress until finally the spotter announced, "They're on their way!" We did five more minutes of scurried tidying and then came out to greet our guests, steadying their dinghy while they climbed over the gunwales and into the cockpit. It felt strange to be the hosts. For once, our boat was the biggest. We moved on below, out of the wind, and settled everyone around our table. Carolyn had made chowder in their pressure cooker and she glanced enviously at our oven as she set it on a burner. The smell of bread filled the cabin and we wasted no time serving up the feast. Bryan stayed near the companionway to keep an eye on the grill but after the second batch of lobster was done, herbed butter glistening on the meat in the shells, he relaxed and ate as well. Before long, Will had joined the party, and we all shifted around to make room at the table. Bryan settled into his seat on the companionway steps, Hannah sat on her pillow, her berth within arms' reach of the food. The guests scooted in around the wobbly table and Meira pulled a bag of dirty laundry into the space between the head and the stores locker and perched on top of her improvised seat.

Working together across the cabin, hands reaching and retreating like a minuet, we cleared the dinner dishes and produced mugs for after-dinner drinks. Cocoa for the crew, rum for the guests. I curled up on the edge of the settee with a cup of tea. Just as everyone was getting settled again, Meira spoke up from her spot toward the bow, "I think I should go check on the dinghies."

"No, sweetie. They're fine. You're just nervous because of *Splitpea*. Besides, you're all the way up by the V-berth. Everyone would have to move to let you out."

Meira insisted, and we wanted to reward her initiative a bit, so we slipped out from our spots at the table and she do-si-doed her way to the cockpit. We'd started to settle back into our conversation when we heard her.

"Did somebody move Will's dinghy?" A quick glance around the cabin and Bryan was up the steps.

"No. It should still be right ... hmmm." By now David and Will were dashing for the cockpit and soon Bryan stuck his face back down.

"Will's dinghy is missing. It must have worked loose in this wind. It can't have been gone long." He quickly shifted into action. "Beth, flip on the compass. Let's get a reciprocal course to the wind and go after it. David, Carolyn, do you want to head back to your boat before we take off or do you want to come along for the ride?"

The *Crazy Love* crew volunteered to stay and help, a couple more sets of eyes searching the dark water. On a whim earlier in the day, Bryan had plugged in our big spotlight to charge and we passed it up to Will who stepped to the bow. Dave grabbed our twelve-volt work light and traced a wide arc behind the boat in case we passed the dinghy in the pitch black. Bryan held the helm, both eyes on the compass, steering straight downwind, and I flipped on our running lights and our red cabin light, for all the good it would do with our wrecked night vision. The crescent moon had already set and the wind-blown clouds blocked out the stars.

After the initial rush, I stood below with nothing to do but panic. "I can't believe this is happening again!" I said to Carolyn. "I think one of us tied Will's dinghy up. Do we need to offer to pay for it?" I didn't want to shirk any responsibility, but I didn't know how we were going to recover from our own loss, much less make right the disaster we'd caused our friend.

Carolyn locked eyes with me in the narrow walkway. "Let's just wait and see. You don't owe Will anything. These things happen." Her calm kindness quelled my rising anxiety and I headed up to help. I knew spotting the dinghy wasn't our only concern. The wind didn't feel too high now, while we were moving with it. But if we were to stop or turn up into it, the apparent wind would increase dramatically. We hadn't had time to drink more than a few sips of rum but we didn't want to ignore the possibility that reactions might be impaired by that or the stress of the situation.

Bryan passed David a life jacket and I reminded the kids to grab theirs before heading out on deck, though they were already buckling them on. We spread out around the boat, Bryan and David in the cockpit, Will and Meira on the bow. Carolyn and Hannah stayed out of the way down below. I knelt on the stern, center of gravity low, spotlight held high. I didn't know what to feel—hope, despair, fear? I ignored my emotions and focused on the job at hand.

We'd spent forty-five minutes of searching about three miles across the bay when suddenly we heard shouts from the foredeck.

"There it is!"

"I see it!"

I took a moment to feel the relief, then took a deep breath to remind myself the job wasn't done. Losing a dinghy was bad enough. But losing a crew member while trying to retrieve it would be horrific, senseless. I held on tight to every handhold as I worked my way up the side deck. Meira handed me the boat hook and then planted herself on the deck, secure and ready—more my fellow sailor than my child. Bryan and David maneuvered *LiLo* alongside the dinghy. I knelt on the starboard side and reached out with the hook for an attachment point.

"I got it!" I couldn't grab the painter, but I held the pontoon tightly against *LiLo*'s hull and waited for help. Will reached long arms down toward the water and snagged the floating line. I held my breath while he and Meira hauled the dinghy aboard and, in a victorious fight against the gusts, lashed it firmly to the cabin top.

Bryan turned the boat slowly to wind and pointed us back toward the trio of anchor lights across the bay. I stepped below to get out of the cold and started some hot water in the kettle. As we neared the other boats, Bryan began the tricky process of anchoring in the dark. We didn't want to end up too far away—our friends still had to row home through the choppy water—but we didn't want to end up too close either and risk tangling our anchor lines or drifting into a collision. On our first attempt we crowded *Lazy Days*, the other boat in the anchorage. I stood at the ready in the companionway until Bryan settled on a better location, then stepped to the helm to help set the anchor. As we drifted back into place, we congratulated each other on a job well done.

We praised Meira's intuition. "If you hadn't insisted on checking, who knows when we would have noticed it was gone?" We told and retold the story of the evening, each person's perspective adding depth to our shared adventure, the tale already shifting from experience into legend.

After a few minutes of high-energy debriefing, our adrenaline faded fast. Will headed out in his salvaged dinghy and *Crazy Love* paddled northeast, into the wind, back to their little boat. They quickly faded from view in the dark so we waited on deck, squinting toward their anchor light, for a sign they had arrived safely. I imagine they took a minute to tie up their dinghy extra tight before flashing their headlamp our way. Hannah rushed below to blink our anchor light in response and the anchorage subsided into stillness.

Chapter Fourteen

TO THE BOTTOM OF THE SEA

Bahía Santa Maria, Bahía Magdalena, and San Carlos, Mexico
December 2013; Waxing Crescent

I waited, as if the sea could make my decision for me.
—Sylvia Plath

I sat out in the cockpit in the morning light. Once, it had all the comfort and welcome of a warm front porch. Today it felt more like a prison. A wet, salty prison. We'd stayed aboard for longer than this before, but always by choice. This day, I couldn't escape the helplessness of our situation. I tried not to think too far ahead. *How many more days before we need fresh water? How will we find someone to help us? What if I have to make Christmas merry with only what we have on hand?* Staying present to the moment offered little solace.

Hannah stuck her head through the doorway, hair still rumpled from sleeping in her cluttered bunk. Her eyes mirrored the sadness I felt, so I made an effort to smile believably. "It'll be okay, sweetie," I said, speaking a promise I was almost certain I would break. She grinned courage in my direction, her young trust undimmed by experience, and then she disappeared, back to her book, where disasters are always just precursors to happy endings.

But here in real life, sometimes disasters are just disastrous. Sometimes things break and can't be fixed, even the things you care about most. Sometimes people leave for good, treasure sinks to the bottom of the sea.

I couldn't pretend I knew what to do. I had no idea how to be a safe place for our kids to grieve, didn't have a suggestion for a plan to offer Bryan, couldn't add anything but worry to the day.

I moved to the bow, the most privacy I could find on our floating home, buried my face in the head sail and, as quietly as possible, cried my heart out. The fear and sadness didn't go away but the tears gradually dried up. I sat rehearsing our options—inflatable dinghy or hard dinghy? Back and forth, I considered again first one, than the other. The holes in either plan gaped large—size, weight, cost, accessibility—and I struggled to peek through, looking for a third choice on the other side, trying to formulate a Plan C. But nothing presented itself and finally, weary of my own thoughts, I gave up and went back to the cockpit.

Bryan and I had worked together well through the initial aftermath of *Splitpea*'s disappearance, but we hadn't been saying very much to each other. Without a clear plan to pursue, our reality felt too raw to process aloud. At one point, when I thought the kids couldn't hear me, I attempted to articulate how I was feeling, "Even with all the tough stuff on the northwest coast, I never seriously thought about quitting. I know there's no real way to give up and go home but if there was, this is the first time I might actually consider it."

"I'm not giving up yet," Bryan said, and I was glad at least one of us had the will to continue.

Later that day, we finally managed to flag down a panga and they graciously transported us over to the estuary, through the surf to shore. I searched for the words to explain what we were planning and hoped I communicated our need for a ride back to *LiLo* a little later in the afternoon. In the warmth of the day, I resisted my fears of getting stranded on shore, and focused on the task at hand, searching the sand and the mangroves beyond. The topography was dimpled with low spots, puddles and hollows and we found our way to high places and scanned the natural landscape for the sharp-edged shapes of constructed things. We split into pairs, Bryan and Meira to the east, Hannah and I searching the west, and hauled our light day packs up and down the rolling dunes. A couple of times we dead-ended into a thicket or a stream that seemed unwise to cross. We worked our way semi-methodically, trying to keep our hopes up, trying not to get our hopes up. We'd spotted each other's heads across the way, knew we would have heard the yell if *Splitpea* had been discovered.

After an hour or so, we met back up, empty handed. It was time to give up. Just as we started to walk back toward the fish camp to rustle up a ride, we spotted a couple of fishermen unloading their panga at the water's edge. Bryan wanted to go ask them if they'd seen anything. I had already moved on. But I gave in and walked over with him while Hannah and Meira waited in the sand, making the best of today's annoyances with songs and stories.

The fisherman said he'd seen our little boat leave the bay with another sailor the day before. This seemed unlikely but he was so confident, nodding at our photo and gesturing toward the sea. Even false hope could be a gift if it would get us moving. We walked back toward the estuary, hoping to stumble on a ride back to *LiLo*.

The panga driver who had brought us to shore must have been watching from the fish camp on the other side of the river. By the time we'd called the kids from their shady spot in the sand and assembled ourselves on the edge of the current, he was already motoring across to retrieve us. Meira rode in the bow the way she always had in *Splitpea* and took each wave as a gift, grinning. Hannah huddled nearer the middle where the ride was steadier. I sat there with her and tucked her under my arm to block the breeze and spray. We couldn't make small talk over the noise of the outboard but we smiled our thanks to the driver and crew.

Back on the boat, we did some quick math. If another boater had picked up our dinghy, Bahía Magdalena, the next bay south, would be the most likely place to find them. Though only a few miles as the crow flies (or here, should it be the pelican?) we had to sail out and down, then in and back up again—about thirty miles before dark. And the darkness was not just scary; it could be downright deadly. Anchoring in strange locations without clear vision was never a good idea, especially not now, tired and stressed. We plotted a course, estimated the current, located a bail-out option, and set our sails.

Once out past the mouth of the bay, we picked up the northwest wind and caught the tidal current south in an exhilarating ride, maybe the best few hours of sailing all year.

After we settled on a tack I spoke up, "At least it feels like we're moving *toward* something instead of just running away."

"I feel the same," Bryan said. "We don't have a much clearer plan, but at least we know we did everything we could before moving on."

Before our fresh energy faded, we reached the mouth of Bahía Magdalena. The wide entrance held few obstacles and we breezed in and turned to port, working our way back north into the bay. We eyed the little cove marked on our charts as a decent anchorage. There was already another boat anchored in the lee of the spit and the space that remained didn't look terribly inviting. I glanced at the sun, noted our speed and our distance, and then estimated.

"Yeah, we've probably got enough daylight left to get to the main anchorage." We motored north in the fading light, our high spirits beginning to give way to fatigue. I guarded myself against rising hope. *What if Splitpea is there when we arrive? What if we pull into the bay and we see her trailing behind another boat?* I didn't dare wonder aloud but I knew the whole crew was wondering the same thing.

We reached our destination with barely enough daylight to anchor safely away from the other boat in the cove. We had heard that *Purusha*, who we'd met in Bahía Tortugas, had been having engine trouble. We'd even heard a few one-sided conversations on our VHF as they communicated with someone in nearby San Carlos, just beyond our radio's reach. So we assumed that the anchor light off to the northeast was theirs. We could only spot one dinghy on their bow and it wasn't *Splitpea*. No big surprise, but still disappointing.

The next morning, we spoke on the radio and they confirmed our fears. No word of a dinghy found, and they'd been around for several days working on their balky motor. They almost certainly would have heard.

A few minutes later they zoomed over in their dinghy with consolation gifts—Snickers bars and a surfboard.

"If you need a way to get to shore, you could use this as a paddle board," the captain offered. "It's not ours, but the guy who owns it won't be around for a while and you can get it back to us later." We were eager to accept their chocolate but reluctant to take an expensive piece of equipment that would require careful coordination to return.

"We probably need something that can carry all of us, actually, but thanks anyway."

They were heading into shore in a few minutes, and asked if we would like to come along. We all jumped at the chance to get off the boat and were ready in moments. We piled into their large inflatable and zipped across the shallows to the beach where we moored the dinghy, panga-style: a large loop of rope ran through the eyelets of two stakes planted in the sand on shore and then a few yards out through the loops in a couple of makeshift mooring buoys. We tied the dinghy painter to this system of ropes and anchors and then hauled the loop around until the dinghy floated freely.

Smooth, white whale ribs arched together at the other end of the small beach. Several dusty lanes angled away from the shoreline. Cement homes lined the streets, each one unique, clearly custom built. A woman came out on her porch and called after her son just as a truck drove through, crushing the toy he'd left in the road. We caught her attention and she stopped to speak to us, answering our questions as best she could. Yes, you can leave your garbage in the barrels. No, there's no charge. You want to what? Buy a boat?

On an earlier excursion to shore, *Purusha*'s captain, David, had spotted a deteriorating dinghy in an empty lot and was convinced we could buy it for cheap. We were dubious, but he persisted.

"Who owns this boat?" He wanted to know. "My friends need a new dinghy. Is this one for sale?"

We hadn't seen the fishermen use a boat this small and this one—overflowing with a tangle of fish nets, sporting a few holes in the hull—didn't seem to have seen the sea in a long time. It looked heavy, but approximately the right size and holes can be patched.

The woman on the porch shook her head, "No, the owner is in La Paz with a sick family member. I don't know when he'll be back." David seemed more disappointed than we were. I think he was tired of engine troubles he couldn't fix and was excited at the possibility of solving our problems instead.

David and several women who were visiting aboard *Purusha* had made arrangements with a local charter fisherman to tow them up to San Carlos's small commercial port, so the next day we watched as their help arrived and pulled them away, the little boat leading the big one on the long winding passage up the estuary. We'd heard the port was not set up for small boat access, so we decided to stay put for the day. Our cruising guide gave information about getting fuel from the port captain and cruiser chatter, the coconut telegraph, confirmed that we should expect a visit from him soon after our arrival in this small bay. "Invite him aboard for coffee before you ask for what you want," they suggested.

We waited around the first morning, getting us and the boat ready for visitors, but when yet another morning passed with no sign of the port captain, Bryan got busy. "We can't just wait here using up all our food and water. Let's go on up to San Carlos too and see if we can figure out how to get to shore for fuel."

The safe channel wound in a long, loose "S" through the shifting shoals of the estuary's delta. We followed the markers and watched the depth sounder carefully. To say that San Carlos was unprotected is quite an understatement. A fleet of large commercial boats fought for space against the tall piers jutting out into the wide open water. *Purusha* bucked at anchor in the middle of the channel and, after a few minutes of searching for a better place to stop, we understood why. Anything outside the channel was too shallow, the docks were full and too big besides, the water between the pier and the shore shoaled alarmingly fast. The tide had been with us on our way north but was beginning to turn against us, kicking up a nasty chop.

We anchored as close to the edge of the channel as we could, then radioed over to *Purusha*. Even with an anchor watch, it had been a perilous night. Their anchor rode had gotten tangled around their keel and threatened to drag them ashore. But today they had a mechanic aboard and he'd offered to take several of them to town for fuel and water. Did one of us want to go along?

With the current and wind as swift as they were, Bryan needed to stay with *LiLo* in case her anchor started to drag. I grabbed the last of our cash, threw on my life jacket, and watched as a little motorboat peeled away from *Purusha*'s hull and rushed across to me. The crew helped hold the two heaving boats together and Bryan tossed four fuel cans, two water jugs, and one startled wife over the gunwales and into the other boat.

First stop: the mechanic's house where we picked up his wife and infant son to take them out to lunch. Guillermo had been helping the sailors on *Purusha* for several days and they wanted to express their thanks. I hadn't had a relaxed meal in what seemed like weeks, so I disregarded thoughts of how miserable it must be aboard our boat and decided to enjoy myself. Next we went for a fuel run to a gas station that actually accepted Visa so I saved my cash for groceries.

On our way to the grocery store the women from *Purusha* stopped in a little variety store for toys and art supplies to give away to local kids. They giggled and chose as I wandered the aisles resisting worry. *Was LiLo dragging anchor while I was safe on shore? Would they still be there when I got back?*

At the grocery store, I grabbed tortillas and fruit, bread and cookies, just a few essentials to tide us over. I calculated carefully and held back the last of our cash just in case. We walked our groceries across the street to the truck, where all the sailors climbed up the trailer wheels and piled into the motorboat for the ride. We pulled out into the street and drove a few blocks before stopping again, this time right in the middle of the road. The man going the opposite direction was the son of the owner of the local desalination plant and, yes, he hollered back to Guillermo, he would be willing to open up for us, even though it was a Sunday.

A few minutes later, we met again at the plant. He and Guillermo teased the women from *Purusha* as they filled their collection of 5-gallon blue water containers—"150 gallons of water? Really? How big is your sailboat?"

They turned to me next, and I held out a pair of water jugs and spoke into the eruption of laughter. "Just twelve gallons, please."

Purusha knew we were short on cash, so they waved away my offer to pay.

"For only twelve gallons? Never mind."

We stopped by Guillermo's house once more, to drop off his wife and son and pick up a weather report. His years of experience along this coastline were reassuring as we looked over the forecasts together.

"Leaving for Cabo today or tomorrow? Looks good!"

Finally ready to head out to the sailboats, we drove our heavy load back through town. As we neared the beach, the truck started sputtering, one cylinder not firing. We had barely enough time to exchange troubled glances when the trailer lurched and listed suddenly. I glanced over the side—sure enough, a flat tire.

Our driver didn't seem to care, just bounced the whole wobbly circus down to the shore, whipped a slick U-turn, and backed the motorboat into the water. He parked the truck and climbed into the cockpit with us.

His cheery, "I think we'll be okay," was maybe not as reassuring as intended, as he shuffled water jugs and passengers to balance the weight in the overloaded motorboat. I buckled my life jacket securely and took shallow breaths all the way back to *LiLo*. Bryan was waiting for me on the side decks and we performed a reverse of our previous maneuver. He hauled now full jugs over the sides, as I navigated the step from motorboat to sailboat, careful not to get any part of me stuck between any part of them.

As soon as the motorboat was clear, Bryan announced, "We're leaving. Right now. I can't stand this anchorage one second longer, much less all night." Bryan had calculated how late we could take off and still safely clear the tricky S-curve before nightfall and had been watching the clock all afternoon, increasingly worried for me. He and the kids had been waiting for hours, bucking up and down and watching the daylight slip away. They'd tried to raise me on the handheld VHF but the reception was poor between the buildings in town. His self-imposed deadline had passed five minutes before I arrived. In seconds, the anchor was up and we were once again riding fair winds and following seas away from a miserable memory.

On our way back toward Bahía Magdalena, Bryan asked, "Any reason why we can't just take off tonight? If the weather looks good—does it? We could be in Cabo in thirty-six hours. We've got fuel and food and water. What are we waiting for?"

And that's how we ended up sailing from the worst anchorage of the trip into the biggest storm of my life.

Chapter Fifteen

IF IT DOESN'T GET ANY WORSE

In the ocean off southern Baja California, Mexico
December 2013: Waxing Crescent

*The floor seemed wonderfully solid.
It was comforting to know I had fallen and could fall no further.*
—Sylvia Plath

All night and most of the next day the ride was smooth and calm but as evening fell, the wind rose with an intensity that demanded attention.

"I checked the weather online in San Carlos and Guillermo said it looked great for days. I don't know what's going on."

"Well, it doesn't matter what it was *supposed* to be. This is what it *is*."

"We're more than halfway to Cabo. It won't do us any good to turn around. I think we're just going to have to ride it out."

They say that by the time you wonder if you should be reefing it's too late. So before it got dark, Bryan braved the foredeck to pull down our sails and put up the storm jib. He set the autopilot on a safe, offshore course and lashed it to the tiller, checked the sheets for chafe, and then stood on the companionway steps sliding each drop board securely into place. We usually traveled with the doorway open, sometimes covered in a canvas for warmth. On bad days we'd put in one or two boards, enough to keep the water out if the cockpit got swamped. Tonight he dropped in all four slats and shut the cover firmly, checked the hatches on all the ports, and sent us to bed for safety.

"Take a book if you want, but I don't want you crashing around in here." He spoke calmly, but firmly, and the kids and I crawled under our covers. *If he's not panicking yet, maybe we're still okay,* I thought. *If it doesn't get any worse, and nothing breaks, I think we'll be all right.*

Storms in this part of the Pacific typically approach from the northwest or the west, the winds stirring up high-wheeling waves as they bluster across the surface. This storm flew in from the east, from the land side, but even with the shorter fetch, the swell was already knocking us hard to starboard. *LiLo* lifted to each crest and swayed into each trough. The gunwale rolled down to meet the sea, rebounded as the iron keel answered the pull of the earth beneath.

Bryan came up to the V-berth and braced himself between the hanging lockers. "The wind is high, but it's directly on the beam and I think we've gotten the little sail set just right to balance the boat in the swell. The autopilot is doing a great job of keeping us on course. I'll stay up and keep watch. You try to rest."

"Okay. Let me know if you need me to get up to help."

"I will, but I think you're safer out of the way."

As he turned to head back toward the stern I reached out to touch his arm.

"Hey, it's going to be okay, right? Tell me it's going to be okay. Lie to me if you have to. I just need to hear you say it."

He straightened his shoulders and turned back my way. "It's going to be okay, Beth. It's all going to be okay."

But I knew he might be lying.

The night dissolved into a haze of fear and holding on. Waves beat down like a pestle, crushing the breath from my lungs. Every time we slid off a crest, I gulped for air in the weightlessness. Everything that could fall had already fallen.

Bryan laid on the floor in the debris and the damp and Meira dozed over him, braced across the salon. With each swell that hit the beam she gave a shove to keep the settee cushions in place, back up onto the high side. Over and over, I heard her whisper, "It's been ten minutes, Dad. Time to check for ships."

The wind-blown spray made the duty more obligatory than helpful. If there were other ships nearby, we might not be able to see them until too late to avoid a collision. This was the least hospitable stretch of coastline so far, with not even a curve in the land to tuck behind for shelter. We harbored hope we were the only ones foolhardy enough to be out in this mess.

Already lulled into numbness by the passage, my body's primal response to the dark overtook me completely. I laid on the low side, half on the berth, half on the wall as the wind knocked us out toward sea. Water rushed past the starboard window with solid inky depth. Waves leapt over the boat crashing into the porthole above me.

I moved in and out of awareness through the long night. When panic rose to join the screeching wind, I drew on familiar thoughts for comfort. *This is going to be a story. Let's just hope it's an autobiographical one.*

I rehearsed what was going right to stave off all the what-ifs. *The autopilot is holding for now. Everything is holding for now. In this moment—and this one—everything is okay. Maybe it will stay that way.*

The racket of the storm melded into a steady din but a sound began to assert itself above the fray. *Clank. Clank-clank.* I kept hoping it was only my imagination. *Clank.* But no. *Clank-clank.* Something on deck had definitely worked its way loose.

Bryan stepped into view again, his face weary in the red light. "I'm going to have to go up and see what that is."

"Should I come out on deck and watch for you?" I asked, reluctantly. *I shouldn't let him go out there alone.*

"Don't worry; I'll tether in. You just stay here and I'll be right back."

My fear for his safety lost out to my fear of the storm. I strained to hear every move he made as he suited up, slid out two of the drop boards, and hoisted himself over the others and into the cockpit. *I'm sure he tethered in before he ventured out,* I thought, but I couldn't drag myself from the bunk to double check. I listened for the beat of his shackle on the lifeline as he made his way up the high side to the mast. I listened hard, my whole body tense, as if I could keep him safe if I heard him fall. The tether stopped amidships and presently the clanking stopped as well. The first moment of silence came as a relief. *It must have been a halyard coming loose. It's all good now.* But the longer the silence stretched out, the worse I felt. *What's going on up there? Why is he not coming back? How long should I wait before I get up to check? What if I check, and find him gone?*

My limbs felt heavy, as if caught in the water that held us up. I tried to will myself from the bunk, but didn't even manage to turn over before I heard the welcome sounds resume. A pair of careful steps followed by the drag of the tether, another cautious step, another pull on the jack lines. I followed every move from beneath. *And there, now he's back in the cockpit. And there, now he's opening the cabin hatch.* I glanced up and watched his hands grasp the hatch rails, his strong arms lift his frame over the drop boards, his feet reach down to the steps below. He sealed the opening and moved carefully to my side.

"It was just the main halyard coming loose. The sail looks great and the autopilot is still hanging in there. But, whew, it's wild out there." He grinned a little, his drenched face lifting in exhilaration. "I've heard folks talk about 'angry seas' before. Now I know exactly what they mean."

"I'm sorry I didn't come check on you. I was scared when it got quiet."

"I just needed to take a minute to look around. I may never see a sight like this again."

"I'd go look but I just can't."

He let go of one handhold for a moment, laid his cold hand on my warm one. "It's okay, Beth. It's really all going to be okay."

The harbor at Cabo was still hours away and the storm had yet to ease, but I began to breathe again. I had already made my way to refuge.

Chapter Sixteen

To the End of the Earth

Cabo San Lucas, Mexico
December 2013: First Quarter, Waxing Gibbous

You have come to the shore. There are no instructions.
—Denise Levertov

As we rounded the southwest corner of Baja and started to head east toward the Cabo San Lucas harbor, Bryan called down to the crew, "We're going to need all eyes for the entrance. Anyone who's not dead tired come make sure we don't screw this up."

Pangas and charter boats, water taxis and catamaran tours all buzzed around the arches at the entrance and we worked to navigate safely. We motored slowly past El Arco at the southern tip of the peninsula and picked our way through the charter fleet in the outer bay. I pulled out some cruising guides and made a couple of calls to the marinas listed. Without gestures and facial expressions, my language skills disintegrated almost completely so I wasn't totally sure I'd understood correctly.

"I think we have a slip waiting for us but it sounds like it's … " I stopped for a minute to do some quick mental conversions, " … it's going to be about eighty dollars a day."

"Ouch! That's going to take a bite out of our budget."

"I couldn't tell if there was a cheaper option but once we get in we can do a little looking around."

We followed the harbor map past the fuel dock to the rows of gleaming white fishing boats near the wharf and turned into Dock D where we'd been told we could find an empty slip. About halfway down the fairway toward the sea wall, a security guard stood waiting at the end of a dock finger. We nosed in and handed him the stern line. I jumped down and hauled the midline around a cleat to keep us from swaying across into the neighbor boat.

It had been more than a month since Ensenada, where we last tied up to a dock. More than a week since we had been able to get to shore under our own power. Bryan killed the engine and tossed a few things below while I exchanged introductions and got instructions from the guard, Mauricio. "The marina office is closing soon. You'd better get up there in a hurry!"

"Do they close at four?" I asked, a bit confused.

"No, they close at five, but it's quarter till now."

I glanced below at the ship's clock, still set to 3:45.

"We must have changed time zones since we left San Carlos." I called below to the crew. "Get shore-ready in a hurry. We've got to go get checked in!"

Mauricio walked us up to the embarcadero on the seawall and pointed us down the walkway toward the restaurant strip.

"The office is just around the corner. You'll find it!"

After weeks in rural Baja, I was overwhelmed by the noise and bustle. Glitzy shops blared Christmas music from giant speakers. Street vendors worked the crowd selling cigars and silver bracelets. We made our way past the busy outdoor tables and turned the corner by a giant green ATM.

"That must be it," I pointed and we rushed over to the modest entrance and filed inside, filling the small office.

A kind face looked up from the front desk and took in our sea-weary expressions. "Are you here to check in?"

"Yes, please."

"How many nights?"

"Just one for now but we may need to stay longer if there's room."

"Yes, no problem! A lot of boats are here waiting for the northers in the sea to die down."

As we started in on paperwork, I made a mental note. *Storms in the Sea of Cortez. We only checked the weather on the west side of Baja. I wonder ...*

Sure enough, when we stopped to look, we found the storm we'd sailed through had started up in the northern gulf, rushed down the narrow sea and funneled through a dip in the mountain range, accelerating on its way. No wonder we hadn't seen it coming.

It felt rude to inquire about a cheaper marina so we decided to walk around the docks and see for ourselves.

We headed around the harbor's perimeter toward where we'd seen another marina on the map. After almost a mile of restaurants, T-shirt kiosks, and time-share booths we decided to ask for help. I spotted a friendly face in one of the shops and asked, "Can you tell me where the marina is around here?"

"Just follow the green arrows on the sidewalk. They will take you right there."

We stepped back out into the crowd and found the first green arrow. Hannah and Meira ran ahead looking for the next one and we followed behind, increasingly confused.

"I'm not sure the marina would be big enough to have all these signs on the sidewalk."

"Yeah, me either. Maybe this is something to do with the cruise ships in town?"

The farther we followed the more certain we became: we were lost.

"These are taking us out to the end of the wharf where the ships drop off. He must have thought we were here on a cruise."

I looked down at my sundress, so different from the sailing gear I'd worn not long before, and my skin, still pale despite all these months at sea.

"I guess we do look like we could be here on vacation, right?"

We stopped to regroup and I heard a voice call out, "You need some help?"

I turned and looked, a little bewildered. A man about my age stood bouncing on the balls of his feet, on his face a broad grin. "You need some help?" he repeated.

"Maybe," I hedged. "We just came in on a sailboat and are looking for a marina with a slip available. Do you know where the marina office is on this side of the harbor?"

"Oh, yes! Follow me!" He took off back the way we'd come and then turned south away from the water a bit. My tired legs strained to stay close enough to hear his cheerful chatter.

"I know everything about this harbor, everything! You need anything, you just ask Endy, that's me!" We stopped to shake hands and share our names in turn.

"I'm here every day, all the time! I can help with anything you need!" He walked as fast as he spoke, nodding a greeting to shopkeepers along the way.

"There's no cruise ship in today so I'm not very busy but when there is—whew!—it's *really* busy here." I imagined a shipload of visitors added to the melee.

"This way." He led us around another corner and up to a security booth marked with official looking decals. The guards seemed to recognize him and they waved us on through. I hung back and whispered to Bryan, "I think we're headed onto a Navy base. This doesn't really seem right either."

"No, but I guess we'll find out soon enough."

We walked down another street and back toward the water. Endy led us out to the end of a wide pier, pointed at the last building to the right.

"Here you are! The marina office."

The inside air cooled my face as I stepped through the door. I explained our situation again to the agent at the front desk and waited while she conversed in high-speed Spanish with the other employees.

She turned back to me and slowed her speech. "I'm sorry. This marina is just for commercial boats, not small ships like yours. There are no cheaper options, just the marina where you are."

Back out on the wharf, we explained the whole story to Endy–how we had lost our dinghy and needed to save as much money as possible while we figured out what to do next.

"I know all the people!" he said. "I'll try to find something for you." He walked us back through the streets to the main wharf. We gave him our thanks and headed down the embarcadero.

As we walked, Bryan said, "Well, no matter what happens next, we're here now. We made it all the way to Finisterre—to the end of the earth, they say. To the end of Baja in any case. And that deserves celebrating. We'll have lots of time to think about what to do later. This afternoon, we're going to pretend our problems don't exist for just a few hours. Let's go find some tacos!"

We walked all the way back around the harbor to a beach on the other side. We wove through the beach chairs in the sand and found a balcony restaurant still serving lunch. From the cabana next door came the amplified sounds of compulsory fun. "Come on up to the stage and bring your tequila! But watch yourselves on the steps. If you hurt yourself, this is Mexico and you can't sue us!"

Bryan and I smiled at the crew and we raised a toast to ourselves, finding ways to celebrate even in the middle of the uncertain journey.

On our way back, we stopped to talk to several of the sidewalk vendors. We were still trying to explain to one of them, a cheerful restauranteur named, Ivan, that, yes, we really had sailed a little boat all the way from Los Estados Unidos, when we heard a distinctive holler.

"Leeelo, Leeelo, Leeelo!" We turned to look—*who knows us here?*—and finally spotted a water taxi, nose bumping the rocky seawall, Endy in the bow waving wildly. "Come! Come! I have a friend with a boat for you!" Bryan and I exchanged a loaded glance, smiled our apologies to Ivan, and stepped to the edge of the wharf. Hannah went first, then Meira and Bryan, each one climbing over the guard rail and working their way down the boulders to the panga. I held my skirt in place as I followed and found a seat. As we pulled back out into the maze of docks and floats we worked to understand what we'd just agreed to.

"Who has a boat? What's going on?"

Endy was more concerned with getting us into bulky orange life jackets, saying, "The patrols have been out today." Eventually he explained, "I have a friend who has an inflatable dinghy for sale, maybe even two. They are very new, very cheap. But we have to find him before he leaves." We rushed across the harbor to where we'd met Endy earlier in the day and pulled into a dock loaded with other water taxis. Endy and his friend helped us out onto the dock and we followed them down to the end of the finger.

"He's gone," Endy said, but ever the salesman, continued, "Here's one like the one he has to sell. Maybe he has two. Very new. Very cheap!" We looked over the inflatable obligingly but, even if the "very new" one was "very cheap" it wouldn't be a good fit for us without an expensive outboard, an electric pump, and a bigger mothership. We made tentative plans to meet him and his friend the next day just in case they could find something suitable and then taxied back to *LiLo*.

Bryan and I left the kids to get ready for bed and walked up to the marina patio for internet access.

"I've been thinking," he said. My ears perked up. After all these years together, I've never known him to follow those words with anything dull. In fact, I'm pretty sure our first conversation about this whole wild adventure started with that very statement.

"Yes?" I smiled.

He went on. "So if we can find a spot. And if we can get all the materials we need. And if you're up for it ... " He took a deep breath and rushed to the point.

"I think we can build a new dinghy in five days."

My mouth started shaping protests even as my mind was jumping ahead to agree.

"But the last one took us nine months!" I said.

"We'll be faster this time,"

You were looking for a Plan C.

"Do you really think we could find fiberglass and epoxy?" I asked.

"I don't know, but don't you want to find out?"

This could be the perfect solution.

"Do we even have the tools we would need?"

"Probably not but I think we can make it work with what we have."

Think of the story this would make if we could pull it off.

"You really think we can do this?"

He nodded. "I really think we can do this."

"Okay, then. Let's build us a new dinghy."

Chapter Seventeen

When We're Done, She'll Float

Cabo San Lucas, Mexico
December 2013: Waxing Gibbous

Floating is not the only reason to make a boat.
—Holly Wren Spaulding

We started planning immediately. Bryan downloaded a digital copy of a boatbuilding book he'd used before and started making lists of the materials he needed to source. I listened and took notes, wrapping my brain around the unexpected solution. *Of course we'll build a boat in a parking lot. How could I ever have imagined this DIY family would find any other solution to our problem?*

We made a game plan for the next day and went to bed. But the city didn't sleep and neither did we. Dockside restaurants turned up the volume and boisterous partiers reveled until well after midnight. At dawn, charter fishermen broke the brief silence as they piled aboard and motored out for the day. We shook off our weariness and started planning, tea and coffee close at hand.

"If you can talk to the harbormaster or the marina manager, maybe you can find us a place to build," Bryan said. "I've done the math again and again. I really think we can do this in five days. We'll spend a day gathering materials, cut and assemble the frame the second day, tape and fiberglass the third day, finish the fiberglass the fourth day, and on the fifth day, paint!"

Put that way, it seemed simple, though I knew the actual work wouldn't be easy.

"We had a full shop and nine months to build the last one. Can we really get this one done in a week?"

"Five days," Bryan corrected me. "And yep. We spent a lot of time joining plywood together to make extra long sheets. This plan was written to make use of the standard eight-foot lengths, so we can skip that whole step. We'll buy quick-cure epoxy and it'll harden fast here in the heat. And we'll just paint the whole thing, inside and out. No days of sanding and fancy varnish. It'll be closer to wood-butchery than woodworking, but when we're done, she'll float."

As the shops began to open, he headed out to locate fiberglass, epoxy, tape, and tools. Hannah, Meira, and I walked up to the marina office.

"Maybe you can help us," I began, and explained our situation.

The receptionist listened but shook her head. "I think you need to talk to the boatyard. They're right around the corner."

So we headed out the door and around the corner, aiming toward the masts and antennas towering over the waterfront buildings. I walked in through the open gate and stopped short. The boatyard took up less than half a block. Every speck of spare ground was covered by a tarp with a boat on top. Workers buzzed through hollering above the din of power tools. I finally caught someone's attention and explained again. He looked around as if a gap might suddenly open up for us.

"I'm sorry, no. Every spot is full and we have a waiting list for weeks. We just can't help you here."

We walked back out into the streets and looked around. In this tourism-driven environment, every bit of land not taken up by high-rise hotels or beach-front restaurants was jam packed with shops, booths, and taco stands. We only wanted a few square feet of space but here even parking spots were rare. We went back to the boat to get some food and let our minds untangle a bit. Refreshed, I stood up and made a decision.

"Kids, let's go back to the office to try again. Maybe they know of another place to send us."

We walked back up the docks again, past the gate guard and the street sellers who were starting to recognize us as regulars. I pushed open the office door again. This time, Chuy, the local manager, was standing behind the receptionist's desk.

I repeated our plea, letting them know what the boatyard had said.

"We really only need one little parking spot and we just don't know what we'll do otherwise. We can't build a boat on the docks."

The manager stepped around the desk and measured us with a look. "Well, the big boss is in from out of town today but he's leaving tomorrow. If you can wait until then, I can give you a spot next to the shop for the desalination plant. They've got power if you need it and can make big cuts for you if you don't have tools. Come back in the morning and I'll show you where it is." He shook his head and grinned, "A family of gringos building a boat in five days in my parking lot. This I've got to see."

I knew we wouldn't have much time for Christmas shopping once we started construction so I made plans to bus up to a shopping center with friends from *Vales Valeo,* who had come in a day or two before us. The kids and I ran back to the boat, left a note on the drop boards: "WE GOT A SPOT! Be back later." And off we went.

Back at the boat that evening, Bryan and I shared stories from the day. I showed him my Christmas haul while tucking it into the locker under my pillow and then pulled out the Skilsaw and clamps I'd borrowed from another sailboat in the marina.

He bragged about all the materials he'd gathered—the fiberglass cloth, fiberglass tape, and epoxy resin, each from a different shop—and all the wood, which he'd somehow talked Home Depot into delivering immediately.

"They said they'd bring it next week," he said, "and I just kept saying, 'Can you bring it today?' until they said, 'Okay.' Then I asked if they could deliver me too. It saved me the three-mile walk back and now I'm getting started on the lofting plans. See?"

He held up his sketches and the sheets of paper he'd taped together for full-sized patterns.

"I have all the measurements planned out here. There's just a couple of numbers I couldn't read in the digital version of the book but I asked on a boatbuilding forum if anyone could take a look at their copy and send me the accurate numbers. I'm betting I'll hear back any minute."

We talked over the plan for the next day and he stayed up late tracing lines piece by piece on our small table.

In the morning Chuy walked us to the build site, the first of many treks along that portion of the wharf. We hauled all our tools—the Skilsaw, three hand saws, a cordless drill, and a hammer—and got to work right away. By lunchtime, we'd cut and assembled all the panels. We drilled small holes along the edges of each one and used tiny zip ties to stitch the boat together. Since we didn't have sawhorses, this part of the project required someone to lie under the boat to drill the holes and feed the ties back up. The crew cheerfully volunteered to work on the shady side of this task, and the lines of the boat began to take shape.

After lunch and a cooling dip in the tiny marina pool, we got back to work. The sun set about 5:30 p.m. so we pulled out our headlamps and soldiered on. By bedtime we'd finished joining the interior seams with epoxy and tape, one person mixing epoxy according to Bryan's instructions—"until it looks like peanut butter"—and the rest spreading the fiberglass tape in place before the resin hardened. We thickened the epoxy with wood flour Bryan had brought for repairs and, when we ran out of that, with whole wheat flour from the back of *LiLo*'s pantry.

As we cleaned up for the evening and packed up our tools for the walk back to the boat, Bryan said, "Technically, if everything cures well tonight, we could float the boat tomorrow. It wouldn't be a good idea but we could do it." We walked back and celebrated with gelato all around.

Saturday, the kids and I tracked down breakfast pastries and then walked over to the marine store to look for oars. We knew these might be tricky to find so far away from the mega stores in the US so we weren't too surprised when the shopkeeper shook his head. On the walk around to the build site, we tried to imagine other possibilities.

"Could we make some?" Meira asked.

"I don't know. Probably. I'm sure we'll figure out something."

Bryan had gone over to the build site early to sand the exterior seams and cover them with more fiberglass tape. The plywood and fiberglass were both thinner than we'd like and we knew we were going to be tough on our dinghy, so we decided to spend the extra time to add some reinforcement.

While we waited for the epoxy to harden, I connected to the marina internet and sent an email to Cameron, who we'd met back in Eureka, California. We hadn't crossed paths since, but had kept in touch along the way and we knew he was already up in the Sea of Cortez enjoying the snorkeling there.

When he first heard about our loss, he searched Craigslist all up and down the coast and sent me links to a few possible replacement options. None of them would work for us, which was almost a relief. I wasn't sure how we could get to San Diego and then bus back carrying a dinghy.

After he heard we'd decided to build, he reached out to say he'd be near Cabo on Sunday and would be happy to bring us equipment we needed from the more sailing-centric La Paz. I asked if there was any way he could find oars and the space in his rental car to carry them.

He replied right away, offering us his spare set of oars complete with the oarlocks necessary to attach them to the boat.

After lunch and a little more sanding, we started in on the fiberglass cloth, spreading the fabric over the upturned hull and gluing it into place with sticky epoxy. Meira and I held the dinghy in the air while Bryan frantically smoothed down the edges.

We finished one half in good time but when we rolled out the second length of fiberglass, we were a yard short. The crew and I worked to finish up what we had while Bryan ran to the fiberglass store to see if they were still open. Too soon, he was back with bad news. Not only was the shop closed, they would likely not be open again until Monday.

Just a minute or two after he got back, we ran out of epoxy.

"That's the last of it?" Bryan hammered on the pump nozzle. "Shoot, we're really out."

I hovered over the dinghy where the dry edge of the fiberglass cloth stuck up in awkward crinkles. "We can't let it cure like this or it'll never lie flat."

"Beth, what time is it?" Bryan was already reaching for his phone, "It's 5:15 but the epoxy place is all the way on the other side of the harbor. Let's just hope they're open until six."

We left the crew and our mess behind and took off race-walking through the tourist zone in our grungy clothes and sticky shoes.

We got to the shop at 5:32 and read the hours on the door: "9:00 a.m.-5:30 p.m." We caught our breath and tried the door. It was still unlocked, so we went in and explained our situation.

The proprietor kindly responded, "I'll sell you some epoxy, but I've shut my computer down for the day and can only take cash." He agreed to wait five minutes while we found an ATM. Almost all the machines on the waterfront charge high fees and only give out US dollars. We ran from one ATM to another and finally, feeling very out of place inside a glamorous hotel lobby, we found an ATM with pesos.

We sprinted back to the store, sure the shopkeeper had given up on us. But he was still there and we pushed our bills across the counter.

"That's a little over," he said apologetically, "but I can't open the cash drawer for change."

"No worries," I replied. "We're just grateful you were still here and willing to wait."

On the way back, we recalibrated our plan for Sunday.

Bryan said, "So now we can't work on the hull tomorrow, but we need to build the seats anyway. Let's flip the boat and get going on that. We still have gunwales and flotation to figure out as well."

"Ugh," I sighed. "I think Meira and I are coming down with a cold. I hope we are up for all of that."

"Why don't I clean up with the kids and you go grab some dinner. We'll meet you back on *LiLo* in a bit."

On every trip through the tourist zone, we passed the same vendors and restaurant workers. The first day of our build, I decided it was faster to stop once and offer a full explanation than to walk by rudely multiple times a day. Each person we met responded with concern and interest. Some looked at me with utter amazement.

One man in a time-share booth stared at my face in disbelief. "A lady? Is building a dinghy?" He mimed an explosion from his head at the thought.

"Yes, with my kids and their dad, but yes."

"Well, you're going to need to eat well," he said and gave me directions to a food cart up the way.

"You don't order off the menu. You need to tell them you want two kilos of birria and they will give it to you in one of those, you know, the white cups with the lid and they will give you tortillas and everything you need to eat for a couple of meals."

Our traveling philosophy is to say yes to just about anything suggested by someone from the area, so this evening I wandered the streets to the food cart and parroted the script I'd been given. Sure enough, I came back with plenty of food—salsa, tortillas, and delicious meat stew—and we spread it out on *LiLo*'s table and dug in.

By the time we were done eating, the dinghy was ready for another coat of epoxy. Bryan and I left the crew on board, walked back together, and finished up by headlamp in the dark. Every time I leaned over, my sinuses ached so Bryan suggested I stand to mix epoxy while he bent to spread it on the hull.

We finished quickly, gathered up our tools, bagged up the day's garbage, and walked back around the harbor to *LiLo*. After checking in on the crew, we walked up to the Starbucks on the corner. Here, where everything was open late, we'd gotten into the habit of going out for an evening cup of tea and internet access.

Bryan did some boat-building research and I updated my website with the day's events and sipped my English Breakfast as the pictures uploaded. So many friends had heard of our loss and were following our progress closely. My inbox contained several supportive emails including one from a friend who had put out a call for financial support and gathered enough to help defray the cost of our boatbuilding materials.

We lingered over our drinks, reading and responding to each message then walked back on the wharf past a motorcycle convention beginning to gather at the Harley Davidson Cafe next to our dock.

I breathed through my stuffy nose and spoke over the din, "Looks like we won't be getting much sleep again tonight."

Chapter Eighteen

Nothing is Going to Look Quite Like the Plan

Cabo San Lucas, Mexico
December 2013: Full Moon

*Faith is not protection from the storm.
It is knowing that you will either find shelter
or become it.*
—Leigh Standley

I slept a little in the quiet hours after the parties wound down and before the dawn fishing excursions picked up. I woke tired, sick, and worried. *What if we don't get done in time for Christmas? What if the weather doesn't clear for crossing the Sea of Cortez? What if all this extra expense means we run out of money before we get home?*

Bryan sensed my tension and reached across the gap in the V-berth. "I've got to go cut the seat panels this morning. You and the kids stay here and get a little more rest."

"You sound like you're getting sick, too," I said.

"What? Me? Sick? Never!" He sniffed, grinned, rolled out of bed, stepped over the laundry bag, and started a cup of coffee. A few minutes later, he grabbed a pencil and the Skilsaw and headed out.

By the time Hannah, Meira, and I made it to the parking spot, Bryan was ready for a break. He showed us what he'd done and how all the seat panels were going to fit into the curves of the boat.

"Nothing is going to look quite like the plan," he said, "but I wanted to have room for all of us to sit. I rough-cut the seats and then trimmed them to fit, see? I think there'll be room for my knees even with Mom and Hannah in the stern. And there's a spot for Meira in the bow just like in *Splitpea*. Now all these pieces and the interior need to be waterproofed. Can you do that while I make a hydration run?"

We worked in the heat until Bryan returned, downed the cold drinks he brought us, and tossed the empty bottles into the pile we were saving for flotation. Theoretically, filling the seats with the empties would give us positive flotation—enough buoyancy to keep the dinghy afloat even if it was completely swamped with water. We hoped we wouldn't one day find out we were wrong.

We knew our five-day plan was audacious and depended on nothing going wrong. We also knew at some point, there would be a day when it felt like everything was going wrong. This was that day.

I made another run to the hardware store for gloves but it was closed for the weekend. Then Bryan had to walk back to the boat for some tools we'd forgotten. Then we ran out of garbage bags so I walked back to the boat for those. I turned the corner by the ramp and the day turned with me. Our friend, Cameron, was standing by the gate. His face brightened when he saw me.

"It's been a long time and a lot of miles, huh?"

I spoke over his words. "It's so good to see you! Thanks for coming down and bringing the oars."

I grabbed what I needed from *LiLo* and we fell into step on the walk to the dinghy.

"How have you been? How was your trip south? Where did you stop in Baja? Where are you headed next?"

The questions tumbled out of my mouth and we exchanged stories all the way to the build site.

"Look who I found on my way to get garbage bags!" I announced as we walked into the parking lot. The crew was ready for a break so we cleaned up quickly, showed off our work, and walked back along the pier and up the street for lunch.

Cameron was in town to pick up his sister who was flying into the Los Cabos airport. He didn't have much time to hang around and we needed to get back to work anyway, so after lunch we walked him back to his car and picked up the gear he'd brought for us.

The eight-foot oars were oversized for our little dinghy but we were grateful to have any at all. Hannah and Meira paraded back to the boat, each holding an oar, paddles high above the curious crowd.

"Careful!" I called. "You could knock someone off the seawall with those things."

Just as we got back to *LiLo* our friends from *Vales Valeo* pulled up in their dinghy and the kids stood at the end of the dock to chat.

"I've got to go fit the interior panels," Bryan said. "But it'll be easier if I do it alone. Why don't you and the kids do a little souvenir shopping and join me later."

On our way out, we ran into David from *Purusha* and followed him back to his boat to borrow a few more tools. When building *Splitpea* we'd used almost fifty clamps to glue the gunwales into place. Here, after asking everyone we knew in the marina, we had collected seven.

"Well, it's better than none!" I said to the crew as we headed toward the shops. "I'm pretty sure your dad will be able to figure something out."

After choosing a few treasures we showed up at the build site ready to work, but Bryan wasn't quite ready for us. A board had broken while he was installing it, and it sat on the workbench, fiberglass tape Band-Aided across the break.

"Back home, I would have just pulled a new piece out of the scrap pile," he said. "But here, there isn't a scrap pile. This will cost us a few hours but when it's dry, it'll be stronger than ever."

We'd planned to install the gunwales during our evening shift but when Bryan pulled out the wood he'd bought for those reinforcing strips, it wasn't flexible enough to bend into place along the upper edges of the dinghy. By this point in the day we were getting cranky, most of us were sniffly, and all of us were tired. This latest setback felt enormous. We sat down on the ground by the boat in the fading daylight.

"What if," I began. "Umm, what if … " I'd hoped my mind would supply a solution, fill in the blank at the end of my suggestion, but there was nothing there. I felt flat and empty. The quiet moment grew into an uncomfortable silence.

I recalled Bryan once reading that the most important tool in a boatbuilder's arsenal is a good pondering chair in which to sit when solving a problem or recovering from a mistake and I laughed a bit at the thought. No chairs here. I shifted to the curb and stretched my weary hamstrings.

"Can you find some thinner wood? Something that would curve around the rim?"

"No, this is the best they had at Home Depot. Back home I could run it through the band saw to trim it down but here, no."

We subsided into silence again.

"And we have to have the gunwales to hold the hull in shape, right?"

I'd learned to offer even bad suggestions. Sometimes while Bryan explained to me why they wouldn't work, he'd stumble over an idea that just might.

"Actually, we don't *have* to have gunwales on this design. The inner frames hold the hull shape stable. They're just there for added strength so maybe … " As he spoke he moved to a crouch next to the little boat.

"What if ... ? Okay, yes. I think this might work. Let's cut sections of wood and glue them into the inside between the frames. We can use the clamps until we get each section screwed in and then move on to the next strip right away." His voice rose as he talked his way to a solution. "That will solve our problem with the wood *and* our issue of not having enough clamps."

I was still mostly in the dark about his plans but I could see the clarity dawning for him.

"I know we already had a lot on our list for tomorrow," he said. "Still, I think we should wait to try this out until we're a little more fresh. We can't afford to make foolish mistakes at this point."

After another short night's rest, we got to work implementing our plan for the fourth day—finish the interior support and the gunwales, patch the fiberglass, install the skeg. Even with the quick-cure epoxy, the boat needed hours to dry after every step. To stay on schedule we needed to be ready to paint by morning, but there was no way to rush the waiting.

We spent our downtime on an unsuccessful search for more gloves. The glue we were using ate through the latex in just a few minutes so we rationed the few we had by giving the kids most of the day off and working one-handed when possible. On one of Bryan's errands, he found a flotation motherlode—an empty lot with a huge pile of plastic bottles, enough to fill the last of the seats to the brim.

I stopped in at the marina office to give them an update and pay our moorage. With the dinghy this close to complete, we were starting to watch the weather for a good time to cross to Mazatlán and at the high daily rate, we didn't want to spend one more night than necessary. I paid up through Thursday and checked with the manager about the latest rumors in the marina.

"What's this I hear about boats getting impounded? Do you need any extra paperwork from us?"

Before we left the United States I'd read everything I could find about the legalities of boat travel in Mexico but since then there'd been a flurry of surprise raids on various marinas on the west coast.

Sailboats without the necessary permits had been confiscated. Some boats with the proper paperwork were taken if the captain wasn't on board to display all the required documents. We'd heard rumors that boats were being held for even minor discrepancies in documentation.

The manager reassured me. "We've got you covered. All your papers are in order. Just make sure you check in and out with the port captains along the way and you should be fine."

I still wasn't sure I understood the port captain requirement but it was at the bottom of a long, long list of things we were figuring out along the way.

That night we worked by headlamp and the light of the rising full moon. I stood often to stretch and moved slower as the evening went on.

Finally, Bryan said, "Okay, this'll be the last cup of epoxy I need."

"Really? We're almost done?"

"Just the painting and the rub rail to do tomorrow. We should be able to launch on Wednesday."

Tuesday morning came early after Monday's late shift. I'd lost my voice in the night and Bryan woke up feeling awful. On any other week, we'd declare a sick day and stay in bed, but we had a boat to finish.

Bryan made a cup of coffee and headed off with the sander to knock down the worst of the epoxy drips. The kids and I followed shortly with wet rags to wipe down the dust.

Then it was time to paint. Bryan applied a ceremonial bright red brushstroke on the bow and we left the crew working and walked to the market for cold drinks. On the way, a now-familiar vendor called out to us.

"Let us know when you're going to move your boat. We'll get some nice strong men to help you!"

I smiled and nodded but I knew the look on Bryan's face. *We built it. We'll carry it.*

When we got back, Hannah and Meira were just finishing the paint on the stern and the bow was already dry.

"Let's put on another coat and then move the boat into the sun," Bryan said. "We'll have to flip it before I'd like but the bottom is going to get scratched up on the beaches anyway."

I walked to the store for clean paintbrushes so we didn't end up with red paint on our white interior. I bought a large brush for the big spaces and two smaller ones for the tight corners. It seemed like a good idea until I got back and realized our big brush didn't fit into the paint can or the cups we were using as paint trays. Bryan thought for a moment, grabbed a pair of scissors, and made me a dish from an old Pepsi bottle. He and Meira taped a scrap of wood to it so I could set it down without it rolling away.

Just as we finished the first interior coat, Chuy showed up to check on our progress.

Bryan proudly showed off our work. "One more coat of paint and we'll be down to the final fittings—just the oarlocks and the rub rail to go. We should be out of your hair tomorrow."

Later that day, Chuy caught me on the sidewalk. He shifted his feet and held out a small envelope.

"I heard you were talking about taking your kids to see the latest *Hobbit* movie. Well, I think what you and your family are doing is simply sensational and I wanted to give you some tickets to the movie to celebrate. A little early Christmas gift."

We'd come into the harbor exhausted and discouraged, drained of money and hope. In just a few days, we'd rebuilt more than just our lost dinghy. We'd dug deep for strength, stirred up new energy, and pieced together a community strong enough to see us through.

"Chuy, you've been such a huge help all along the way. The security guards, the restaurant recommendations, the parking spot—I simply don't know what we would have done without you. Thank you for everything. Gracias."

We made plans to see the movie that evening and rushed through the final coat of paint before dark.

"We don't really have enough for a full second coat inside," Bryan said, "so just touch up the parts that look really bad and we'll call it good."

With the very last bit of white paint, he freehanded some letters on the transom, across the cherry-red stern.

"I know we didn't really talk about what to call her," he said. "I've always thought it would be fun to have a dinghy named *Rover*. It didn't seem right for *Splitpea* but I think it's just the right fit for this little boat."

"We all worked hard on her but all of us know there's no way we'd have even tried this without you. I'm happy to give you naming privileges. And *Rover* seems just right."

Hannah feigned a radio call. "*LiLo, LiLo, LiLo,* this is *Rover,* over."

Meira joined in. "*Rover,* over. *Rover,* over. That's fun to say!"

"What's the T/T *LiLo* for?" Hannah asked.

"That stands for tender to *LiLo*," Bryan explained. "She's not going to be the same as *Splitpea*, but she's a good little boat. We've got a dinghy again."

Chapter Nineteen

BUOYED ONCE AGAIN

Cabo San Lucas, Mexico
December 2013: Waning Gibbous

Trust that water will bear you up
Trust the moon to keep faith
With ebb and flow
Trust the leafing
The chrysalis, the seed
And every other way
Death gives birth to resurrection

Wednesday morning, I woke sparking with excitement.

"Today is launch day, kids," I announced. "Where's your dad?"

A few minutes later he returned with buzzing energy and the last of what we needed—some stainless washers and morning coffee. We gathered up our tools and set out for the last walk to the build site. We'd grown accustomed to this daily commute—past the shops and restaurants, up the stairs, through a parking lot, around the corner to the desalination shop.

We passed a red pickup and the workers lined up to buy breakfast from the tailgate.

"The food truck is here today!" Hannah said.

"Yay!" I responded. "And we even have cash with us. We'll get red-truck lunch to celebrate the launch!"

The week before, on our way to the build site the first time, Chuy had pointed out the spot to us as the best place for authentic food.

"It's where all the workers eat," he said, eyeing the truck sadly, "If my wife didn't have me on a diet, I'd be eating there every day. But you should eat there! He's not always here but if you see the truck, don't wait. Get in line!"

I slipped into the queue and chatted with the other folks who were waiting, feeling like I had been given a VIP pass to a behind-the-scenes Cabo club.

"Order 'Poco de todos,'" one recommended. A little of everything. So I did.

I came back with more food than even hungry boatbuilders could eat. We spread it out and stood around shoveling in tacos de papa, arroz con frijoles, sopes, and huevos con chorizo, all topped with salsa de nopales.

Meira spoke around a mouthful of taco. "I think this is the best thing I've ever eaten."

"You know what?" I said. "I think I agree."

Bryan wiped his hands and got back to work on the final touch—a rope rub rail.

"I hope we have enough of this rope," he said. "Did I tell you about buying it? I asked for seven meters and the shopkeeper started measuring sections in arm lengths. When he noticed my look, he just grinned and said 'It's Mexican meters.'" We had more than enough.

I whipped the ends of the rope. Bryan installed the oarlocks. Hannah and Meira bagged up the tools and trash.

"That's it." I looked around the parking lot. "We're really done."

We sat down for a few minutes to let the sense of accomplishment sink in. Soon, Bryan was back up fiddling with our GoPro.

"Okay, I think the camera's ready for the big walk. Are you?"

"Ready!" Meira stood and moved to the starboard bow.

"Me too!" Hannah took her place on the port side.

"All right," Bryan said as he and I stepped up to the stern, "if anyone is getting tired or needs to readjust your handhold just say, 'Set,' and we'll all put the boat down right away. You can change sides to give your arms a rest. We'll take lots of breaks so we don't hurt ourselves."

"And all our friends on the embarcadero are waiting to see our work," I said. "I'm betting we'll have plenty of chances to stop."

"Got everything? Here we go ... and up!"

We hoisted *Rover* between us, stood for a moment balancing the load, and then we walked away. With my free hand, I waved our thanks to the shop workers and we began the last walk back along the familiar path. Around the corner, down the steps.

"Set!" someone called, and we stopped at the bottom of the stairs. The first of the vendors came over to look.

"You really were building a boat this week!" They'd listened to our story and asked for daily updates but it still seemed like a shock to see our fully completed work.

Well-dressed tourists eyed us with confusion and one stopped to ask, "Why are you carrying a boat up here when," he gestured over the railing to the harbor, "there's all that water down there?"

After we explained and turned to walk away Hannah whispered, "Do you think he's going to be telling stories about us at home tonight?"

"I saw the strangest family today!" Meira parodied.

I laughed. "Yeah, I'm betting that's being said about us a lot these days."

Slowly we made progress, took a few more breaks to rest. We turned the last tricky corner by the ATM and stopped in shock. The sidewalk was full of friends—all the marina office workers, the manager, several security guards—so many people who'd helped along the way and a few we'd never met.

Chuy stepped forward as we set *Rover* down. Cameras flashed in the bright sun.

"We saw you coming and had to come out to meet you. We've all been talking about you and how great it is that you've done this as a family. We wanted to see the big launch day." He lowered his voice and grinned. "Okay, and yes. Some of us are wondering if the boat will really float."

Bryan spoke up, "It might not float well and it might row crooked but it's made of wood. It's not going to sink."

Surrounded by the gathering crowd, we walked the last few yards to the boat ramp.

"Quick, before someone else needs to launch, let's get her in the water."

"Wait!" Chuy stopped us again and held out a tiny blue bottle. "I looked for some champagne for the christening but all I could find was tequila."

"It'll be a truly Mexican christening," I said.

Bryan splashed a little on the bow, took a sip, and poured a shot into the sea. An improvised ritual for our DIY dinghy.

We stripped off our shoes, slipped on our life jackets, and slid *Rover* into the water.

"It floats!"

"¡Que bueno!"

The calls from the pier faded as my focus narrowed. Bryan rolled up his pants and fitted the oars into place. "Meira, go ahead and hop in. We'll hold the boat steady."

Hannah stepped in next and took her place in the stern. Bryan pulled the boat a little farther out to keep it from banging into the ramp.

"Now you, Bethany."

I tossed my shoes into the bottom and hiked up my skirt. The crew leaned to starboard as I settled in on the port side.

"Okay, watch your knees." We held ourselves still as Bryan jumped in and sat on the center seat, feet dripping onto the fresh paint.

"And, we're off!" The oversized oars stuck out awkwardly as Bryan maneuvered us out into deeper water.

"Well, she's less stable than *Splitpea* and she doesn't track quite as well but she rides plenty high enough to carry us and our gear. I think she'll get us where we need to go."

I glanced back at the wharf where our new friends stood smiling and I waved and smiled in return.

That first horrible day after *Splitpea* went missing, I'd told myself I didn't want to live through the next part of my own story, didn't want to have to walk the difficult way to the resilience on the other side of loss. But here we were, carried through by our ingenuity and grit, buoyed once again by the kindness of strangers.

Bryan woke me with a plan. "If we take today off, go snorkeling on the other side of the harbor, and then leave tomorrow for Mazatlán, we'll still get in before Christmas. What do you say? Want a little break?"

The kids overheard and chimed in.

"Yes, please!"

"I'm not ready to leave just yet."

"I agree," I said. "A rest day sounds like just what we need."

Meira and I swam in the sun all afternoon. Bryan snorkeled out beyond the surf and took some video footage with our underwater camera. Hannah sat on the beach, knitting. By evening we were too relaxed to move. We walked the embarcadero slowly around the harbor, resisting the urge to take a water taxi. Partway back on the long seawall, we ran into Endy.

"Endy, Endy, Endy!" I called.

"LeeLo! Where have you been? I've been looking for you!"

We explained what we'd been up to, that we'd decided to build a dinghy instead of buy one.

"Oh, you are having the boatyard build you a boat?"

"No, we built a boat."

"Someone built a boat for you?"

"No." I pointed at the crew. "*We* built a boat."

I dug into my bag for the camera, pulled up photos from the week and showed them off, proud as a new parent.

"Look! Here's the wood from the first day. And here are the kids piecing it together. Here we are putting in the seats. And here's the day we painted. Today we just came across the bay to relax, but tomorrow we're taking off for Mazatlán."

Endy's mouth gaped in astonishment and I couldn't blame him. I could hardly believe it myself. We'd come in only a week before, weary and disoriented. Though he hadn't said so at the time, Bryan had been almost sure our journey was over, that we would have to abandon our boat and fly home. Yet here we stood, undefeated.

Only few hours later I wasn't feeling so invincible. We'd left Cabo on the tail end of a gale and were racing along under menacing skies toward a lightning storm ahead. We had a few more miles to change our minds and find an anchorage on the south end of Baja before we'd be out in the mouth of the Sea of Cortez, a long beat back to safe harbor.

"Maybe I made the wrong call," I said. "I thought the storm would have blown out by now."

"No, I think this is just right." Bryan came up on deck to take a look around. "The lightning is running with the storm up ahead. If we get too close, we can always reef and slow down. But for now, with this tailwind, we're making fabulous time!"

I shifted my grip on the tiller, reacquainting myself with the motion of the sea after so many days on land.

"We shouldn't be anywhere close to the lightning but we're the tallest metal thing for miles," I said. "Meira here, put all the handheld gear into the oven. If we do get struck, it might save our GPS from frying."

"You got it, Mom."

My mind knew the storm would blow itself out, that we'd likely make it across this big water to Mazatlán in a couple of days, come in tired but safe and sound. But my body held all the primal fear of the dark I thought I'd left behind in childhood.

Years before, on my very first night in the ocean, I felt this specific terror for the first time. We were sailing south off the coast of Washington and I was hand-steering through high waves singing in the dark to calm myself, to fool my body into courage.

Suddenly, I heard strange noises from the night. Not the flutter of bird flocks taking off before our bow—I knew that sound. And it wasn't the hum of the sails or the whir of the wind in the lines.

I looked around in every direction, a little panicked, and finally looked down. On both sides of the boat sparkling green shapes torpedoed through the water, chattering, clicking, and whistling.

As soon as I realized they were dolphins swimming through phosphorescence, I woke Bryan to come up to see them, but by the time he came on deck they were gone.

I went back to steering and singing and they returned. I called him onto the deck again, and again they swam away.

It took us three times to realize they were approaching because I was singing. By then, Bryan was too tired to come above again so I just stood on the deck and steered and sang and sailed through the night, accompanied by the dolphins.

I was surprised to find that they didn't make me feel any less afraid. But they made me feel less alone.

Chapter Twenty

ALL IS CALM; ALL IS BRIGHT

Mazatlán, Mexico
December 2013: Third Quarter, Waning Crescent, New Moon

*You're not doing courage wrong
If it doesn't feel brave*

It didn't feel like Christmas Eve to us. Of course, for the local residents, it was always this warm in December. As the sun set, we decided we'd head downtown with Will, our friend from *Thallasea*, to attend a service and join the celebration. We splurged on a taxi instead of waiting for the bus and piled the five of us into the tiny, open pulmonia, more like a golf cart than a car. Hannah and Meira tucked in next to the cheerful driver and Bryan, Will, and I gave up all pretense of personal space across the back bench.

When we arrived, the cathedral was bustling, a press of worshippers all filing in together. We'd planned to get dinner first and then go to the midnight mass but stopped by the cathedral to get our bearings. I stepped up to the entry and read the sign.

"Misa: 10 a.m., 12 p.m., 4 p.m., 8 p.m. Hey, what time is it?"

"It's five to eight."

"Well, it looks like we got here just in time. There isn't a midnight mass. The last one starts in five minutes."

We flip-flopped our plans and joined the parishioners packing into the sanctuary. There were still a few open seats here and there but no place we could all sit together. We stood with the crowd in the back, nudging Hannah and Meira to the front so they could see.

Understanding surfaced from the depths of shared traditions as familiar stories and themes emerged in the songs and recitations. By the cadence of the priest and the restlessness in the pews, we could tell when the service was drawing to a close. At last, the cantor stood and led a traditional tune.

"Noche de paz, noche de amor … "

By the second line, we'd joined in.

"All is calm, all is bright."

My ears reached out to hold the sounds of those around, families and friends, the old and the young, singing of the light that spreads through all the world.

"Entre sus astros que esparcen su luz."

From behind me, Bryan's deep bass and Will's rough German swelled.

"'Nur das traute hochheilige Paar."

"Holy infant, so tender and mild."

I blended my alto into the mix, Hannah's soprano to one side and Meira's on the other, and sang the last lines through the tears in my throat, caught for a heartbeat in a moment that answered our universal prayer.

"Sleep in heavenly peace,

Sleep in heavenly peace"

The last note echoed from the walls and drifted down into the hush below. An instant later we found ourselves on the leading edge of the wave of bodies moving out the door. We stepped out into the square and huddled for a minute to make a plan while the crowds evaporated.

Will pointed. "I think the main plaza is that way."

On an evening this warm and beautiful, who would care if we took the long way? We walked a few blocks south until the road turned into Plazuela Machado. Sidewalk seating spilled out into the streets and we found what looked to be the last empty spots in sea of tables packed so close, we had no idea which restaurant we'd chosen.

We lingered over our late-night dinner. Thousands of lights sparkled on the trees. Fire jugglers lit up the gazebo in the plaza center. No one seemed in any rush to move on from the magical evening, but eventually we couldn't put it off any longer. We headed north, away from the city center, in hopes of finding cheaper taxi fare. I hung back to capture one last look at the radiance. *All is calm; all is bright.*

Despite the late hour, once back at the boat, we still had presents to wrap.

"Head to bed, kids," I said. "We don't have stockings to fill, so hand me your pillowcases and close your eyes!"

We uncovered gifts we'd squirreled away over the last few weeks, turned our backs to the quarter berths, and balanced a roll of wrapping paper on the settee. Bryan covertly cut and taped paper around symmetrical packages while I knotted scarves and sarongs around the lumpy ones. We pulled down the paper stockings we'd hung from the bulkhead and set them up against the pillowcases, now full of treats. Finally, he shooed me off to bed.

"If you don't go away, how will I ever be able to wrap your presents, too?"

By the time he crawled in next to me, I had already drifted off, but I surfaced when his hand found mine.

"Good night," he said. "Or, good morning, I guess. Merry Christmas, Love."

Some things about Christmas morning with my family are the same everywhere. I woke first and made coffee, loudly. Hannah and Meira opened sleepy eyes that widened in happy recognition.

"It's Christmas!"

"Merry Christmas!"

"Can we open our stockings now?" Meira asked.

"Let's let Dad get out of bed first, okay?"

Hannah plopped onto the floor and the rest of us found spots to perch around the pile of presents. Bryan had sneaked away for a little shopping and bought variety packs of local sweets. We tore them open and shared them around.

"Ooooh, this one is my favorite," Hannah said, with a mouth full of marshmallow stickiness.

"I like the Emperadors," said Meira, "especially the lemon ones."

I made a mental note of everyone's preferences for future provisioning and reached for my gift from Bryan. He'd found a local silversmith and chosen a pendant and bracelet, silver with red coral accents. I slipped the bracelet on right away and showed it off to Hannah. She'd just opened a new skirt and was tying it on over her pajamas. Meira immediately started building with a new toy set.

We stretched the morning festivities out as long as we wanted and then, to fill the long afternoon without our traditional family gatherings, we motored out to Isla de Venados, rowed to shore, and jumped into the water for an afternoon of snorkeling. Tourist boats and other traffic came and went in the channel. Bryan and Meira decided to swim back to *LiLo* so Hannah and I rowed nearby to wave off any boats that came too close.

We'd made plans to celebrate again with Will, so back at the marina I spent the warm afternoon coaxing pie out of unconventional ingredients and our recalcitrant oven. Just after dark we walked up our dock, up the ramp to shore, and down the wharf to the next dock over, carrying our offerings like modern-day magi.

Will's German Christmas tradition called for sausage and potatoes and he had done his best with what he'd found in the market. No one complained about the stubby sausages, which tasted as bland and strange as they looked, all rubbery and mauve in the candlelight. The potatoes were served boiled, peeled, plain and I was too timid to ask for salt or pepper.

The company was good though and the pie was near perfection—apple, with a hint of the tropics from the coconut oil crust.

We spent the next couple of days doing boat chores and relaxing in the marina pools. The marina adjoined an all-inclusive resort and, although we didn't sport the colorful bracelets of the resort guests, the servers were so used to giving out food and beverages that we often found ourselves with chips and salsa, "En la casa." "On the house." The prices on the menu were outrageous, printed mostly, I suspect, to make the all-inclusive customers feel like they got a great deal.

"2-for-1 during happy hour," the bartender said, winking, "and *every* hour is happy hour!"

After months of travel and the shifting schedules a sailing life demands, I had found surprising direction and stability in our structured days in Cabo San Lucas: build all morning, eat lunch and take a break, run errands, work all evening. Stay hydrated, eat ice cream, and end the day writing a blog post at a cafe. Not a bad way to live, actually, at least not for a week or two. The shift back into unpredictable days plunged me back into a melancholy I thought I'd left behind in Baja.

One night I lost it. "I know I should feel better. We built the dinghy and made it to the mainland and we're here in this resort marina where everything is supposed to be relaxing and easy, but there aren't any groceries close by and all the food is so expensive if you don't have the all-inclusive wristband. I'm tired of cooking from cans, and sitting by the pool in the sun is so hot. It's all just too much."

We'd walked up the ramp to some oversized rocking chairs overlooking the harbor. Bryan sat quietly beside me and waited for me to wind down.

"I know. If we were on vacation here, it would be lovely. But we didn't choose a vacation kind of traveling."

"It really is a whole different thing isn't it?" I said. "This probably isn't ever going to feel easy."

"This might not be the best time to have this conversation but I think ... " he paused and my heart began to sink at his tone. "When it's time to head back, unless we want to just sell the boat here somewhere, I think we're going to have to sail straight back up the coastline to get her home."

We'd left without a solid plan for our return but it was nearing time to make a decision. I ran through all the options in my head. Some sailors we knew were preparing for a crossing to the South Pacific and another year or more of cruising. Some planned to move to New Zealand or Australia or sell their boat there and fly home. We didn't have the time or money for those choices.

Most sailors from the Pacific Northwest travel home by way of Hawaii, riding the tradewinds across and circling with the currents around the North Pacific through the Gulf of Alaska back to the west coast of the US.

On such a small boat, without a desalinating water maker, we simply couldn't carry enough water for all four of us to make the crossing to Hawaii. And even if we bought a manual desalinator and took turns pumping every day, we knew that a couple of months away from land, with only one short stop in Hawaii, would be enormously difficult on a boat as small as *LiLo*.

We couldn't leave Hannah and Meira somewhere and sail to Hawaii alone, and we'd become such a well-tuned crew, it was hard to imagine *LiLo* without them. Some families split up, the mother flying home alone with the kids while the dad took on crew for the trip back. Some people hired a delivery captain. None of these choices seemed right for us.

"We could try to leave the boat here in a boatyard," Bryan said, "but at some point, we will have spent everything she's worth just to store her here in a hurricane zone. You know we probably won't make it down here again while the kids are in high school. That just seems sad. I think our best option is to bash back."

Our logical conversation flowed over my swirling emotions. I closed my eyes to keep the tears from falling and spoke into the night.

"It was all we could do to get here, going *with* the wind and current. I just don't think I'm strong enough to do it again backward. Everybody says how hard it is to bash back up Baja but that's just, what? A third of the way?" My navigator habits were taking over. "And we have to make it back around Point Conception and Cape Mendocino."

"I know. I have myself on video vowing to never again sail that coastline in my lifetime," Bryan said. "But delivery captains do it all the time, right? No one knows our boat better than we do. And somehow it feels important for all of us, even *LiLo,* to get all the way home again. I think we can do it. I think we have to try."

We sat on the edge of the water in silence but my thoughts were anything but quiet.

"We don't have to make the choice tonight," Bryan said, though we both knew we had already decided. "We still have months to go before we have to turn around. Let's enjoy every moment."

I opened my eyes and looked at him. At least for this moment, I was right where I belonged.

The next day, I felt the boat rock as Bryan came back aboard from a walk. He poked his head down and caught my eye. "Guess what I just found by the dumpster? You know how the guy on the boat across the way is doing some repairs? Well, he pulled out an engine heater just like the one we had, and it's there, free for the taking."

"Really?" I'd already started to adjust to the idea of a bash back home, but this felt like confirmation.

We walked up the dock to check it out. "See, it looks like it's in good shape."

"I think he's working on board today," I said. "Let's go ask him if it works."

We knocked on the hull and our neighbor popped his head up from below.

"Are you really getting rid of that heater by the dumpster?" Bryan asked. "We had one just like it on our trip down the coast but it corroded in southern California and stopped working. Now that we're heading back up we're going to need something for the cold."

"You're more than welcome to it. It still works great; we just decided to switch it out for a forced air system. In fact, wait just a second." He dashed back below and emerged in a moment, carrying an identical mechanism. "We had two and we don't need either one."

Bryan glanced my way. "Is this good news or bad news?"

I laughed and shrugged. "We'll take them both," I said, "and thank you. It looks like we're going to need them."

We spent the rest of the holiday week on the southern edge of Mazatlán in anchorages near the commercial harbor. After celebrating the New Year, we spent a day preparing for an easy overnight run to Isla Isabel.

The island is a world heritage site, protected for its abundant bird population and nicknamed "The Galapagos of Mexico." But the anchorages there aren't very well protected and, because of the rocky bottom, are known for their iffy holding and tendency to snag anchors. I was concerned that weather might blow up while we were there and cut our visit short. I tried to get a weather report from the cruisers' radio net in the morning but we were too far away to pick up the weak signal.

After breakfast a trio from a neighboring boat came by on a swimming tour of the bay. They climbed up our swim ladder and sat dripping in our cockpit for a short visit before heading off to another boat. They too were planning to head to Isla Isabel and I asked if they'd pulled in the morning forecast.

"Nope, we couldn't get it today. Let us know if you hear anything and we'll do the same."

"Will do."

That afternoon we were still debating about the weather when our morning visitors sailed by heading south. We called over to the captain, "Did you ever hear the weather report?"

"No, but it's blowing eight knots right now," he said.

I'd fallen into the trap of valuing the weather forecast over the weather conditions. I took one last look at the steady barometer and decided.

"I guess it'll be what it'll be. Let's go."

Chapter Twenty-one

INTO THE LUMINOUS

Isla Isabel and Chacala, Mexico
January 2014: Waxing Crescent

*On a day when the wind is perfect,
the sail just needs to open and the world is full of beauty.
Today is such a day.*

—*Rumi*

I slipped a long-sleeved shirt over my tank top and buckled into my life jacket, untwisting the harness straps to lie flat around my torso.

I called up to Bryan in the cockpit, "I'll be up for my watch in a minute."

"Take your time." I could hear the smile in his voice. "It's a beautiful night. I hung a crescent moon just for you."

I grabbed a granola bar and stepped to the companionway for our watch-swap ritual. Bryan picked up the spare tether and hooked the locking carabiner through the D rings on my chest. He yanked hard twice to test the shackle and the harness tugged at my ribcage, each pull saying without words: *I love you. Be safe. Be here when I wake up.*

We traded places, careful to avoid tangling our safety lines. I spun back around to face Bryan through the doorway, reached for his harness, and loosened his tether. *I love you. Rest well. I'll be here when you wake up.*

I turned around in the cockpit getting my bearings. The crescent moon dangled underneath the dim shadow of the whole moon, just visible as a starless sphere in the spangled sky. I kept an eye out for fishermen and watched the glow of Mazatlán fade behind us.

A couple of hours after the moon slipped below the horizon, I woke Bryan for his late evening watch. He had warned me that he might want to take a long night watch alone, so I wasn't too surprised to wake up six hours later and find him still awake, enjoying the peace of a silent night at sea. He'd been working on a few projects during his watch and wasn't quite ready to be done. I gladly went back to bed and slept until the sun came up.

When I peeked out in the morning, what I initially thought was a large boat low on the horizon was actually Isla Isabel. The approach was clear, as indicated in our maps and guidebooks, but the charted location was off by several miles. The last hour or so, I stopped checking our navigation equipment and just pointed us toward the island itself and the pair of pinnacle rocks to its east sticking up from the ocean floor like a hitchhiker's thumb.

As we approached the eastern shore, *Vales Valeo* shouted across to us from their spot in the anchorage south of Las Monas, the pinnacles. We'd been together on New Year's Eve and discussed our plans to head south about the same time, so we weren't surprised to see them here. They confirmed our plan to skip the southern anchorage. While slightly more protected than the eastern one, it was also surrounded by dangerous reefs, and an underwater, unmarked rock spire threatened keels and peace of mind.

The limpid water magnified the sand and rocks below as we motored slowly in, looking for a place to anchor. Bryan walked to the bow and waited for us to drift over a large patch of sand, then tossed the anchor over. After we set it well, he and the kids snorkeled around

LiLo's swing area looking for any rocks tall enough to bump our keel. We knew better than to get complacent; the sand lay in a thin layer over rock and in strong winds or current, we could easily drag. But the winds and seas were calm, so we relaxed a bit and celebrated the accomplishment of this long-awaited landfall.

Our friends from *Vales Valeo* motored over in their large dinghy and offered us a ride around to the southern anchorage. They zoomed around for a few minutes to give us time to dry off and pull together some snacks for an excursion.

We carefully balanced in their not-quite-overloaded dinghy and motored around the southeast point of the island. We landed the dinghy and hauled it safely up the beach. As we walked past the row of fishing huts a panga full of eco-tourists landed and we followed them and their bulging backpacks up the trail a few yards to an old research station, now a campsite for visitors and iguanas. The air was humid and heavy with the scent of avian guano, though not overwhelmingly so. We marveled at the varied iguanas hanging out together in the sun. Our group was already moving on so we followed them back through the fish camp to a trail leading to an inland valley. Bryan and I lagged behind until all sound receded but the sounds of the jungle, the howls and clatter from the trees, and the beat of powerful wings overhead.

We climbed a flight of concrete steps up out of the valley and scrabbled down the other side to the watery caldera at the heart of the island. The small lake seemed stagnant, green with algae, but otherwise lifeless. A bird carcass lay on the bank near bare limbs of driftwood. We teased the crew, telling them not to toss rocks or disturb the monsters hiding in the gloomy water, but the only monster we saw was a tiny hermit crab scuttling along his busy way.

Weariness from the overnight passage was catching up with all of us so we scurried too, back to the beach, back out of the bay, back to our boats on the eastern shore. Our friends planned to leave the next morning so the four kids spent the evening on the bigger boat, playing games. A twitter of giggling voices on the radio broke the silence on *LiLo* and Bryan rowed over to retrieve our happy crew.

A couple of hours after dark, after the moon had set over the island, Bryan took Hannah and Meira out on deck for some spectacular stargazing. Light pollution from even small population centers travels miles out to sea. But here, more than thirty miles out, the stars lit up the night. I enjoyed listening to them exclaim as I savored some rare alone time below.

About three in the morning, I woke with middle-of-the-night clarity, the kind where you know right away you might as well give up on going back to sleep for a while. I got up to check our position but our anchor had held right where we'd been all day. I took a couple of drop boards out of the companionway and stepped out into the warm, still night. Familiar constellations swung in unfamiliar patterns. Orion, usually a friendly presence toward the southeast on winter evenings back home, now hung by his feet on the western horizon. The abundance of stars, many typically too faint to see, made it difficult to pick out the well-known groupings. Our anchor light wobbled in a gentle circle somewhere east of Ursa Major. In just the starlight—no moon, no clouds, no hint of dawn—I stared at the pinnacles, the horizon to the east, the dark island sleeping out to sea.

I woke early to birdcalls outside and spent the morning in the cockpit hypnotized by the swirl of countless birds overhead and the gentle sounds of surf and sea.

We'd heard there was a population of blue-footed boobies on this island, but hadn't spotted a single blue foot on our first trip to shore. We packed a lunch and all our snorkel gear and rowed over to the beach.

Not only were there colonies of brown and blue-footed boobies on the eastern shore, it was mating season and we spotted some birds already brooding over eggs in the sand. Others were obviously still in the courting stages. We even witnessed a couple of pairs perform their pompous, ridiculous mating dance.

We walked north up the beach and discovered several unusual formations where the sea had eroded the volcanic rock. Slender skulls, hollow breastbones, and tiny bird vertebrae lay scattered in the sand.

We met a couple of wary iguanas and stepped carefully around so many herds of hermit crabs we became convinced they aren't solitary at all but misunderstood party animals.

Hannah wasn't in the mood to snorkel but the rest of us suited up and jumped in. The water was shallow and a bit murky with surf-tossed sand, but several yards past the breakers, the bottom dropped away and the visibility cleared. We'd heard people describe good snorkeling as swimming in an aquarium but, until today, hadn't had that kind of experience. Schools of fish of every color and size swam beneath us in all directions. Blue ones with yellow fins, silver ones with blue fins, green ones with white polka dots, black ones with purple eyeshadow. My favorite was a slightly pudgy, iridescent black one with white dots and silly, floppy fins. I followed it for several minutes wondering what it thought of the orange and black creature above it, the one with the bright yellow foam jacket and those gangly, inefficient arms and legs.

I got out to dry off and rest up and Bryan and Meira soon followed. We sat near the dinghy and ate our lunch, staying well clear of the nesting birds nearby.

We spoke idly of the wonder of the underwater universe. We'd been floating over it for months now, but were no closer to being a part of it. Our snorkels gave us a mere glimpse into the aquatic life so different from our own.

Suddenly, a great splash out past our boat signaled the presence of humpback whales. Our track and timing mimicked their annual migratory patterns and we'd seen quite a few lately. This day, as always, the sight was breathtaking. Two whales surfaced multiple times, breaching and crashing back into the water with great energy and commotion. They swam south of our boat, then turned back and came closer again.

I found myself hoping the whales would come a bit nearer, dance a little longer, then I sank completely into the moment, grateful for this glimpse of their essence, no matter how brief.

After lunch Bryan and I left Hannah and Meira relaxing in the sand and walked down toward the rocky southern edge of the beach.

We met colonies of crabs, accidentally startling several into a leap from their rocky perch. Their claws skittered across the black rocks as they moved sideways, then shifted—quick-as-a-blink—forward or backward. Red and blue shells stood out against the pitted stone and black shapes hung almost invisible on cliffs and under outcroppings. Brown boobies with greenish beaks and feet stood out among their more prevalent blue-footed cousins.

Bryan climbed down the cliffs for a better view of the green and pink chitons. I found an easier way down and joined him in marveling at their hard, articulated shells and their textured circumference. Streaks of color in the black rock reflected their strange hues.

We stepped quickly past several apparently barren tide pools, but a closer inspection revealed hundreds of minuscule snails, each with a slightly different shell pattern.

We couldn't stop exclaiming at the dense abundance of life, calling back and forth across the stones, "You have to come look at this!"

Convinced there would never be enough time to take it all in, we finally walked back to the crew and launched the dinghy across the rocks and through the surf. We rowed back to the boat in a daze of gratitude, humbled by the wealth of wonder.

Our first morning back on the mainland we rowed to shore with a short to-do list: check in with the Chacala port captain and find a laundromat. The port office was located in a little house just up from the dinghy landing and I took in our paperwork and stumbled our way through the process while Bryan stood back bewildered. On the path into town, I filled him in on the conversation.

"It's hard to be sure, but it sounds like the port captains don't actually communicate with each other much if at all. So technically, we checked in and out at both Cabo and Mazatlán but this guy didn't know or seem to care. He took our paperwork, though, and I pointed out *LiLo*. He said we need to check out when we leave so I asked what we should do if we ended up needing to leave in the middle of the night or on a weekend when he wasn't here. He said, 'Well, officially, you must check out when you leave. But if I come into work one morning and you are not in the bay—'" I mimicked his hand wave and mischievous smile, "'*Mágico.*'"

We walked on into town and got our bearings. The main road ran parallel to the beach and we strolled the few blocks to the other end of town and back again. We found a laundromat and picked out some restaurants to try. The streets were dusty and quiet. Everyone we met was cheerful and chatty and we soon learned of a local attraction—a caldera from an extinct volcano just a short hike away.

The next day we packed snacks and water and walked through town toward the slopes beyond. We found a narrow path into the jungle and followed it along a creek past a couple of isolated homes. We came out on a road near a three-story security tower. I stopped to ask permission from the guard and he waved us on through.

"Enjoy the caldera and stop by on your way out."

We hiked up through an orchard, stepping off the road when a truck came whizzing by. It stopped and backed up. The driver introduced himself as the orchard owner, and invited us to eat any of the fruit that looked ripe.

"The guanabana only grow in a few areas," he said, proudly, "but this is one of them. We sell most of them for ice cream but they're good raw too. Enjoy!"

We wandered through the orchard, poking at the prickly fruit and examining the blossoms and buds. The fruit didn't seem quite ready to eat so we found a spot at the edge of the caldera for our lunch. With my back to all signs of civilization, the wide, grassy bowl seemed primeval. I almost expected a brontosaurus to step out of the trees, out of the past.

Toward the end of the hike we ran into a pair of fellow hikers. We exchanged pleasantries and then paused to engage in actual conversation. They were interested in our travels and we in their purpose here—a universalist Sufi retreat at a local spiritual retreat center. They invited us to join them that night for a Sufi dance circle, the week's highlight.

After we got back to the boat and got the kids settled for the evening, we decided to take the hikers up on their offer. I had read some Sufi poetry, had been fascinated by many different religion's mystical traditions and we didn't know when we would get another opportunity like this. We rowed to shore and walked the path to the beach, then across the sand to the retreat center. As we got close, I got nervous. *What if we couldn't figure out where to go? What if we weren't really welcome?* But right away, we spotted our new friend Roger on the patio. "I'm so sorry," he said, "I got my dates wrong. It's actually tomorrow."

So we headed back up the beach in the moonlight. I carried my shoes and a headlamp in one hand, scuffing my feet in the warm surf. About halfway back, I shifted my grip on my shoes and realized I'd dropped one somewhere along the way. This pair was quick-drying for wet landings, comfortable enough for a hike, not too ugly for a date, so they were the only shoes I'd brought on the trip. We walked back to the retreat center with light from a couple of dim headlamps and the bright, bright moon. We finally turned around and headed back to the boat. The shoe hadn't been there on our first pass but all the way back, we kept hoping we'd find it on the shore. And then, there it was, tossed up by a big wave, sandy and sopping, but still usable.

The next day was a quiet day aboard. We read and tidied and hung out together. Meira changed into swimwear and shuffled out to the end of the boom to dive in from there.

Partway through the day, we got an email about some fraudulent charges on one of our bank accounts. Bryan checked his wallet and his credit card was missing. He realized he must have left it behind the last time he used an ATM. Our bank's fraud department required claims to be made by phone so we rowed in a little early that evening to try an internet call. It turned out that the fraud was on *my* card and Bryan's missing card was just a coincidental piece of bad luck.

For security reasons, the bank would only mail new cards to our temporary home address, at Bryan's mother's house, which meant that they'd show up in Oregon a few days after she and her sister planned to fly into Mexico for a visit. We'd have to wait for them to return home and forward the cards on to us, wherever we happened to be. We canceled both our cards and hung up in time to make a second attempt at the dance circle.

I tucked my shoes safely into Bryan's backpack and didn't put them on all night. We walked up the beach to the retreat center again. This time we didn't recognize anyone on the patio but we asked directions from a small group of women and they led us to the recently completed temple, describing along the way a little of what we could expect from the evening.

Sandy flip-flops lined the entryway as we stepped into the luminous room. Wood floors shone golden in the soft lighting and candles on an altar added to the radiance. The western wall was made up of glass doors, which were partially folded back to let in the sounds of the surf and the evening jungle. I had expected to sit and watch, but right away, we were swept into the swirl, walking barefoot on the smooth floors around the small band of musicians in the center.

Within a few minutes, the dancers shifted to form a circle. We couldn't resist their welcoming encouragement, though we stood a little closer to each other in our uncertainty. One woman prayed in Spanish to officially open the evening and then a willowy brunette sang the prayer again in haunting Arabic. I inhaled the gift of music, the immediate connection to humanity, and dropped into the present.

From around the circle, a different person led each dance, repeating the words and steps until we were all comfortable joining in. The band began together, with no obvious leader. The songs were familiar concepts if not familiar words or tunes. "Soli Deo Gloria," we sang, "To God be all the glory."

Bryan and I separated and met again in a spinning circle dance. Step in, step out, spin to the right. Sing of the light that shines in us all. Turn to the right and sing to your partner, palm to palm, face to face—"Shine, shine, shine."

Each face held a unique story, each body bore a different shape. Dark skin, light skin, women in flowing scarves, white linen and bright colors, men with kindly smiles.

We danced through the evening, singing, whirling, bowing down together. Over and over, we sang to new partners, as the brilliance of each soul shone out from bright eyes—"Shine, shine, shine."

We walked back in the moonlight—for once just exactly as romantic as it sounds—and rowed out to the boat. It was late, almost eleven, and, once we did the math on how soon we would need to leave to get to Puerto Vallarta before dark the next day, we decided to take off right away.

We worked together silently to haul up both of our anchors and motor out of the crowded anchorage. But as we passed the first line of boats on our way out, our oil pressure alarm sounded. I took the helm while Bryan went below to check the levels. We were a bit low, but he had some extra oil stashed away. With a little push from the ebbing tide, I kept the boat angled out to sea while Bryan tore the engine compartment apart and added fluids. I watched the boats and the bay fade behind us, and breathed a sigh of relief when we cleared the islets at the entrance and fired the motor back up in the still ocean.

After all the evening's excitement, I found it hard to sleep. I dozed off and on, but was awake about 3 a.m. when Bryan came up to the V-berth and whispered my name. His voice was filled with excitement, not weariness or alarm, and I swung quickly out of bed and followed him to the cockpit. He took my shoulders and turned me around, pointed to the sky past the bow.

There, just above the horizon: the Southern Cross. I'd read many sailor's accounts of their travels in southern waters and wondered if we would get far enough south on this trip to see this epic constellation.

I grew up watching the Big Dipper dance across the northern night, traced its lines to the northern star. And now we were following the southern equivalent, an unmistakable guide pointing the way ahead.

Chapter Twenty-two

Grandma's Dishes

Puerto Vallarta and Bahía de Banderas, Mexico
January 2014: First Quarter, Waxing Gibbous

Some years ago—never mind how long precisely—having little or no money in my purse, and nothing particular to interest me on shore, I thought I would sail about a little and see the watery part of the world

—*Herman Melville*

Some sailors cross the Columbia River Bar, head straight to sea, and knock out the trip to San Francisco in a week. We took almost a month to journey the same distance. It took us two and a half months to reach Mexico. We'd stayed longer than we expected in Cabo San Lucas and now we planned to spend a couple of months in the Puerto Vallarta area, hosting family and friends and resting up for the journey north. It was clear we weren't even going to make it to southern Mexico, much less to Central America or beyond.

One day I talked this over with Bryan.

"I mean it's not like I'm disappointed I can't see Scotland on this trip, right?" I said. "That was never in the plan. So what if I can't see the port just south of here? How is that any different?"

"I feel the same way," he said. "I don't want to spend so much time and energy pushing to go new places and see new things that we can't even enjoy where we are. We pushed ourselves hard enough on the northwest coast and we know we have a tough run ahead getting home. Let's take it easy for a while and see how that feels."

We put out the word to family and friends: if you are serious about coming to visit us, now's the time to make it happen.

Plans came together for Bryan's mom, Michele, and her sister, Trina, to fly into Puerto Vallarta and stay three weeks. They made reservations for the first three nights but figured they'd hop from town to town after that, following our wandering ways from the land.

Ryan, a friend from our years in Alaska, planned to join us for a couple of weeks as well. In the years that we'd known him, he'd become a friend of our extended family and he arranged his visit to overlap the end of Trina and Michele's by a few days. We didn't know where we'd be by that point, but we knew we'd be within reach of the Puerto Vallarta airport, and he decided to squeeze aboard with us instead of finding lodging on shore.

We warned our visitors to be prepared to enjoy themselves alone. Storms and breakdowns and many other circumstances could keep us from arriving on schedule. Everyone decided a trip to sunny Mexico in the middle of winter was worth the risk, even without the certainty of meeting us.

We pulled into Puerto Vallarta with one day to spare, just enough time to turn our seafaring mess into a hospitable boat. We found a laundromat on the wharf and dropped off a heap of washing. I spotted the open flames from the propane dryers and timidly attempted to ask for special care for my delicates.

"Could you please hang dry my … " I stopped. I didn't know the Spanish word for bra.

Bryan was not at all shy. He cupped his hands around giant, imaginary breasts and bounced. "These," he said.

"Sí, claro. Sus brasieres." I blushed and the proprietress and Bryan laughed at my discomfort.

"I will take care of you," she promised. "Come back tomorrow and all will be finished."

She sent us off with directions to her favorite taco stand. We had almost all we needed for dinner aboard but stopped by for some fresh salsa. The women at the taco stand gave us two different kinds, warning us that one was very spicy. We tried the mild salsa first.

"This is the not-so-spicy kind?" Hannah said after an experimental taste. "Not to me, it's not! It's full of the spicy!"

In a crew brave enough to sail the Pacific, no one was willing to taste the spicy salsa.

The next day, we couldn't put it off any longer: our settee was saturated with salt and grime and always felt a bit damp, even when dry. We wrestled the foam out of the tight-fitting covers and dunked them in buckets—first in soapy water, then rinse after rinse of fresh. They dried quickly in the tropical sun and we worked together to wedge the cushions back into the upholstery.

We finished our chores just in time to set off for the airport. Michele and Trina had planned to bus to their hotel and meet us the next day, but we couldn't wait to see them. While we waited for their flight to disembark, we chatted with a few other folks in the terminal. One man struck up a conversation with me and asked why we were there.

"We sailed here from Oregon and are waiting for our family who are here for a visit."

"What part of Oregon? I lived in Portland for fifteen years!"

We chatted a bit more and he asked about our family.

"Are they staying with you on the boat?"

"Oh, goodness, no! It's far too small. They've got a hotel in Mismaloya."

"Yes! Mismaloya! I grew up there. It's such a beautiful town. You're taking the bus down, yes? Here's what you need to know to find your way there."

I tried to commit his instructions to memory, even though they didn't make much sense without his frame of reference.

Soon passengers began to emerge from the tunnel past the security gate. All conversation ceased except the happy reunions blossoming throughout the lobby. We kept a careful eye out since Trina and Michele weren't expecting us. We didn't want them to slip out and catch a taxi while we weren't looking. Soon their familiar faces appeared in the crowd. I hopped impatiently while they wrangled their suitcases through the throng and then I flung my arms around them.

"Mom, you're here!" I said to Michele.

"*You're* here!" she responded. "I thought we wouldn't see you until tomorrow!"

"We didn't think you'd mind. Let's get out of here. It's a short walk to the boat and we can get some dinner and catch up before you head to the hotel."

We walked back through the maze of parking lots and waiting taxis down the street a mile or so to the marina. We stopped by the boat to stash the suitcases and our guests pulled out mail and small gifts from home. We took a few minutes to open the cards and the chocolate, admired drawings from the cousins, and tucked away the tea and treats for later.

Back up on the embarcadero we asked a couple of security guards for a dinner recommendation. They pointed out a restaurant just down the wharf. As we headed that way one of the guards ran ahead of us to let the proprietor know we were coming. We found spots around an outdoor table just as a warm rain began to fall. Waiters rushed around adjusting umbrellas and reseating uncomfortable patrons, but we stayed put and the heavy raindrops tapered off almost immediately leaving the patio sparkling in the evening light.

After dinner we sent the kids back to the boat and walked our guests and all their bags to a waiting taxi. They were willing to navigate the public transit system, but we weren't sure how late the buses ran and didn't want to take any chances this time of night. The next morning we knew we'd made the right choice. It took the four of us almost two hours on two different buses to get to the hotel in Mismaloya.

The directions we'd gotten at the airport came to life as we rode and walked through town: "Get off five blocks after the second tunnel, walk toward the Oxxo, ask anyone you meet for the bus stop to Mismaloya." We finally found our way to the right hotel. We walked through the gate at the entrance, past a pool full of sunning turtles, and rounded a corner into a beautiful courtyard. Michele and Trina were waiting there for us, and we went up to their room and shared the pasta salad we'd packed for lunch.

After spending the afternoon in the shade at a nearby zoo we decided to cook dinner at the hotel so Bryan and I walked to the market for ingredients. The stove in the kitchenette didn't work, but the hotel staff brought us a portable hot plate and we heated up a simple family meal and sat around the coffee table telling stories and sharing photos.

Through long years of juggling family and career, Michele and Trina had kept their dreams of travel alive and now were wasting no time in making them come true. Since we'd left, they had traveled to southern Africa and Amsterdam, and a trip to the Galapagos was in the offing. We were as thrilled to hear about their adventures as they were to listen to ours.

I stacked the dishes on the corner of the table. Not knowing how the kitchenette would be stocked, we'd carried our own plates from the boat—hand-me-down Corelle from Bryan's grandmother, Thelma, the family matriarch.

"She would have loved this, you know," Trina said. "She loved adventure and she would have been so happy to know that her daughters, her grandson, her granddaughter-in-law, and her great-grandchildren were all sharing food and travel stories over her plates in a little town in Mexico."

Finding our way back the next morning was a bit easier. But this time the buses were more crowded—standing room only—and we'd brought not only our backpacks with lunch and water, but all our snorkeling equipment and an unwieldy bundle of life jackets as well.

By the time we got off the bus we were ready for a dip in the ocean. Our guests had come prepared with rash guard suits and prescription snorkel masks and we carried all the gear down to the beach.

The swell was high in the bay and we weren't sure we could get through the breakers to the calmer water on the other side. We talked with the panga drivers who offered to take us out to Los Arcos, a pair of nearby islets known for their marine wildlife, but we thought the women would find it easier to snorkel for the first time from a beach instead of over the side of a boat. We walked down the coastline and found a rocky cove where the swell seemed lighter. It was still quite challenging to get out into the ocean and the turbulence lifted sand from the sea floor clouding the water.

We paddled around together anyway. Bryan showed both women how to clear their snorkels and masks and they got some practice at breathing underwater. Before we all got exhausted we decided to head in. Bryan pointed out a route through the surf, in between two boulders. He led his mom in first, staying close as she lost her footing and ended up on her bum with her back to the shore.

"Can you just pull me in?" she asked, and he did, grabbing her life jacket straps and tugging her in a little more each time a wave lifted her off the sand.

"Have you ever seen anything so hilarious?" Trina asked, pointing to her sister, who was bouncing through the surf and making faces at us.

I laughed until I started going under, came up for air, and laughed again.

Once she reached the safety of dry land, Michele called back to us, grinning. "Don't laugh too hard. You have to come in the same way!"

Eventually, we all made it back to the beach and, after showers and a little break at the hotel, we walked back down for dinner on the shore. As dusk fell at the beachside palapa the waiter brought out candles nestled into sand-filled margarita glasses. He pointed over his shoulder at the almost-full moon, hanging freshly-polished over the treetops. Pelicans dove for their dinner in the breakers and a young fisherman stood silhouetted on the shore, tossing out a hand line to see if he could catch something too. The rising tide lapped at the legs of our table, the water as warm as the connections between us.

The next day, I spent a couple of hours at a nearby coffee shop writing, sipping tea, and staring out the window—a rare solitary morning in this season of togetherness. About the time I wandered back to the boat, Michele and Trina showed up, bags in hand, for water transport to their next vacation rental. We spent a beautiful afternoon sailing northwest across the bay to La Cruz de Huanacaxtle and dropped our anchor in the twilight.

Bryan lowered the dinghy and he and I held it still while Michele and Trina lowered themselves and their suitcases down into *Rover*. I watched them row away in the dark and waited to see their light slip behind the breakwater on their way to the dinghy dock at the marina. I kept an eye out for Bryan's return and finally, an hour and a half after he left, I heard the quiet sound of his oars in the water and spotted his light—a headlamp worn backward to keep his night vision clear.

We slept well, but the next morning Bryan woke up nauseated, wishing he was anywhere but a crowded boat with a tiny head. Then an east wind kicked up in the bay and set *LiLo* to rolling. It didn't take long for us to decide to splurge on a slip in the marina.

I called ahead on the radio and got instructions—dock nine, side B, slip fifteen, north side, starboard tie—and kicked on the engine. Hannah hauled up the anchor and Meira gathered in the anchor rode while I drove. We pointed the bow through the sea wall and toward dock nine. At the last minute, we spotted slip fifteen on the south side, a port tie.

"We're coming in on the wrong side," I called. "Quick–switch the fenders to the port side and drop the dock lines."

The crew scrambled around on the deck, sure-footed and secure. Bryan wobbled up from below.

"Let me take the tiller so you can take the midline."

"If you're sure you can manage."

"Yeah, I'm okay for the moment. Too late to argue; we're turning in now."

I handed Meira the boat hook in case we got a little close to the neighboring boat and coiled up the midline in my hand. I reached for the shroud with my other hand and stepped over the lifelines to perch on the edge of the toe rail. As soon as the side deck neared the dock, I stepped down and wrapped the line around a cleat, levering the boat into place and slowing her momentum. Hannah jumped off the stern and looped her line around the rear cleat. Before Meira had the bowline down Bryan had shut off the engine and disappeared below.

I hollered after him, "We got this! Get some rest!"

We checked into the marina, brought Bryan a bucket of ice and some soda, and spent the day with our guests to give him the boat to himself.

By the next day, Bryan was fully recovered and ready to take on another snorkeling adventure. We'd passed up the opportunity to snorkel at Los Arcos that first day at Mismaloya, but now we wanted to try going there ourselves.

The trip over was beautiful with perfect wind for sailing. Michele and Trina settled in on the bow of the boat enjoying the gentle motion and the shade of the big nylon drifter. At one point we spotted something shiny in the sea. We slowed down, circled around, and found ourselves face to face with a giant sea turtle floating along unperturbed by our presence. Our conversation stilled and even my breathing slowed at the quiet grace of its motion on the sea. We waited until it floated back past our wake to pick up speed again.

We neared the islets, careful to miss the tour boats and snorkelers already in the water, and found a place to anchor. We all jumped in but, even here past the surf, the visibility was terrible. We could only see a foot or two in front of our faces and there was no way to get into water shallow enough to see any fish. We finally gave up and decided to explore the sea caves by dinghy. Trina and the kids stayed behind on *LiLo*, but Bryan, Michele, and I rowed through the islet's namesake arch. As we entered, I wondered aloud why none of the pangas take this route on their tours. About halfway through, I started to figure out why. The ocean floor shoaled quickly from one end of the arch to another, and out the other side, breakers frothed white on an submerged reef. Steeper and steeper swells caught us from behind and sent us rushing toward the reef. Bryan backstroked skillfully, holding us away from the tunnel walls. I leaned forward from my place in the bow to keep us balanced on the waves. Suddenly a steep wall of water lifted *Rover's* stern. Michele clung to the seat, mouth wide, almost directly above me as we fought to stay upright. We surfed the front edge of the wave the rest of the way through the rock and out the other side, missing the reef by just a few feet. The dinghy resumed a horizontal position but my heart raced for minutes.

"I can't believe we didn't capsize!" I said.

"I thought for sure I was going over," Mom said, grinning now that the danger had passed.

Bryan grinned back at her, "Well, that was exciting."

We headed back across the bay, motoring this time in calm seas and no wind. Michele and Trina headed back to their house for the night and the kids settled in for a quiet evening aboard, but I'd heard that the local German restaurant hosted live flamenco and jazz on Friday nights, so Bryan and I quickly changed out of snorkeling clothes and walked up into town.

We arrived just a few minutes before the music started and snagged one of the very last tables. The waitress greeted us in Spanish and brought us a Spanish menu. I'd gotten pretty good at translating menus into English if the food was Mexican. But translating the German menu through Spanish into English was more than my skill could handle. Soon the server was back with a flurry of information beyond my grasp.

"I'm sorry," I said in Spanish, "I don't speak much Spanish."

"No problem," she returned in English. "Would you like English, Spanish, French, or German?"

We laughed, "English is great, thank you!"

All our dates on the trip so far had been side-by-side internet surfing and frantic podcast downloading at nearby coffee shops. This was an honest-to-goodness date, so we splurged on drinks and sat back to enjoy the night. The musicians were superb and the food, absolute perfection. When a new server came to offer us dessert menus, he took one look at Bryan's deep tan and my freckles, handed Bryan a Spanish menu and me an English one. Bryan held his up studiously, but glanced over at mine like a cheating third grader looking for the right answers.

We sat through the entertainment and beyond, lingering late into the evening over one last cup of coffee. As we stood to go, I slipped my red scarf over my bare shoulders and stepped out into the breeze off the water, completely awake to the moment, the perfection and gift of now.

Chapter Twenty-three

No Boring Stories

Islas Marietas and Chacala, Mexico
January 2014: Full Moon

Adventure is the child of courage.

—*Jonathan Lockwood Huie*

"Rule number one:" I announced hauling suitcases over the toe rail, "We can only promise you one thing—no boring stories."

Michele and Trina laughed as they climbed aboard. They'd made reservations in Chacala for the last few days of their trip and we all agreed we could cram aboard overnight to get them there by sea.

"The rest of the rules are really just a subset of rule number one," I continued. "Something will go wrong. You will be asked to use skills you do not possess to salvage a situation you do not understand. And you will almost certainly want to do it again."

The kids ferried the suitcases up to the V-berth and got our guests settled. I started the engine and steered as Bryan pushed us off the dock. He hopped aboard and took over for the short trip out to Islas Marietas. These three islets sat in the entrance to Bahía de Banderas and would serve well as an overnight destination.

I'd read reports of uncharted, unmarked rocks in the area and navigated with care as we approached the largest island. There were a few orange buoys bobbing in the cove and we anchored to avoid them. Bryan rowed his mom and Trina into shore for an attempt at snorkeling, but they returned without landing.

"The swells seem calm out here but they're wild in by the beach," he said. "And there are too many rocks to swim safely. We decided to just paddle around the boat."

The visibility wasn't great but Michele and the kids jumped in and swam laps around *LiLo*. Trina and Bryan and I chatted in the cockpit in the deepening twilight. Just as the sun touched the horizon, a large sailboat pulled into the cove and picked up one of the orange buoys.

Bryan rowed over for a quick chat and returned with a plan.

"These buoys are apparently part of a national park system. We could hook up to one but I think it makes more sense to just drop a stern anchor so we don't swing in the night."

"Sounds good," I said. "You deal with the bow and I'll take the stern."

Up on the bow, Bryan loosened the anchor rode and gently fed it out as we slowly drifted astern. Once we had swung back to the full length of line, I dropped the stern anchor and he hauled us forward again toward the bow anchor, hand over hand, until we were centered between the two. He winched the stern anchor line hard to set it in the sand and went below to dry his hands.

"Babe, you've got to come see this!" I called down.

An enormous, four-story power yacht was approaching the anchorage. Several crew members jumped into a panga and peeled away from the stern to attach lines to the two remaining mooring buoys in the tiny cove. I eyeballed our position and estimated the play we had in our anchor rode. The yacht blocked what remained of the sunset and cranked up their loudspeakers, making it hard to feel very neighborly.

Michele, just getting ready to take a fresh-water rinse from our solar shower on the cabin top, joked, "I could just start taking my clothes off. That would clear the cove for you."

After only a few minutes though, the yacht crew emerged from the cabin, dropped the mooring lines, and motored back toward the mainland. We settled into the cockpit and watched the light fade until the stars brightened the indigo sky. Down in the water, spots of neon green phosphorescent glitter collected into swirling spirals and then winked out. Solitary blue sparks floated by. No one could find the energy to go below and cook dinner; we just sat and soaked in the beauty. Bryan passed around glasses of rum and we raised a toast to the end of the day.

By bedtime a slight swell had kicked up from the north, but our anchors held our bow to the waves and *LiLo* rode each one with ease. After midnight though, a strong east wind picked up and set us to rolling—up and down, side to side like the ropes in a game of double Dutch.

Seasick, Trina left the cabin for the fresh air of the deck. Michele stayed tucked in on the settee but she soon found herself sharing the bunk with items formerly secured on the shelf above. When Bryan and I stepped into the cabin to make a plan, I glanced over to see books scattered on her legs and a spindle of CDs tucked just under the covers, her eyes shut determinedly against the onslaught.

"I kept putting things back on the shelf only to have them fall right back down on me." She spoke up over the rising wind. "I decided just to let things lay where they fell."

For the first time in weeks, Bryan and I dug out our jackets. We moved into the breezy cockpit to check on Trina and come up with a plan.

"No one's getting any sleep anyway. We might as well just take off and get a head start on tomorrow's travel," Bryan said.

I nodded slowly, considering. "The moon's almost full. I can lead us out how we came in so we miss any rocks around."

Trina chimed in as she and the boat continued to rock. "Anything would be better than this. I think I might throw up."

Michele couldn't resist teasing her sister and hollered from her bunk, "That would be a waste of good rum!"

With the wind primed to blow us west as soon as we loosened the first line, we didn't want to risk floating into the sailboat or the rocks behind us. So we talked over our escape plan: drop the stern anchor on a floating fender, motor up and pull in the bow anchor, and circle back to retrieve the stern. Just as we were ready to begin we heard the unmistakable exhale of whale breath. Even in the bright moonlight I couldn't see our nighttime visitor so we stopped and listened until the sounds faded to the south.

Bryan repeated his work from the afternoon, releasing the line at the bow as I hauled us closer to the stern anchor. He snagged a fender from the side deck and brought it back to me to tie onto the anchor line. We untied the rode completely and tossed the bitter end out into the dark. I squinted to see the bobbing fender, took a quick visual sight of our position. I reached around Trina to start the engine and quickly eased it into idle. Back on the bow, Bryan slid us closer to the bow anchor.

"We're straight over the top and I'm going to haul it up now. Be ready to head back around."

I shifted gently into forward and waited for his call.

"Okay, we're free!"

A sailboat has no brakes. To drive up to a floating object close enough to pick it up, the helmsperson must find a balance between forward and reverse, taking wind and current into account, as they steer to a stop near a buoy or mooring. And to make matters even more difficult, in the last few feet of the approach, the bow blocks the helmsperson's view. We typically use hand signals, the bow watch waving wide to indicate direction, speed, and distance. But in the dim light, we found it hard to see each other, much less the bobbing fender. I eyed the island, the moon, and the mainland and worked to recreate our previous position from memory. Soon we were close enough for Bryan to spot the float and I slowed our approach for him to catch the line with the boat hook.

Slipping the engine back into idle, I waited for his word and stilled my body to feel the anchor breaking free. Nothing. Several moments passed and I grew anxious. I forced my mind back to the rational. *I guess if he can't get the anchor up, we're safe. We're not going anywhere.*

Bryan stepped back to confer. "We must have hooked a fluke under a rock or some debris. I can't get it to budge at all. I think we'd better wait out the night and try again after dawn."

"Okay, Let's see. We shouldn't swing much as long as this wind is up, but we don't have room to drag." I glanced behind us toward the jagged coast. "If we do come loose, we'll be on the rocks in seconds. I think we'd better tie up to that mooring buoy off our stern and stand an anchor watch just in case."

Meira poked her head through the companionway. "I'm awake anyway. You want me to help?"

I glanced at Bryan's weary face. "Yeah, I'm not too tired, but why don't you keep me company for a couple of hours while your dad gets some sleep."

She bundled up and came out on deck as Bryan tied us off and he and Trina went below. The boat bucked at the anchor, but the head-on swell was an easier ride. I stared at the mooring a few feet off our stern.

"As long as that buoy is still the same distance away," I said to Meira, "we haven't moved. But if you see it coming closer, that means we're dragging anchor. The buoy will probably hold us but we'll want to reset the anchor in a hurry in case it doesn't. We can't risk getting blown onto the beach."

She nodded solemnly and we found comfortable seats. I set her mind to solving our problem.

"So the best way to free a stuck anchor is with a trip line attached to the front of the anchor shank." I gestured to illustrate my words. "You can use that to pull the anchor out from the other side, easy. But we didn't drop ours with a trip line and now we need to send a line down the anchor rode to the front of the shank. Without a weight, the line would just float, so the books say you can use a circular weight called a kellet. Lots of sailors have dive weights they can hook around the line to slide down and onto the shank, but we don't have dive equipment. Can you think of anything we have onboard that is heavy and waterproof and round, like a donut?"

We brainstormed cheerfully for a bit, naming all the ridiculous ideas we could think of.

"Let's use Hannah. She can just hold her breath."

"She might not like that plan"

"How about the seat from the head!"

"It's not round. It's U-shaped."

"Oh, yeah."

"Ooh, ooh. I know!" I smiled at the certainty in her voice. "What if we wrapped the dinghy cable around and around and duct-taped it into a circle. I bet it would be heavy enough to carry a line down to the anchor!"

"I think that might just work."

In the morning, we put our idea to the test. I wound the cable and held it tight while Bryan taped it into shape. He tied an extra length of line to the makeshift kellet, carefully loosened the bitter end of the anchor rode, slipped the kellet over it, and tied the anchor line back to the bow. He shook the trip line a bit to encourage it to sink and cleated off the end.

If we pulled our jury-rigged trip line straight up, it would just slip back off the anchor shank, so Bryan dropped the dinghy off the deck and rowed around to the bow. I uncleated the trip line and handed it down. He paddled forward a few meters and stood to heave the anchor free. *Rover* started rocking in the choppy bay and I wondered if she would tip him out. He sat down hard and rowed back.

"I can't get enough leverage in the dinghy. We're going to have to drive forward and pull it out from the bow."

The whole crew had crowded into the cockpit.

"Meira, can you loose the stern line from the mooring buoy?" I said. "Thanks!"

As I started the engine again, I spoke a warning.

"This might get tricky for a minute, but everything should be okay. Just please don't move around or I'll trip over you in the fuss. If I need anything, I'll ask. Be ready to help."

Bryan climbed aboard, tied *Rover* off, and carried the trip line back to the bow. I drove dead slow up over the anchor and just beyond. Trip line in one hand, anchor line in the other, he hauled hard and lifted his arms high.

"We're free!"

"Good! But get back here quick," I hollered. "We're drifting into shore!" The wind had blown us off in an instant, *LiLo* headed past the mooring buoy on one side, *Rover* swung west on the other. I revved the engine to keep us in place until Bryan pulled *Rover* back around.

"The anchor's up on deck and we're clear of the mooring," he said. "Let's get some sea room before I pull *Rover* up."

"Sounds good to me!" I watched our depth increase as I drove away from the island. Within minutes we were in safer water and Bryan stepped to the side deck to pull *Rover* up for the day at sea. Just as he lifted her out of the water, a wave splashed into the dinghy and knocked her out of his hands. She settled back into the ocean, filled to the brim but still floating. Our guests gasped, but Bryan called back reassuringly.

"Flotation check! Looks like it works just fine!"

While I drove slowly into the swell, he rolled his pants up and hopped into the dinghy with a bailing bucket. He bent and straightened like an oil derrick. Water flew as he lightened the load. When *Rover* was mostly dry, Meira went up onto the bow and the two of them wrestled the dinghy to the cabin top.

Bryan checked all the lines and tied the deck gear tight. I handed the tiller off and went below to make breakfast. Only Hannah had gotten a full night's sleep, but the sun was warm and once we cleared Punta Mita at the north end of the bay the choppy seas gave way to a gentle swell. The crew sprawled around the deck and cockpit and we traded off, taking short watches. Even our visitors steered for a while, sinking into the slow pace of the day.

I broke the stillness. "Last night was one of the most miserable nights we've ever spent at anchor, but this—" I turned to look over one shoulder and then the other, blue sky meeting blue sea and not another soul in sight, "—this makes up for the hard days in a hurry."

Just then the ocean rippled. A great, gray ridge broke the surface and rolled, raising a giant flipper to the sky.

"Look there!" I pointed out to sea. "Whales!"

The boat shifted under me as everyone turned to stare. The flukes of the humpback's tail were just descending but several other pod mates had emerged.

Meira called out a count from the bow. "I see one, two, three, four, maybe five; it's hard to tell!"

Bryan grabbed the camera from the shelf below and I dropped the throttle and gave the whales some space.

"We've heard a couple on night watches and seen a few surfacing to breathe," I said to Trina and Michele, "but nothing like this."

The whales swam lazily north, spiraling on the surface. Fins rose and slapped the sea, explosive breath misted the air. Droplets sparkled from the tips of tails as one after another whales dove to gather speed, disappeared for a moment, and then launched their gigantic frames into the sky.

Bryan added some perspective. "Those whales are half again as long as our whole boat and probably weigh six times what we do."

I eased the rudder to starboard just a bit, away from their course. I didn't really want to meet them any closer.

Off to the left the whales still danced. On my right two more emerged. Here, on the surface of the water, we had invaded their home. I dropped the engine into neutral and waited for them to make their course clear.

Suddenly, two whales breached in unison, their powerful bodies slipping into the air—free, just for a moment, of the weight of the sea.

They flew, hung, succumbed to gravity. The sound came a split-second after the splash.

We turned to each other in wonder.

"Did you see that?"

"I can't believe it!"

"Dad, did you get that on video?"

Bryan held the camera under his chin, aiming the lens to follow his gaze.

"I have no idea! I didn't have time to set up a shot, and there was no way I was going to look away to check. This is too amazing to miss!"

We drifted along with the whales for an hour or so. When they finally turned to swim out to sea, I let out a breath I didn't even know I was holding.

"My cheeks hurt from smiling so much," Hannah said.

"Me too." I reached for the chart to get us back on course. "What a gift."

Even with the welcome delay, we came into Chacala with plenty of time to anchor before dark. We drove through the anchorage and looked for a space. "There's *Thallasea* and *Crazy Love!*" I said. "Is there room for us between them?"

"Looks just about perfect," said Bryan. He leaned down, pushed the gear shift into neutral, and stood up again, surprised.

"So, we might have a little problem."

I whipped around, no idea how to predict his next words.

"Looks like something let loose in the shift linkage. I can't get the engine to go into neutral or reverse, only forward."

He moved the tiller to the side to send us into a wide, slow circle.

"We have to drop both anchors here. Let's make a plan for how to do that without reverse." I kept my voice calm for the crew and for our guests, who were already on alert.

"Okay, how about this." I could see the wheels turning as Bryan calculated. "The wind's offshore, but we want to end up with our bow to the ocean swell. If we drop the bow anchor while we're heading toward shore, we can cleat it off at the proper scope and kill the engine. The momentum should swing us around as it sets." I followed along as his mind worked through each step. "Then if we let out more scope, we should be able to drop the stern anchor and set it with a winch. We'll center ourselves between the two, just like we did last night."

"Don't remind me," moaned Trina, "I never want to think about last night again!" We laughed and moved to take our positions.

"Should we go down below?" Michele asked.

"No, just sit still and we'll work around you."

Across the way a sailor stepped down into a dinghy and began to row toward us.

"Isn't that the man we met in the anchorage in Mazatlán? The one who swam over to our boat?" I asked.

"Looks like it," Bryan said. "I'll drive as slow as I can. You call over to let him know what's up."

I hollered from the stern as he came close. "We've lost neutral and reverse. We're going to try to set our anchors without them but we might need some help if you don't mind sticking around."

"No problem," he said, backpaddling. "I'll just stay out of your way."

The crew stepped to the side decks to fend us off if we drifted toward another boat. I took the tiller and called out depths until Bryan raised his fist and tossed the anchor over. Just as I reached down to cut the engine, it choked and died.

"Shoot! Leave it off!" Bryan called, already on his way back from the bow. "I should have thought to tell you to cut it right away. We must have driven right over our anchor line and caught it in the prop."

Our sailor friend had grasped the situation and was rapidly approaching. The current swung us slowly his way.

"How about you toss me your stern anchor and an assistant and I'll pull you straight and get you set?"

"Sounds good," Bryan said.

Meira moved to the stern and grabbed our friend's dinghy painter. She handed down the anchor and Bryan double checked its line to make sure it was cleated off securely at our end. Then she hopped down into the little inflatable and shoved against our hull. Bryan fed the anchor line out as they headed toward shore. When our stern pulled around straight, he yelled to Meira—"Okay, now!"—and she dropped the anchor with a splash.

"Thanks so much," I called out as the dinghy neared again to transfer Meira back. "I don't think we would have had time to drop our dinghy without drifting into someone."

"Anytime," he said. "You'd do the same for me."

Bryan stripped off his shirt and grabbed a snorkel. "I'd better go see what sort of mess we've got down there." He jumped in and dove, bobbed back up right away, smiling. "I'm going to need the camera. That's quite a sight! But it doesn't look like we damaged the line or the prop. I should be able to unwind it by hand." Sure enough, a few dives later I felt us swing free. Bryan climbed aboard and pulled in the slack. We winched both anchor lines hard to check our set and finally sat down in the cockpit.

"That's boat life for you," he said.

"Is it always like this?" Michele asked.

I draped my head back over the lifeline and let out a relieved exhale. "Well, we promised you no boring stories."

Chapter Twenty-four

WE'D COME TO LOVE

La Cruz de Huanacaxtle, Mexico
February 2014: Waxing Crescent, First Quarter,
Waxing Gibbous, Full Moon

*Love doesn't just sit there, like a stone, it has to be made,
like bread; remade all the time, made new.*
—Ursula K. Le Guin

If this journey was a film, the following days would be the photo montage, filled with images of cold drinks in coconuts and afternoons on the beach.

Picture the snapshots as they flash by. Fruit served in a pineapple. Salsa dancing in the sand. Crocodiles at the water's edge. Our friend, Ryan, arriving at the airport. Waving goodbye to Trina and Michele at the bus stop in Chacala. Blue-footed boobies nesting on the shore of Isla Isabel. Sailing into Bahía de Banderas, sunset off the stern.

Back at La Cruz de Huanacaxtle, a vibrant cultural center and a crossroads for many long-distance sailors, we nosed into our assigned moorage at the marina, secured our lines, then looked up and laughed.

Just across the finger to port sat *Thallasea*. Two slips to starboard, *Crazy Love* lay tucked in and quiet.

"Hey, Will!" I hollered down into *Thallasea's* cabin. "It's *LiLo*. Hope you weren't trying to get away from us!"

We spent a few days exploring the town, enjoying the company of old friends and new ones before Ryan had to return to his regular life in wintry Alaska.

The day he left I converted his bunk back into the dinette and started in on some long-postponed chores. By afternoon the boat was a wreck—dishes piled in the sink and laundry pulled out and sorted on the settee. I grabbed my phone and took a couple of photos.

"Everyone somehow seems to think it's minimalist to live in a space this small," I said to the kids, who were folding laundry on their bunks, "but when you have all the things four people and a boat need for a year, it's mostly just various stages of messy. I've been messaging with Charlotte from *Rebel Heart*, you know—the one who started the women's sailing forum? She said she'd call me after the radio net tomorrow and arrange a time to finally meet. I can't take her a hostess gift but I thought she might enjoy seeing what it's really like with all of us on board."

We listened together to the cruisers' morning net. The official announcements ranged from weather and sea conditions to information about the night produce market and which bands were playing in town that evening. Afterward there was a steady stream of sailors hailing each other and flipping away to open channels for more conversation. In the past we'd sometimes followed along to eavesdrop on any chats that sounded interesting. Today, keenly aware of all the listening ears, I picked up the mic.

"*Rebel Heart, Rebel Heart, Rebel Heart*, this is *LiLo*, over."

Charlotte responded quickly and we switched channels and made a plan.

I called toward the V-berth where Bryan was still nursing a cup of coffee. "I'm going to go for breakfast with Charlotte and her family. I can't tell if we're going to a friend's house or a restaurant. Either way, I'll be back later."

"I know," came the groggy reply. "Everyone can hear everything in here."

By the end of breakfast at Lupe's, which turned out to be both a private home and public restaurant, Charlotte and I had made plans to meet again for a trip to a doctor in nearby Bucerías. She spoke fluent Spanish and had located a physician who she said would see me too. My autoimmune disorder had been pretty well-behaved on the trip but I needed to get some blood work done and refill my prescription.

It took a week of mornings to finish our tasks—multiple trips on public transit together, where we traded off carrying her baby, Lyra, and caring for her preschooler, Cora. She helped me find my way through the medical system and we shared stories of our journey, the joys and struggles of raising a family aboard.

"Oh, yeah," I said at one point. "I took these pictures to show you what it really looks like to have four full-sized people in a small ship."

She looked over my shoulder as I swiped through the photos.

"If I didn't already like you, girl, this would do it."

We soon felt at home in the welcoming community. We settled on a favorite taco stand on the edge of the plaza and made friends with the couple who ran it—Leno and Alejandra. We connected with many other sailors in the marina, which served as both a gathering place and a jumping off point for long-distance cruisers. I found places to write—the marina cafe and a coffee shop called the Octopus's Garden, which, in addition to offering a shaded courtyard location, hosted an art gallery and various classes for kids and adults.

Despite all the new friends, the safety of the harbor, the ease of fresh food, and tacos for dinner almost every night, I found myself in tears most days. I'd struggled with depression a few times before in my life, always as a response to trauma or a difficult transition. I took advantage of our steady internet access to look for more information, hoping there was some explanation for why I still felt so emotional.

"Situational depression or adjustment disorder is a short-term condition that occurs when a person has great difficulty coping with, or adjusting to, a particular source of stress, such as a major life change, loss, or event. A person with an adjustment disorder develops emotional and/or behavioral symptoms as a reaction to a stressful event. These symptoms generally begin within three months of the event and rarely last for longer than six months after the event or situation has ended."

"But what if your whole life is major change?" I sobbed to Bryan later that night. "When do I count from? The day we moved out of our house? The day we left? The day we left the next port? The day we left again? Do I blame the stress of losing the dinghy or the constant fear of what will go wrong next?"

This life of incessant beginnings also brought more endings than my system knew how to handle.

One day I caught a glimpse of myself in the mirror. My right shoulder hung crooked, an adjustment I'd unconsciously made to handle the pain of my old injury in a life of heavy demands. My smile was crooked, too, and unconvincing.

"This is supposed to be the easy part," I said to my reflection. "Why are you still so sad?"

We'd heard through the sailor grapevine that there was a night produce market on Tuesdays and Sundays. Friends who were getting ready for a Pacific crossing had put in special orders for boxes of unripe vegetables, but anyone could go shopping among the newly delivered crates on the loading dock if they knew when and where to arrive.

One Tuesday I grabbed my grocery bags and went on a mission.

"Bring avocados!" Hannah said, as I headed up the ramp.

I walked the streets to the tienda on the corner by the pizza place, ducked through the hallway in the back, and slid past the pile of boxes through the doorway into a produce paradise.

My eyes went first to the piles of mangoes, red tomatoes, and ripe bananas. I had room for only a few delicate items at the top of my bags. I looked beyond the fragile fruit for hardier choices. Cabbage, grapes, apples, and onions all hold up well without refrigeration. Too many of these, though, and my bags would be too heavy to carry.

Already several friends were browsing among the boxes, produce bin in hand. I looked around for the stack of empty bins and joined the quest.

I passed up the mushrooms, strawberries, and lettuce; settled for grapefruit, limes, and potatoes. I chose four rock hard avocados, one perfectly ready to eat. I made plans to tuck the green ones, one at a time, into a dark place to ripen and to elicit the crew's help to remember to pull them out before they rotted. *We can always find a use for some cilantro, right?* I tucked a bunch on top of my haul. *One more mango,* I decided. After so many days of cans and packages, it was hard to resist the abundant freshness.

The cashier weighed out my choices from top to bottom, lightest to heaviest, and I mounded the grapes, cilantro, and mangoes next to the chewing gum rack while I waited to line my bags with the heavier goods. I filled the backpack with the weightiest items and made one bag extra light for my weakened right arm. Even so, I had to stop several times to rest and readjust my load before I reached the docks. I left my bags in the cockpit and went straight to bed.

A few days later, we gathered at the marina plaza for a birthday party for Charlotte's youngest, Lyra. *Rebel Heart* had invited all the cruisers from the marina and all their friends from town. I looked around the party and found Lupe and her family near the buffet. I got some food and asked if I could join them. Though the conversation mostly flowed over my head, the more I chose to interact with non-English speakers, the better my Spanish became and the more I learned about the people and places we'd come to love.

I looked up to see a couple about our age peeking through a cut in the hedge.

I waved to get their attention. "Come on in! There's plenty of food to go around and everyone's welcome." They looked a little familiar so we exchanged boat names and listed ports of call to see if we'd crossed paths before. Because so many sailors travel in similarly-sized boats through the same weather systems, we often ended up in the same harbors.

"You left from Oregon too? I can't believe we didn't meet up before this. We must have been leapfrogging each other all the way down. I'm Bethany, by the way."

"I'm Darren and this is Jodi." He wrapped his arm around her tan shoulders. "We're traveling slow on a shoestring budget on our thirty-six-foot Pearson, *Gratitouille*. If there's no wind, we just bob around at sea playing cards until it comes back."

"Nice," Bryan said. "We're hoping to still like each other when we're done. If there's no wind, we often end up motoring a bit so we don't end up with cabin fever. We're not purists about this. We're just glad to be out here."

"Hey ... " recognition lit up Jodi's face. "When were you in San Diego? Did you stay in the cruiser's anchorage?"

As we compared our routes, a memory surfaced. "Wait—I think I remember seeing you there. The anchorage was packed when we got in and we were motoring around, looking for space. Were you the one tucked up near the rocks?"

"Yes! I remember you driving by!"

We were talking over each other now in our excitement. "You smiled at me so warmly I almost cried when we ended up on the other side of the anchorage. It had been so long since I'd been around another woman sailor—the whole trip, in fact."

"Yes, and I was sick and couldn't come visit you but I sent Darren over to meet you. I knew as soon as I saw you, we were meant to be friends."

"I thought the same about you. I can't believe it took this long to find each other!"

Jodi took my hand and pulled me close into a long hug.

"Well, we're here now and I'm not losing you again!"

Chapter Twenty-five

COLD WATER, SWEET BREAD

Soyatán, Mexico
February 2014: Waning Gibbous

Tourists are pilgrims who don't know they are pilgrims.
—*Jonathan White*

It came together the way the best plans do: last minute and full of room for serendipity. One evening Bryan was hanging out in the Octopus's Garden and one of the waiters overheard him talking to a woman about taking a trip to see some petroglyphs. We'd heard there were some in a couple of hours to the north and had talked about going to see them from there. She offered us a day trip out with lunch for "only $300 US dollars." That seemed reasonable enough, it just wasn't in our budget.

The friendly server, Kevin, who was on a tight budget himself, told Bryan he knew someone who could rent us a cheap car. Kevin was willing to drive if we'd pay for the rental. So we made plans to meet on Sunday morning for an adventure and invited some friends to come along.

Saturday afternoon, Bryan and Kevin went to pick up the Suburban. They bussed to the rental shop, exchanged money for keys, and drove away, no paperwork required.

The next morning we met Jodi and Darren in the marina parking lot and loaded up the Suburban. The release lever to flip the center seat forward was broken, so the kids and I crawled into the back seat from the way back. On our way we stopped to pick up our friend Will, who was staying in Bucerías while his boat was being worked on in the boatyard, and Michelle, a Canadian friend of Kevin's.

We turned off the main highway onto a smaller road and soon turned onto an even smaller road, a one-lane dirt track that wound up into the mountains. We navigated steep slopes, deep ruts, and oncoming traffic—some on horseback. Thick dust swirled and settled revealing one beautiful vista after another. We'd been told to drive until we thought we were on the wrong road and then keep going. Eventually we reached a pass in the mountain tops and headed down into in a peak-ringed valley. Hints of spicy earth and green growth blew in through the open windows and we spotted a collection of rooftops low in the basin.

We drove into the outskirts of the community and stopped to ask directions from a couple of older men. Michelle spoke excellent Spanish, so we elected her to interpret. We followed the instructions into town, past a small store and the local church. On the other end of town the road got too narrow for the Suburban and we decided we must have missed our stop. A woman near the lane sent us back to the crossroads and told us to ask any of the men sitting there to show us around.

By the time I crawled out of the car, the first of our group had already introduced themselves to the men and were following one of them up the hill. Just a few meters up the road, our guide pointed out a boulder near the path. We walked around to the downhill side and turned to look up at the ancient carvings. Sinuous and geometric at the same time, the curved lines snaked across the black stone. A woman walked up, baby on her hip and child by the hand, and added her interpretation of the carvings.

"We think this petroglyph represents the three streams that nourish this valley." My eyes traced three distinct grooves running down the face of the rock surrounding a honeycomb pattern in the center.

"Some people think the honeycomb represents a treasure hidden in the valley," she said. "Many people have come with metal detectors to look, but no one has found any."

Someone mentioned more carvings up the hill and we crawled under the barbed wire fence and walked to where they pointed. I stood in front of one of the petroglyphs, awed by the weight of history present in this place.

"Did you bring your lunch?" Our guide recalled me to the present. "You must take it up to la cascada" *The waterfall.*

We crawled back under the fence and emerged to see an older man riding down the road on a dust-colored donkey. He'd been to the waterfall, he said, and was on his way to Celia's house to take her some water. Would we like to come along?

"Why, yes, please!"

"And would you like to ride the burro?" As he spoke, he dismounted and slipped his water jugs off the saddle horn. Meira didn't take much convincing to accept. I turned around to collect the abandoned jugs and when I turned back they were halfway up the hill, her glossy head bobbing above his gray one. Hannah and I took turns, too, riding up to Celia's house where she and some friends were working on a massive batch of sweet rolls. We spoke for a few minutes and quickly found common ground. I admired her outdoor oven, so much more elegant than the clay pizza oven we'd once built in our backyard at home.

"I love to bake, too," I said. "In fact, sometimes I teach bread-baking classes."

Celia's eyebrows shot up. "You teach bread baking? Doesn't everyone in your hometown know how to bake already?"

While we'd been talking, Celia and her friend had been expertly portioning dough, rolling and shaping it under cupped palms, and placing it in rows on baking sheets. From the mound remaining in the bowl, it was obvious we were getting in the way of a serious production. We offered grateful goodbyes and, her hands never pausing in their work, Celia invited us to come back later for the finished product.

"But first, you must have lunch at la cascada!"

The local church was the next stop on our unofficial tour of the town. On the way Jodi took a turn on the donkey at the owner's insistence.

"The burro should not walk in vain," he said. On our way to the church, we exchanged names, butchering the unfamiliar syllables a few times. We finally got his name on paper—Anecito. We asked his burro's name too and he looked amused by the question. "I call my burro, Burro."

We asked him about the waterfall, and he spoke affectionately of the landmark, its beauty and provision, the way it changes from season to season. It sounded nice, but Oregon is home to hundreds of stunning waterfalls and I didn't expect to be very impressed.

At the church one guide took us inside while Anecito waited. We walked past the skillfully carved cross at the entrance and through the stout wooden doors. Blue and white streamers hung from the arched brick ceiling and simple wooden pews lined the cool tile floor. The man with us shared what he knew about the intricately carved altar, saying it was made from the strong, rot-resistant wood of the huanacaxtle tree.

He also told us the story of the miracle at the church of San Miguel.

Before the town had electricity they lit the sanctuary with oil lanterns. One day, one of the lanterns started to flame up and glow. Worried the lamp would explode or set the building on fire, the parishioners tossed dirt on the flames to no avail. They eventually gave up and evacuated the church, fully expecting it to burn. After a while, when nothing happened, they cautiously went back into the church and found the oil lamp, with plenty of oil still in it but no longer burning. In the center of the lamp, they found a sword that had fallen from the statue of San Miguel on the altar above. The woman showed us the tiny sword, now firmly stitched to the statue's hand.

We emerged from the cool church into the hot sun. Anecito and his burro were waiting with a friend. We walked back across town to Anecito's front yard where he tied Burro securely to a tree. He gestured proudly at his home and spoke sincerely.

"Mi casa es su casa."

To save Anecito a second hike to the waterfall, we piled back into the Suburban and drove a few minutes up the road. Meira rode in the way-way-back and we tucked Anecito in the front with Michelle and Kevin. On the drive, we peppered him with questions.

"Do you really hike to the waterfall every day for water?"

"Sí."

"How long have you lived here?"

"All my life."

"How many tourists come to your village in a year?"

"Oh, a lot. Very many," he insisted. "Like twenty!"

We pulled over to the side of the road and unloaded. Everyone grabbed backpacks and water and we headed across the field. Anecito pointed to a stand of corn and assured us that the waterfall was just beyond. We walked in the sun for a few minutes, picking our way across hoof prints and irrigation puddles, and then headed straight through the planting. "Knee high by the fourth of July" is only true about corn in certain latitudes. The stalks here stood above even the tallest head and fat ears stuck out in our way.

We followed Anecito's sure steps through what Hannah dubbed a "Mexican corn maze" and came out the other side onto a dirt path. A few more steps brought us to a steep hillside. Anecito stood at the tricky corners and helped us down the switchbacks. A heavy carpet of dry leaves threatened our footing and more than one hiker grabbed for tree trunks and vines as we slipped and slid our way down to the rocky valley at the bottom. During the wet season the water fills the valley floor and rushes on down the slopes. But now, toward the end of the dry season, only one of the two waterfalls was running and it dropped into a tranquil pool at the base of the cliffs. Even this time of year, the cataract dominated the ravine.

I should have known better than to disdain any waterfall. I've explored many in the Columbia River Gorge, from seasonal trickles to the grand Multnomah Falls and I saw echoes of the familiar cascades, but the variations took my breath away. The flora was different here; the ferns from home would be dwarfed under the split leaf huanacaxtle. The earth was different too. There, water flows over and among sharp boulders down ancient landslides to the valleys below. Here, the rushing river fell on a stone slab worn smooth as a water slide. The surface sloped steeply from several hundred feet above to its terminus only a feet feet over our heads. There the water changed directions, freefalling into the pool below.

Several took turns standing under the surprisingly cool spray. First Michelle stepped in, her mass of black curls dripping onto her white suit. Then Darren and Jodi took a turn—Darren, playful as a sea otter; Jodi, blonde and radiant, a tall water nymph. Hannah and I waded around the edges and Meira jumped right in under the flow. At one point, she shook her head to get the water out of her eyes and her glasses flew off into the pool. It wasn't too deep or swift and Bryan waded in near her and found them intact.

Once we were cool enough to consider lunch, we toweled off and found spots to sit on the giant boulder near the base of the falls. Heat from the morning sun still radiated from the stone and we lounged like sleepy snakes on its warmth. We ate sandwiches and chips, washed them down with water or soda.

As Michelle started to pack up her litter, Anecito spoke sharply. I didn't understand what he was trying to say but his hand gestures made it clear. *Throw your garbage on the ground.* He grabbed her chip bag and tossed it down. Michelle picked it up.

"No. I'll take it with me, thanks."

He spoke up again, more urgently this time and she translated.

"We just leave those things here," he said. "The river will carry them away." We exchanged glances with the other sailors, horrified. All rivers run to the sea and we'd seen the impact of litter on the ocean, on the sea life that made it their home.

"No, we'll take it with us and throw it away properly." He finally relented but the moment stuck with me, prompting questions about cultural differences and the quality of my own waste-disposal choices. It was hard not to feel superior about our ecologically friendly habits. But I remained convinced that this community was not careless or ignorant; their choices very likely reflected values similar to ours, filtered through a different reality.

One day at sea, a few weeks later, my understanding shifted. Until very recently, this village would have used only naturally biodegradable wrappings—paper or corn husks—and their relative isolation may have led them to make the choice to send their refuse down the river instead of storing it near their village where it could contaminate the lives in their sheltered community. I wasn't sure I knew enough to completely comprehend their thinking but I knew better than to judge.

We looked around the river bed, almost dry this time of year. Large, curving seed pods the color of rich chocolate lay scattered all around. Bryan picked one up and held it to his mouth, his face a silent question.

Is this edible?

Anecito nodded, shook his head, then nodded again.

"Sí. No. Sí." We were confused and he tried to explain. "Not to eat but…" He turned to the side and pantomimed broadly—first faking belly discomfort, then chewing and swallowing, and finally bringing his hands around behind his outstretched bum in a violent charade of gushing illness. Bryan pulled the pod quickly away from his mouth and the riverbed echoed with laughter. The hand signal for diarrhea is universal.

We finished our lunch and started back up the hill. In the corn field all the cool relief of the waterfall quickly evaporated. Anecito snagged a couple of ears of corn and shoved them in his back pockets. We followed the bobbing tassels back through the fields to the road. Piling into the Suburban again, we drove along the lane, slowing to pass the only other traffic: a father and daughter, each on a sturdy pony, riding slowly by. Sheaves of corn stalks, the ears still attached, balanced across each saddle horn.

Back in town we wanted to find a way to show our gratitude. Anecito turned down our offer of cash but when we suggested the gift of a cold beer, his eyes lit up.

"Yes, please. They sell it at my neighbor's house." So off we went to the neighbor's. We filed through the gate and settled around the patio. Anecito refused to drink alone so Michelle gave in and drank along with him. He introduced us to the ersatz bartender and her son and we all sat around making awkward conversation while the drinkers savored their cold beverages.

We needed to get back to the marina but couldn't resist one more stop at Celia's. While we'd been exploring, her sweet rolls had completed their final rise and the first batch was just coming out of the oven. Celia tested one expertly and flipped the tray around on her rough wooden peel. The heat in the wood-fired oven hadn't yet evened out and the pan dulce in the back was starting to burn.

Even in the open air, the aroma was intoxicating. When she finally declared them ready, we tore in, juggling the scorching rolls between tender fingertips. Celia laughed at us, then waited for the verdict. Mouths full, we grinned our approval and she offered us a second round.

Too soon, we had to go. Celia's warm invitation echoed Anecito's earlier words.

"You're welcome at my home anytime!"

Back by our vehicle, I lingered while the rest of our crew said their goodbyes and then I stepped forward. Through my limited language, across our cultural differences, how could I express my deep gratitude at having been given a taste of the connections between us?

I leaned in for a hug and double-cheeked kisses and poured my heart into my words, "Gracias. Muchas gracias." There was treasure in this valley after all.

Chapter Twenty-six

Courage Expanding

La Cruz de Huanacaxtle, Mexico
February and March 2014: Waning Crescent,
New Moon, Waxing Crescent

*Becoming
takes more courage
than sailing into a storm*

LiLo tilted to port as excited teenagers bounced into the cockpit. Cheerful voices broke the silence.

"We're going to have a sleepover on the beach!"

"Can we use the tarp, Dad? We're going to build our own tents!"

Hannah and Meira had fallen into the pattern of spending most days with a gang of cruising kids—six or eight teens who each lived aboard. We gladly gave them a few pesos a day to spend on snacks or sodas and we connected with the other parents to make sure the kids were following family rules and not taking over any one boat too often.

Unless we needed to find them, we steered clear of The Red Gecko cafe, their favorite local hangout. Privacy might be in short supply on a boat but we could at least offer them independence.

"Be back before 9 p.m.," Bryan would say when they left for the day.

"If you get lost," I reminded them, "head downhill until you find water. You can always find your way back to the marina from there."

The local residents and expatriates in the area assured us the town was a safe place for the wandering kids but a night alone on the beach warranted a little more parental oversight.

"Who's going to have a sleepover?" I asked.

"Eli and Rose and Caroline and Max and ... "

I paused the recitation of the familiar kid names.

"Are any parents going to be there?"

"That's the best part! Mike and Kat offered to stay with us so we don't have to bring our parents along!"

At sea, the sailing life requires extreme independence, the willingness and ability to solve problems alone. But put a group of sailors together in one place for a day or two and community springs into being. Independence turns to friendship as folks exchange spare parts, offer expertise, host potlucks, and pour nightcaps.

Kat, who worked at the marina, and Mike, the owner of the local sailing shop, were young adults in their twenties who were much cooler than any of the parents. If they were willing to keep an eye on the kids, we were happy to let them.

The day of the party I walked up to the Oxxo convenience store for hot dogs and buns. On the way back, I stopped at the marina guard shack to chat with Ezekiel, one of the taxi drivers who frequently waited there for fares.

"What's for dinner?" he asked, noting the bag in my hand.

"Oh, this is for the kids. They're staying on the beach tonight with Mike and Kat and the other teenagers."

"Just you and your husband on the boat this evening?" He wolf whistled at me and elbowed the guard on duty. "Have a great night!"

I blushed but stood my ground. "Actually, the dads are all going out for dinner and the moms are hanging out in the marina and ordering in. If the kids are away, we're going to enjoy ourselves!"

The guard smiled at me. "I will send someone down the beach every hour. We will keep watch on them for you."

Before long it seemed everyone in town was keeping an eye out for all of us. One evening Bryan mentioned to Leno he'd been hoping to find some bamboo for a mast for the dinghy. We still had *Splitpea's* rudder and tiller and wanted to rig *Rover* to sail if possible. We'd popped into the little sail shop up the stairs from the fish market, but hadn't found anything that would work. A nice, straight length of bamboo seemed ideal.

That night on the walk home, Bryan shared what he'd learned. "Leno says there's bamboo in the schoolyard and that if I climb over the wall, I can cut some and toss it back over the fence. I'm not comfortable sneaking into the school and taking bamboo. Someone from the marina said there's another stand of it up in town. Let's go tomorrow to check it out."

So the next morning we wandered up the hill, found the place we thought was right. High cement walls surrounded the compound, but we could see tall bamboo nodding overhead.

We found our way around to the front of the estate. The heavy wooden door was open for a delivery and I walked up quickly to catch the man's attention, suddenly realizing I hadn't prepared my question in Spanish. I fumbled ahead, gesturing, "Sir, I ... we are looking for some bamboo for ... We have a dinghy and want to make a ... "

"¿Un mástil?" he prompted, and I laughed.

"Yes! Sí. Un mástil."

"Welcome! I will have the gardener cut a stalk for you." He waved off my offer of payment. "Don't pay me—no, no, no. But you could pay the gardener."

We followed him back through the entry, past a sparkling pool and shady garden into the main house. He walked us into the red-tiled kitchen, offered cold glasses of water.

"Here's the gardener now." He turned and spoke rapidly. The gardener grinned and motioned us to follow him. Outside again, we stood back while he chose the straightest shoot, lopped it down, and expertly macheted the leaves from the stalk.

"Please, let us pay you for your work," I said. And he shook his head.

"No, no, no. Don't pay me." He smiled and pointed across the way to where a young boy was just swinging open the service gate. "But you could pay my son."

We hoisted the thirty feet of bamboo onto our shoulders, and walked out the gate. This time, I didn't ask, just slipped the boy a few pesos.

I felt as long as a triple-trailer semi on the way back, trying to maneuver the pole through the narrow streets. We chuckled at the sight we made and the odd looks we received. When I paused at the security hut, Bryan stopped short. I explained to Ezekiel and the other taxi drivers what we were doing and they laughed with us at our awkward situation.

We stopped just through the gate at the plaza where every morning Zumba dancers bounced and whooped. Bryan laid the bamboo down and stretched out beside it, measuring six-foot sections against his length. He moved around, up and down the stalk, got up and rolled it over, looking for the straightest part. We didn't want to negotiate the ramps and docks with the stalk between us, so he chopped off the best twelve-foot piece and a spare length, just in case that one didn't work out.

We tucked those under our arms and walked back to the boat. Hannah and Meira celebrated our find with us and we slid the bamboo onto the side deck to dry.

That night, we headed back up to the taco stand. Leno greeted us warmly, but then asked, confused, "Where were you? After we talked, I went to the school and cut a piece of bamboo for you. I threw it over the wall like I said, but when I came out, you weren't there. I followed your footprints in the street and called for you, 'Pablo! Pablo!' but you never answered!"

I tried to clear up the misunderstanding, "We thought you meant Bryan should go alone to the school. And did you think he was named 'Pablo'? No wonder he didn't hear you calling him!"

"I don't have it here tonight," he said, "but come back tomorrow and my son will carry it down to the boat for you." We didn't need any more bamboo, but we weren't about to turn him down.

"Can we pay you for it?"

"Oh, no, no, no!" he said, "but you can pay my son."

"Where did you learn Spanish?"

I was upstairs at the marina cafe, sitting on the edge of the balcony and writing, the only customer around. The server caught a hint of my accent as I thanked him for the lemonade and he stopped to chat.

"Oh, I don't speak it very well but my best friend in fourth grade was from Mexico and I spent a lot of time with her and her family. A few things must have rubbed off."

"Well, you and I will practice together!"

From then on, anytime I went upstairs to write, Rafael took me to task, asking questions and gently correcting my halting answers.

One day, as we chatted over some photos of our family, he straightened and asked, formally, "Would you like some more water, miss?"

I sat confused for a moment until I noticed the man who'd just walked in across the room. He grabbed a bottle from the bar and went back through the swinging kitchen doors.

Rafael relaxed. "That's my boss. He wouldn't like to see me talking to you instead of serving the customers but," he swung his arm toward the rest of the room, "you're the only one here!"

"*LiLo, LiLo, LiLo,* this is *Gratitouille,* over."

I picked up the radio and responded.

"This is *LiLo,* come in."

I could hear *Gratitouille's* engine rumbling behind Jodi's voice. "Darren and I are headed south but we wanted to say goodbye one last time. Come down to the end of dock eleven and we'll swing by."

The few short weeks we'd spent together in La Cruz felt like a lifetime of friendship with *Gratitouille* and with so many other boating friends. We'd shared taxis and appetizers, sunsets and surfing lessons, gone out to the market, stayed in for long evenings of conversation and connection.

We exchanged stories of silly moments and stormy days. We talked about our fears at sea and our uncertainties about the transition back to life on land. We plotted new passages together and tried to forget each boat would be heading out alone. We nodded and said, "I believe in you."

I felt my courage expanding to match the confidence of our community. I was beginning to come out of the depression that had settled in on the journey south and my shoulder had improved with rest but I wondered how I would do on the long, lonely slog back north.

Get-to-know-you potlucks gave way to goodbye parties and every morning another boat slipped away from the fleet. *Gratitouille* was pulling out today, but soon *Crazy Love* and *Rebel Heart* and *Thallasea* and so many more would follow, pointing west to Hawaii, southwest to the South Pacific, or south to Central America. Only one other sailor in the marina was northbound like we were. And not a single other boat we knew was planning to sail all the way back to Oregon.

I stood at the edge of the marina, watching *Gratitouille* approach through the seawall from their anchorage in the bay. Darren steered slowly along the length of the dock. Jodi reached over the lifeline and dropped a small packet into my hand.

"This is for the scary moments on the way back. Open it when everything is falling apart."

Already *Gratitouille* was angling away. I waved and called my thanks across the water widening between us.

The day before we left town Rafael caught me on the wharf. "Are you leaving soon? Don't go without finding me. I have something for you."

So before we pulled away, I tracked him down. "Rafael, I can't thank you enough for the Spanish lessons and all the glasses of limonada."

"De nada. Here, this is for you."

He pulled a leather cord from around his neck and slipped it over my head. I looked down to see a pendant carved with a Tōnalpōhualli, the Aztec calendar.

"This has always brought me luck and now I want you to have it too, to bring you luck on your way back home."

"Rafael," I was trying not to cry, "if I lived here, if I spoke better Spanish, I think we would be such good friends."

"Oh, Betania," he said, "we already are."

Later that day, I showed the necklace to Bryan.

"I knew we'd hoped living like this would give us a chance to connect with people on the way. I just never imagined how many would become such dear friends."

"I know," said Bryan, "I feel just the same. We've met so many amazing people." He caught my eyes and held my gaze. "Don't forget, though, you're the one who smiled and greeted everyone we passed. And you spoke Spanish even when you didn't really know how."

"It's a good thing I don't mind laughing at my mistakes," I said.

"Yeah, and you asked for help when we needed it and said, 'Yes,' when someone reached out. You looked for the similarities beyond our differences and found them every time. Everyone we've met has been so kind. But at least some of that is because of the kindness they see in you."

Chapter Twenty-seven

ABUNDANCE LEADING THE WAY

Isla Isabel, Mazatlán, San Jose del Cabo, and Cabo San Lucas, Mexico
March and April 2014: Waxing Gibbous, Full moon,
Waning Crescent, New Moon

A place to stay untouched by death
Does not exist.
It does not exist in space, it does not exist in the ocean,
Nor if you stay in the middle of a mountain.

—Buddha

Bryan pulled out a marker and drew a map of the coastline along the wall near the head. He marked potential ports of call about every 200 miles all along our 2,500 mile route home.

I stood behind him, imagining the joy of pulling into each of these harbors. "We'll see Chuy again in Cabo and Carlos in Bahía Tortugas, Helen and Glyn and the kids in San Diego, and maybe Ian on San Miguel again." I smiled at the thought of returning to favorite restaurants and how much easier provisioning would be since I knew the streets to the grocery stores. "And then Northern California and Oregon and home."

Meira drew a minuscule *LiLo* on a scrap of paper and we wrapped it in tape to keep it dry. Hannah pulled out some mounting putty to stick the boat to our location.

"That's a long way to go. We'd better get started."

A third stop at Isla Isabel would take us a bit out of our way but, as I told Bryan, "If this trip was about efficiency, we sure wouldn't be doing it in a sailboat." We'd seen the famous blue-footed booby birds during mating season and nesting season. Now, it was baby season and we wanted to go back once more.

After a few days in Yelapa and one last visit to Chacala Bay, we left for Isla Isabel before dawn and rode the morning offshore breezes then the afternoon onshore flow, arriving around sunset. David and Carolyn arrived on *Crazy Love* early the next day and we spent the evening together, cramming in as much time as possible before our routes diverged.

The day we left for Mazatlán, we finally went ashore to look for baby booby birds. We spotted several in the nests on the beaches and hiked inland for a few minutes, past a noisy colony of sooty terns. Meira pointed out baby frigates and Hannah hunted for lizards but my eyes were drawn to the evidence of death beneath and around the lively island.

Half-eaten fish sat rotting in the path. Lobster tails and crab claws cluttered the tide line. Fully-grown birds and ill-fated babies lay sprawled over stones, all the grace of life lost in the twisted pose of death.

We didn't stay long enough to see the complete process, to watch the carcasses provide food for other creatures or dissolve into the ground to fertilize the soil and I didn't come away with any new thoughts about the circle of life. Simply that the contrast was striking: new life hatching out all over, side-by-side with death.

In the afternoon, we rowed over to meet some other sailors who were getting ready to head out for Mazatlán, too. And then, with a last wave goodbye to *Crazy Love*, we pulled up the anchor and headed north.

So far our conditions for the return journey had been great. This day we motorsailed in light winds and calm seas. We laughed ourselves silly over the antics of a group of jumping rays and watched as they flipped and spun through the air, their wings rippling. We sat out in the warm evening as the sun set in the blue, blue sky.

When I woke up the next morning the blue was gone and we were motoring over perfectly calm seas through a thick fog bank.

"Beth, come up here. We've picked up a hitchhiker." When I came up on deck, Bryan pointed out the brown booby on the spreaders. A closer look revealed why it had stopped. Its right foot hung dangling, broken and useless. After a few minutes on the spreaders, it took off, only to land awkwardly again on our side deck. Bryan put on his heavy gloves and went forward to extricate it from the dock lines.

The bird settled in for a few more minutes of rest on the dinghy and we were just discussing how to get it help in Mazatlán when it flew off, trailing its broken leg behind. We'd seen other birds make do with just one good leg, so we knew it might find a way to cope. But the images from Isabel lingered and I chose to face the truths that color the harder side of nature's beauty. There are no beginnings without an end, no hellos without goodbyes. There is no way to live without encountering death.

We spent the first few days in Mazatlán stressed and irritated. Although we were back in the resort marina with several boating friends as dock neighbors, our focus was on getting ready for the long trip north. We planned to use a cell stick to connect to internet access for weather forecasts on the coast of Baja, but first we had to figure out how to get a computer running again. Marine life is tough on electronics and the keyboard on my ancient laptop had given out. Now Bryan's computer was failing, too, and needed a new hard drive.

We left the kids hanging out with friends and took the bus into downtown Mazatlán. We walked from shop to shop looking for a replacement hard drive but returned to the boat empty-handed. Bryan attempted to connect my laptop to a working keyboard but when he restarted the machine, its operating system came up in Spanish. He spent hours guessing his way through the boot menus, struggling to get it converted to English and load the programs we needed.

At one point, heading to the cockpit to clear his head, he picked his way carefully through the mess I'd made cleaning lockers and storing provisions.

Despite his frustration, I couldn't help but laugh as he grumbled, "This boat is such a wreck, you can't even storm out of here properly!"

We finally decided to give in and buy a new computer, but the closest option that would work for us was in Cabo San Lucas, over 200 nautical miles away. In addition to our computer troubles, we had discovered another fraud on our bank account.

Some of our travel guides had recommended that we take multiple credit cards and split up our resources across more than one checking account, since fraud was almost inevitable on a trip such as ours. So we still had access to most of our finances but we needed to let the bank know what was going on. Their fraud department was clearly not set up to deal with folks living mostly off the grid. I spent time in the resort's computer lab figuring out how to print, scan, and fax the documents required to lock our account until we could get back to the United States and resolve things in person.

All through the week we kept an eye on the weather, waiting for a good opportunity to cross back over to Baja.

One evening Bryan and I walked up to the resort entrance. A collection of paintings on easels lined the walkway and I stopped abruptly, stunned by the beautiful colors. Bryan had purchased a glass photo print at the art gallery in Crescent City and we'd picked up a few more small souvenirs along the way but I was still looking for a keepsake to decorate our home.

The artist stood nearby and we asked about prices and suggestions for transport. She couldn't help but notice which pieces had caught my eye, especially one with brightly colored discs hanging from a spacious tree.

"This one is for abundance," the artist said, and Bryan and I nodded at each other. That was just how it felt.

"See?" she continued. "These circles represent coins and the abundance of money."

As she stepped away to let us confer, I turned to Bryan and whispered. "I want to bring the abundance painting home. But I don't see it as money at all, even though that's what she intended."

He was quick to agree, "Right? It feels like the abundance of relationships. Like a family tree."

We purchased a couple of pieces for ourselves and one as a gift. While we waited the artist pulled the canvases from their stretcher bars, rolled them tight, and handed them over, giving us instructions on how to have them remounted to hang once at home. Bryan wrapped them in plastic and then tucked them into boxes and hung them with brackets from the ceiling at the foot of our bunk in the bow, abundance leading the way.

We left Mazatlán late in the afternoon on Monday. The wind was up a bit and we had to rev the motor to get across the small bar at the entrance. We motor sailed in the afternoon chop and then, as the evening calm arrived, took down the sail and motored through the night.

For many reasons, the kids hadn't taken scheduled watches on our southbound journey, just jumped in to help when needed. And until we replaced our autopilot in San Diego we needed to hand steer quite a bit, so our watches were much more tiring. But now, with more understanding of our natural rhythms, we were beginning to find a new routine.

Hannah, Meira, and I split up the morning and evening watches according to our energy and preferences. Hannah loved the sunset shift. Meira liked the starry evenings. I finagled my way into a moonrise watch whenever possible. Bryan came on for a few hours in the afternoons, when the wind was likely to be highest, and enjoyed the solitude and quiet of the long night watches from midnight to 8 a.m. We trusted this healthy pattern of work and rest would ease the long passages on the journey home.

We came into Bahía de Los Frailes, on the eastern side of the tip of Baja, a little after sunrise Wednesday morning. The next day, after a good night's sleep, we motored the few hours into San José del Cabo. We planned to spend one night, just long enough for Bryan to bus over to Cabo San Lucas to order a laptop so we could pick it up as soon as we got into town. We got gas at the fuel dock, called the harbormaster on the VHF for a slip assignment, pulled in, and walked the half mile around the marina to check in at the office. We wandered for a few minutes trying to find our way.

When we finally located the harbormaster I was so focused on our task I didn't notice the group of people we passed until I heard one of them call my name. My brain did a lightning-fast tally of the friends we'd met on our trip. Nope, none of them should be here now. I turned around wondering who could have recognized me.

"Bethany, I'm Toni, Jere's friend." The woman was just locking up a real estate agency next to the marina office. "I've been following your blog this whole year and I can't believe you're here!"

"I'm so glad you introduced yourself. I never would have imagined I might run into you." Our mutual friend Jere had connected Toni and me online and I had considered trying to meet her on our way down, though the dinghy rebuild and busy holiday season conspired against a rendezvous. Now serendipity was on our side.

Toni and her husband, Bruce, gave us a ride back to our boat, and when they heard about our needs, offered to drive Bryan into the computer store as well.

The crew and I hung out on *LiLo* for the afternoon while Bryan ran into Cabo. Meira took advantage of a burst of energy to wash some laundry and do dishes on the dock. While she was out there a fellow sailor from a neighboring boat stopped by and offered to take us to the grocery store. We made tentative arrangements for the next day and I felt great about the hope of getting so many things crossed off our before-Baja list.

Late in the afternoon Bryan came back with bad news. The computer distributor was out of English-keyboard laptops and there was no telling when they would get more in. We took a few minutes to regroup and talk over our options.

Pretty soon it became obvious that our first priority was dinner. We'd seen a little fish shack called The Drunken Sailor on the road near the marina so we walked up and splurged on some fish tacos and came back with renewed energy for our technical difficulties.

Bryan finally verified that a Linux operating system would run the internet from our cell stick. He moved the small hard drive from my old computer—the one with the broken keyboard—to his laptop—the one with the dead hard drive—and got Linux up and running. We couldn't get the touch pad to respond to the cobbled-together system but we had an external wireless mouse that we hoped would get us through until we reached San Diego and could purchase a new device. We installed important software—a word processor for my writing project, an offline blog editor, a few games for long passages—and bookmarked the low-bandwidth interfaces for my favorite weather forecast sites.

The next day, after our neighbor drove Hannah and me to town for provisions, Bryan and I walked over to the marina office to check out. The afternoon wind had picked up considerably and we thought it might make for a good sail once we left the harbor. So we backed out of our slip and headed to sea.

We cleared the breakwater and turned west, into a headwind. We didn't mind tacking for a while, but had just throttled down to raise the sails when we heard a strange sound. It came again, regularly, but not rhythmically. I was trying to identify the source—animal? mechanical?—when Meira poked her head up. "I hear a noise coming from the engine."

I took the helm while Bryan went below to have a look. He quickly identified the trouble, although I wasn't sure I understood his explanation that the accessory drive, a pulley that powers the alternator, had lost its *something-something* and that meant *something-something-something, but we're okay for now.*

I tend to have selective hearing in a crisis and Bryan knows I only want to be told: one—if he knows what the problem is; two—if he thinks he can fix it; and three—if we're all going to die in the meantime. Reassured with "Yes," "Yes," and "That's ridiculous," I stayed at the helm while Bryan raised our jib to head back into port.

The wind, which had been on our nose, was now perfect for a reach back through the breakwater and, though we probably could have safely used our engine for the last few seconds, we didn't need it. The slip we'd been at the night before was empty and perfectly situated for docking under sail.

"The wind is up. We'll be coming in hot," I warned the crew, and the three of us prepped the docklines and fenders while Bryan trimmed and released the jib sheet to keep our speed under control. At the last second he turned us a little upwind and backfilled the sail to spill off more speed and blow us close to the dock. Meira ducked the sail as it crossed the bow and then stepped gracefully down. I followed a second later and fumbled the midline around the end cleat.

"Gently, gently," Bryan called, "we've got lots of room to slow her down." Hannah stepped down when the stern swung in and we eased the boat to a quiet stop.

Bryan and the kids all looked to me, usually the most nervous of the crew. When they saw my wide grin, their faces responded in kind. The wind and slip configuration had been so perfect, the crew so reliable, I hadn't even gotten jittery. We walked the long path over to the marina office again and then, always happy for any excuse to celebrate, took the crew out for gelato.

Later that evening Bryan dangled over the engine compartment, muttering. He had spares for just about every system on the boat—an extra fuel pump, a water pump, gaskets, wires, fuses, even a spare engine head.

He stepped through the cabin to his spare-parts locker and started digging.

"I remember looking at that part before we left and thinking, 'It's just a pulley. That's so straightforward, how could anything go wrong with that?'"

"So that's the one spare you don't have on board?"

"Yeah, but the pulley itself is okay. I really just need a new bolt." He held out his hand with a small collection of bolts in various sizes. "Something here will probably work."

He tested several before finding the right fit and then cleaned it up and reinstalled the drive with a little lock-tite adhesive.

The next morning we got up early and headed back out through the breakwater. This time the wind was easier and the engine ran perfectly. We came into the Cabo San Lucas marina in the mid-afternoon. Pangas, pelicans, and sea lions vied for our attention in the busy entrance.

We'd emailed ahead to let our friends know we were coming, but I was still pleased to see a familiar dock hand on the float as we pulled in. We tied up and greeted each other. "¡Marcilio!" He seemed surprised to be remembered but responded, "¡Betania!" If he was surprised, I was shocked. I didn't expect to be remembered by name; hundreds of boaters come through each month, but I suppose not very many build boats in the parking lot.

When we walked up to the office to check in, the staff was so glad to see us they almost forgot to charge us for our stay. We chatted happily with everyone and asked them to pass along our greetings to Chuy, who was away for a few days. We told stories of our recent adventures and assured them all that *Rover* was doing well. "No leaks!" Even behind-the-scenes personnel we barely remembered came around the counter for hugs.

We reconnected to the internet and pulled in emails and forecasts and some heartbreaking news from the close-knit sailing community. Our friends from *Rebel Heart*, Charlotte and Eric and their two daughters, had experienced a medical crisis at sea. They called a physician on their satellite phone, but as they were getting the information they needed the call cut out. Later they learned their phone provider had abruptly phased out their generation's SIM card without sufficient notification, leaving them with no choice but to set off their EPIRB, the remote locating beacon that would notify authorities and summon assistance. By the time we heard what was happening four medics had parachuted in to assist and stabilize their youngest child, Lyra.

A rescue at sea almost always means losing one's boat, and for Charlotte and Eric and their kids, that also meant losing their home and their plans for the future. The women's sailing forum Charlotte had founded rallied to round up housing, household goods, and finances to support them on their return, and sent messages of encouragement to counteract the negative press and social media commentary.

As we finalized our preparations for the trip up the rural Baja coastline, commonly known as The Baja Bash, we kept an eye on the updates. I was grateful to hear they'd been safely transferred to a Navy frigate, but we grieved at the news they'd needed to scuttle their ship to keep it from being a navigation hazard to others on the same route across the Pacific.

I gathered my courage for our remote journey ahead, trusting that if we needed it, help would be there for us, too.

Chapter Twenty-eight

BEFORE THE SEA CHANGED HER MOOD

Cabo San Lucas, Bahía San Juanico, and Bahía Tortugas, Mexico
April 2014: First Quarter, Waxing gibbous

*water always gets its way
or knows the way
or makes it*
—Juniper Klatt

"What are the chances we can get gas in San Juanico?" At Bryan's question I poked my head up through the companionway and glanced around at the mirror-calm seas. We'd stayed in Cabo San Lucas only until the forecast turned fair and were steadily making progress up the Baja coast.

"It sure seems a shame to waste this perfect weather and spend an extra day to run up to the port in Bahía Magdalena."

"Right? What's the worst that can happen? If they don't have fuel, we could just wait for wind and sail back down. Best case, we grab some gas in San Juanico and head right on north to Bahía Tortugas."

"I haven't seen a forecast since Cabo but the horizon still looks clear and the barometer is steady." I looked up Bahía San Juanico in our cruising guide. "It doesn't say anything about fuel, just that it's a popular surfing spot. I'm not sure we'll be able to get through the breakers to the shore but if we can, there's probably at least a little gas somewhere, right?"

"I'm willing to take that chance. Crew? What do you think?"

Hannah and Meira had been listening in from down below and they chimed in to endorse the plan.

"We always figure it out, right?" Hannah said, "We'll figure this out, too."

In the night Bryan edged closer to land as we passed Bahía Santa Maria and picked up a cell signal strong enough to download the current weather forecast onto my jury-rigged computer—calms through Friday evening.

I woke to another clear day, no boats in sight and land only a distant outline, the glassy swell untouched by even a hint of wind. I did the dishes, taking advantage of the chance to let them dry on the stable counter before the sea changed her mood. I hard-boiled some eggs, chopped the last of a head of romaine, and sliced tomatoes, avocados, and a cucumber for a salad. I improvised a creamy dressing, grated the last of the pepper jack cheese, and pulled out sliced almonds for some crunch. We set up the table and gathered around, grateful for one more easy day heading north.

In the afternoon Bryan hung the solar shower for me and I washed in the cockpit, shivering a little until the sun dried my hair and warmed my skin.

I couldn't tell if it was the ease of a healthy family meal or the joy of being clean at sea, but I was finally feeling at home aboard. All the sailing books I'd read told of the joys of long passages where, once away from the concerns of land, sailors settled into easy rhythms of watches and maintenance, a little cooking, a little rest. The bone-jarring seas of the North Pacific offered no space to feel at home. I was beginning to realize why most of the sailing stories I read had been set in the tropics. Hardly anyone sailing the North Pacific has time to write.

A few years after Bryan and I got married, on one of his parents' visits to Alaska, his mother admitted to me, smiling, "I must say, when you and Bryan got engaged, I breathed a sigh of relief. I thought, 'Eric and Tamarah are settled in Seattle and you never know what Nathan is going to do but at least now that Bryan is married to Bethany, *one* of my boys will stick around. She'd never leave home.'"

I laughed. "I'm as surprised as you are. I never thought I'd leave home either."

Now here, in the middle of an adventure my younger self would never have imagined, her words came back to me. *She'd never leave home.*

What does it mean to leave home? We took our beds with us, had a kitchen, and a place to pee, so had we really left? If all the things they say about home are true—home is where the heart is; home is where you hang your hat; home is the place where, when you have to go there, they have to take you in—we had been home all along. But it sure hadn't felt like home in the middle of the storms. The holidays had only served to heighten how far away from home we were. I couldn't even feel at home in my own body most days. What made today feel like home? And now that I'd recaptured the feeling, could I keep it? Could I manufacture it again? If not, could I keep on living without it?

I was raised under the walnut trees. We dug in the dirt by the cucumbers for night crawlers and pill bugs and buried our pets beneath the blossoming cherry, the arms of the maple an ever present refuge.

Out on the waves my affinities get jumbled. Am I still of the earth? A flag in the soil set adrift in foreign matter?

Or perhaps my lungs feel more at home here with the sponges, each lobe more water than air. The moon calls through my skin with every tide, breath yearning toward the sea since my first gasp. I have never stopped grieving my lost mermaid days.

If I am lucky, I may have a hundred years to make the earth my home. Compared to that, what is one brief turning out here on the water?

"It's been sunny for days," I said. "Do we have enough battery power to watch a movie?"

Hannah scurried to take down the table and prop the laptop across the sink while Bryan checked our course and the set of the autopilot.

"There's no one out here and we're headed straight to San Juanico. If there's room for me on the settee and you don't mind pausing the movie for horizon checks, maybe I'll join you."

"Plenty of room!" Hannah said, scooting over onto her bed to make space.

"Whenever you want, we can take an intermission and I'll make popcorn," I said.

We decided on *Spiderman* and watched it in ten-minute increments, taking turns stepping into the cockpit to look around. After the movie, Bryan stretched out on the settee and got a few minutes of sleep while Meira took her evening watch.

I woke about 12:30 a.m. in sudden silence. Hannah and Meira were both in bed, the cabin and cockpit were empty, and Bryan had just shut down the engine and was stepping forward to set the anchor. He'd eased his way into the outer edge of the shallow bay and, as I watched in the light of the high half-moon, he settled us snug for the night.

In the morning, I woke Bryan with a cup of coffee and the crew got ready to go to shore while I made breakfast burritos. We'd all eaten and were just debating if we should tackle the long row or pull up and re-anchor a little closer when a trio of fishermen drove up in a panga. We exchanged greetings and I asked if there was gasoline in town.

"Yes! Would you like a ride in?"

"Oh, yes! Just a moment, please," I called over. We jammed on our shoes and grabbed the backpack, our cash, a water bottle, and a dry bag with a couple of internet-ready devices in case we found a place to check the weather. Bryan tossed four empty jerry jugs across the water to the waiting fisherman, who tucked them down among the lobster traps and tools. The panga pulled alongside, we stepped across and were off.

On the way in, the spokesman opened the introductions, pointing to his crew in turn.

"That's Marco, he's Luis, and I'm Nacho." They proudly opened a locker to show us the day's catch—four white sea bass.

As we neared the shore the waves loomed enormous.

I leaned over and whispered to Bryan, "No wonder this place is known for surfing. There's no way we could have rowed in through this."

In fact, I couldn't see how we were going to get through the breakers, even in the panga. At the last moment, Nacho whipped the boat around and stalled stern to the beach.

"You wait here," he instructed, and followed his crew as they hopped over the side and waded into shore. We watched, fascinated as they rolled a set of wheels down into the surf and floated the boat into the cradle connected to the wheels. Luis held the boat while Nacho backed his truck down toward the water and the crew expertly tied the boat to the truck bed. The surf threw us into the sand and floated us off again several times before the truck finally hauled us free of the sea.

Once safely ashore we hopped down from the panga, but before we could begin to ask directions to the gas station, Nacho ushered us into his beat up pickup. "Welcome to my fish car," he said.

We found places for the fuel jugs among the crates in the back and climbed into the cab. The crew and I kept our hair clear of the sharp fishing lures hanging from the headliner. The fish car had obviously been well-used. We were all grateful for the ventilation offered by the missing rear window. Of course after several days at sea, it's quite likely we added our own aroma to the mix.

Nacho drove us up the slender road from the beach to town. He'd lived here all his life and talked about how much the town had changed with the influx of surfers from America. "Everything is so much more expensive!" But he seemed quite content with his life. "It's good to live in a town where you know everyone."

We pulled up to an open structure on the side of the road and Nacho asked one of the men there if he had any gasoline. I didn't understand the whole conversation but it was obvious they were out.

"It's cheaper there if they have any," Nacho said as we drove on, "but the gasolinera almost always has gas." We pulled up to a more official-looking station. A series of faded red jugs sat on a raised loading dock, hoses dangling from each nozzle. The sign below read "Gasolinera y Lubricantes."

"¿Gasolina? ¿No diesel?"

"Sí, gasolina, por favor."

The attendant set our jugs up in a row and deftly siphoned twenty gallons into our tanks. The smell of corn from the tortilleria down the road overpowered the odor from the dripping hoses.

Bryan pointed to the tienda next door and spoke to Nacho, "Can I buy sodas for you and the crew?"

"For the crew, sure. I don't need anything."

We took a different route through town on our way back and Nacho stopped in the road to chat with a friend on the way. I spotted what looked like an open ambulance with an examining room in the back. Nacho caught my glance and confirmed, "That's the town clinic."

On the drive, I asked Nacho if he'd seen a recent weather report and he nodded. "The wind looks calm through Saturday," he said. "I have satellite internet and check all the sites every day—twice a day. I have to know what it's like out there. The next week should be the best week of the year," he claimed. "Not like February and March. Too much wind!"

Back on the beach, the men loaded the fuel into the panga. The crew had stayed busy; fish entrails surrounded the boat and we tried to avoid tracking any on our shoes as we climbed up on the tire and over the gunwales.

Bryan joined the fishermen in shoving us back down the gentle slope into the water. The boat bucked in the surf as they pulled the wheels up above the high-tide line and hopped aboard.

We'd anchored half a mile or more off shore, but the panga's powerful engine made quick work of the distance. I stepped back aboard and grabbed our camera to get a couple of pictures of the fishermen, although I didn't need photos to remember their kindness.

I glanced down at the clock. We'd only been gone about thirty minutes. We'd hoped that skipping Bahía Magdalena would work out well, that there would be fuel in Bahía San Juanico, and that we wouldn't end up regretting our decision, but we never expected to get in, get gas, and get out so easily. We quickly added fuel to our main tank and, just a few minutes later, Meira hauled up the anchor, started the engine, and got us on our way again.

The first few hours back out at sea were fueled by leftover adrenaline from our run to town. We put on some music and had a dance party on our microscopic dance floor—watch your elbows!

But as evening came on, reality set in. If our forecast was correct, and the weather began to worsen Friday evening, we could pop into Bahía Asuncion to wait for a chance to day-hop north to Bahía Tortugas. But if, as Nacho had indicated, the weather held another day, we could make it all the way into Bahía Tortugas by dawn on Saturday, more than halfway done with our trip up the coast of Baja in only five easy days. Either way, we still had at least thirty-six hours of motoring ahead. We sent Bryan to bed to get some rest before his night shift.

Toward the end of Meira's watch, in the span of about five minutes, a thick fog bank blew in and surrounded us in opaque mist.

"Mom?" she called. "You might want to come take a look."

Squinting into the void, I listened for engine noises and breathed away the panic. The fog thickened and lightened a bit over the next few hours. I checked the barometer repeatedly and wondered if we were racing an oncoming weather system. Bird sounds flew out of the fog long seconds before the birds appeared, close on our beam. I took comfort in our remote location. No major shipping vessels around, no large fishing boats, and any small panga still out in these conditions should be alert and agile enough to zip out of our way.

By the time Bryan got up for his watch we'd broken free of the fog. I was glad to leave the thick, gray clouds behind. Another night. Another day. Another night. A rising headwind. Bryan put up a sail and pushed ahead.

I woke about dawn and squinted through the cabin to where Meira's feet stuck out across the cockpit. She'd risen early to give Bryan a little rest before our arrival and sat outside, bundled against the morning chill. I got up and helped with the navigation particulars, making sure our course was set to avoid the rocks standing sentinel across the southern portion of the entrance to Bahía Tortugas. Meira moved to the cabin top and perched on the boom with the binoculars.

The pelicans were out en masse, performing their peculiar dives with their last-second reverse. Several dolphins arched nearby. As we passed the point and entered the bay Meira caught the first sight of town.

"I can see Carlos's house. We're back!"

Chapter Twenty-nine

The World is Round

Bahía Tortugas, Mexico
April 2014: Full Moon, Waning Gibbous, Third Quarter

*A tourist remains an outsider throughout his visit;
but a sailor is part of the local scene from the moment he arrives.*
—Anne Davison

"I knew it was you the moment you sailed into the bay!" As if we'd only been away a few days instead of five months, Carlos ushered us into seats, poured coffee, and passed the sugar bowl. "I thought, 'Is that *LiLo?*' and I got out my binoculars and looked. Yes, it is you!" He pantomimed a lookout position and held an imaginary spyglass up to his eye. "I knew you'd come back!" he said. "But what happened to the little boat?"

We jumped in with explanations of *Splitpea's* disappearance and our work to rebuild. Carlos clucked in sympathy and then interrupted himself to say, "But you're here now. And your Spanish is *so* much better!"

In the months since we'd seen him much had changed for us. Our losses had shaped us, yes, but our gains as well. It was a gift to be able to relive the stories with a listening friend and see our progress through his eyes.

"And you came at the perfect time," he said, taking our mugs to the sink. "It's Holy Week, when everyone has the week off. My oldest is still working on the island, but everyone else is going to the fish camp. You should come! Please come!"

"The fish camp, huh?" Bryan's Spanish had improved as well, but it was still hard for him to follow a quick exchange. I filled him in on the way back to the boat.

"Yeah, I'm getting the sense it's a little like a hunting camp. The men live out there during fishing season and any women with small children go along. School-age kids stay here with their moms and go out on the weekends. It's not fishing season, but it sounds like the families use the location as a holiday home too, going up when they can just for the fun of it. I don't really know what we're in for, but it sounds great no matter what!"

"What day are we going?" Bryan asked.

"I didn't catch that part, actually. We'll come in to church for Palm Sunday tomorrow and I'm betting we'll figure it out."

We met Carlos outside the church a few minutes before the service. A few other congregants were milling about outside and we stood off to the side watching the gathering processional—a collection of frond-waving children and an honest-to-goodness donkey carrying a small-girl Jesus, a brown-makeup beard lavishly applied to the lower half of her face. I took the opportunity to check on *LiLo*'s position from the plaza near the doors and raised my eyes to the horizon beyond, white clouds drifting along in the blue sky above.

The church bells rang the hour and continued to peal. We shifted in and found our seats, then turned to watch the children dance up the aisle to the altar rail. From the back, a man led the donkey forward as the children sang, "Hosanna." Over our heads curving beams mimicked a boatbuilder's aesthetic. Stained glass windows along each side wall held shades of blue and green, each mosaic a depiction of the seaside life of Jesus. Jesus calling fishermen to follow, Jesus blessing the fish on the seashore, Jesus walking on the water, Jesus stilling the storm.

The skillful artwork held my attention as the service moved on. No childhood Sunday school teacher had ever brought the stories to life this way. I grew up hearing of the desert wanderers, of Jesus's nomadic life with his ragtag followers—blue-collar workers, thieves, outcasts, and women. First in my memory, though, were the fishermen, who gave up a life on the sea for one around it, who knew enough to be afraid when the storm rose, to be astounded at he who walked the waves. Now I sat surrounded by a community who understood far better than I how to live aligned with the deep.

On the walk back to the beach we clarified our plans.

"Come to my house on Tuesday morning," Carlos said, "and we'll walk over to my daughter Lucia's house together."

We piled into *Rover* and Carlos shoved us off into the bay. "¡Adios!"

Tuesday morning, we packed water and a coffee cake I'd made to share and rowed back in as requested. Carlos passed out cookies and coffee and made cup noodles for the crew, saying, "You need more breakfast!"

Once the spoons and mugs were washed and back in the drying rack, we followed him across town. We cut over dusty slopes and down back alleys. Everyone we met stopped to greet him and meet us. I wondered if we were delaying the day's plans, but when we arrived at the house preparations were still in full swing.

We stood for a few minutes in the driveway, watching the men loading the truck. I didn't have to understand every word to recognize the good-natured bickering. They fussed together to get the coolers and propane wedged into the bed with room for us to ride between.

"Do you have the food ready yet?" one hollered into the kitchen and Lucia hollered back.

"Just hang on! You'll be glad at lunchtime that we didn't rush!"

Young cousins and their teenage counterparts exchanged smiles with our kids. As Lucia and her sister carried out the last of the food, Carlos pointed out seating for each of us.

Hannah's face lit up with excitement. "Is it really okay to ride in the back of the truck, Dad?"

"Well, normally I'd say no but this isn't exactly a normal day. I think it should be fine. Just stay low and don't poke your arms out, okay?"

I climbed into the cab with Carlos's son-in-law, the usually quiet Ruben, who immediately shifted into tour-guide mode. As we barreled north on the dusty highway he pointed out landmarks and vegetation with casual pride and gave me the history of the town's waterlines. Until very recently, acquiring fresh water had required a trip to the arroyos above the village and careful timing with the weather.

Soon we approached the fish camp. The bay here on the north side of the point was almost a mirror image of the southern harbor, but more exposed to the prevailing winds and currents. A small collection of concrete shelters dotted the western edge of the land. Rock-lined stoops, colorful paint, and whale bone fences served to distinguish one from another.

On the ground near new construction sat an oddly shaped structure with one pointed end. Ruben caught my quizzical look.

"That's the bell steeple. We're building a church for the fish camp."

We pulled up to the cabin closest to the sea. "Carlos has been here almost as long as anyone. This is our family's plot."

Cousins piled out everywhere and scattered as parents unloaded the trucks. I stepped inside the cabin and glanced around. A central wall divided the space in two. Through the door I spotted several bunk beds, stripped bare for the off season. The living space sported a central island countertop and a few chairs around the edges of the room.

The women went right to work skinning the chicken they'd packed for lunch. Out of the main window I could see Carlos and Ruben setting up the propane fryer.

"We talked about making octopus for you," said Lucia, her hands moving in sync with her sister's in a well-practiced dance, "but decided on chicken, Kentucky-style."

I nodded my approval. "Anything sounds good to us, thank you!"

The women turned from counter to sink, passing food between them without speaking, as if a single mind shared both bodies. One of the uncles popped in, tickled one of the children, teased his wife, and grinned mischievously in my direction. The women stubbornly ignored his kidding and passed him a bowl of chicken skin to take out to the patio. Carlos and Ruben tested the oil with one small piece and then slid the rest into the sizzling pan.

Bryan helped set up a couple of folding tables and everyone carried dishes and drinks out for the feast. Following our hosts' example we wrapped our "Kentucky-style" chicken in fresh tortillas with beans and salsa, first the fried chicken skin, crispy and searing hot, and then the meat, picked from the bone. We stood around the table and licked our fingers clean.

After lunch, the oldest granddaughter, the younger Lucia, invited Hannah and Meira to go for a walk up the beach. Omar grabbed some fishing gear and took up position on the boat ramp. Ruben Jr. took a panga out past the surf.

Bryan, Carlos, and I headed down to the rocky shoreline, past the white whale skull on the end of the point. We stepped carefully; rocks round as grapefruits covered the sand. Slate gray and white nestled near emerald, sapphire, and ruby stones, glistening where the water touched them. We headed west to the end of the point and then turned south.

Carlos and I stopped and sat in the shadow of an osprey nest. Instead of reeds and grasses, fishing nets and bits of line formed its warp and weft. Bryan picked his way on down the beach, choosing a few of the more colorful stones to bring back to the boat.

I sat with Carlos and listened as he wove together a fuller picture of his life, sharing stories of romance and heartache and reminiscing about his lost love.

At the sound of an engine, we looked up in unison. Omar stood on the bluff above.

"Hey, we heard a whale washed up near here a few days ago. Want to go see if we can find it?"

We did, so we grabbed Bryan and hopped into the truck. We drove along the bluff for a few minutes, staring out to the west for a glimpse of the carcass. Omar stopped on a little point and we got out and walked to the edge and looked over.

Finally Omar turned around. "It must have washed back out to sea. It's probably time to head back anyway."

Hannah and Meira met us at the door with pen and paper in hand.

"They want the recipe for the coffee cake you brought," Meira said, "but the dictionary doesn't have the word for baking powder."

"Yes, and also," added Hannah, "you didn't tell us you were leaving! Where did you go? We've had to look up all the things we didn't know and just nod and smile a lot."

"Sorry about that. We just went for a walk down the beach and ended up on a hunt for a beached whale. I guess we were gone a while."

We'd missed so many family gatherings on our journey but here I'd slipped right back into our big-family mentality. The men around the fryer, the women in the kitchen, the cousins underfoot, even the mischievous brother-in-law—despite the language barrier and the differences in climate and landscape, I looked around and recognized the feeling in my chest. This was home.

By Saturday, it was hard to believe we'd ever been strangers. We'd spent the week with Carlos and his family—eating together, watching baseball, talking by the water's edge, eating again. I didn't want to think about leaving and the months of hard travel ahead, but the taste of home reminded me how much we missed our own community. The pull of the sea hadn't broken the lines that bound us to our family and friends; we felt drawn back as if to the center of our gravity. Along the way, though, we'd picked up new lines of connection, no less powerful for how briefly we held them. The life I was living tugged against the life I'd left. It seemed impossible to integrate the two. And the weather was about to turn.

I looked up from the computer where I'd loaded a low-bandwidth weather forecast.

"It looks like our best bet might be tomorrow night."

"Tomorrow? Already?"

"Well, we've been here a week and I don't think we're likely to see a serious calm streak for a long while." I turned the computer for Bryan to see and flipped through the charts. "I think this little break might get us most of the way back to Ensenada, but we'll have to leave as soon as the wind dies down tomorrow night."

We rowed in the next morning, Easter Sunday, and walked to church together again. On our way back to Carlos's house after the service, we stopped to buy a grilled chicken from the yellow house on the corner. We took it to go and spread out our feast on his kitchen table. Tortillas, rice, chicken, salsa. As we dug in, I broke the news.

"We have to leave tonight, Carlos."

"So soon?"

"I know. We'd love to stay, but the weather is getting better out there and we need to get north while we can."

"The weather—always the weather for the fishermen and the sailors. You must come to Ruben's house tonight for one last goodbye."

We spent the afternoon on engine maintenance and other preparations for travel. I knew it was likely to be a rough ride, so I stowed loose paraphernalia extra carefully and Bryan checked the lines on deck. By evening, we felt physically prepared, if emotionally reluctant. We piled into the dinghy and rowed in one last time. Just as we hit the beach, Hannah's face fell.

"I forgot the dishcloth I made for Lucia. I meant to give it to her tonight."

Throughout the trip, Hannah had spent long hours knitting hostess gifts for the many generous friends we met on the way. She'd chosen a pattern and cheerful coral yarn specifically for these friends and had spent every spare moment all week working on it.

Bryan didn't even hesitate. "You hop out and push me off. I'll row back to get it and just meet you at the other house."

By the time we reached Carlos's door, Bryan's swift strokes had taken him halfway back to *LiLo*. We headed across town in the evening sun.

"Carlos!"

I stopped in the road and looked around to spot the speaker. A smiling face appeared in the doorway of a busy shop. Shelves of paint cans and bottles lined the walls and dented tanks and auto parts lay scattered around the courtyard. We stopped, said hello, and Carlos introduced his friend and proudly pointed out his handiwork.

"He makes boats from oil jugs and bathroom tiles."

"Yes," the man agreed, "to sell to the sailors who come to our bay. But for you, friends of Carlos, I will give a boat as a memento. Stop by on your way back from dinner and I will give it to you."

We hurried away, but still Bryan had beat us. As we turned onto the dusty road in front of the house, Carlos pointed down, "He is already there. See, here are his footprints." Sure enough, Bryan's wide sandals had marked his way through the sandy dirt. We stepped into the house and walked through the kitchen to the table where Ruben, Omar, and Bryan sat together drinking coffee.

"Where were you?" Bryan said. "I thought for sure you'd be here first."

I explained about our unexpected stop and he nodded. "I should have known you'd have stopped to make a friend. Maybe now that you're here, you can explain to them what happened. I tried to tell them why I was here without you, but my Spanish hasn't improved that much." He pointed to his mug and the treats in the middle of the table. "Lucia didn't care, though. She just sat me down and served me coffee."

We spent our last evening together talking weather and ocean safety. Everyone there understood our need to take advantage of the calm between the gales.

"Of course you must go now, while it's not too rough out there. Watch out off Punta Eugenia. It can get really bad after you're past the tip of Isla Natividad." Ruben got out a chart and pointed out a few potential harbors along the way. "If you really need to tuck in out of a blow, you can stop here or here." He pointed and glanced up to make sure I was following. "It doesn't look like much, but this little spit protects the cove pretty well and you'll be safe enough."

We soaked up all the advice we could get and all the presence too. I absorbed everything I noticed—the particular smile from Ruben, Carlos's low, easy laugh, Lucia's beautiful hands.

Finally we had to leave. Everyone stood and walked us out the door. We gave hugs all around and walked away. Our family felt smaller already and we hadn't even said goodbye to Carlos yet.

He broke the silence. "Don't forget—we have to stop for the little boat!"

Bryan slowed his pace, holding my hand to slow mine too, and whispered. "What's going on? We really need to get going. Where are we stopping?"

"Remember I said we met a friend of Carlos on the way over? Well, he wants us to come back to give us a model boat and, I don't know, a send off, maybe?"

"Okay, but let's try not to stay too long."

Carlos led us back to the shop where the craftsman pressed gifts on us. "I make these to sell to the sailors who come through town," he explained again. "See here, I paint—*tu recuerdo*—to remember. But for you, here are two for a gift. Please, take them to remember your time here."

Hannah and I tucked the little ships into our arms as our host walked us across the yard and into the kitchen, where a couple of women and small children sat.

"Meet our new friends from *LiLo!*" he announced and just like that, we were in. The kids and I found seats at the table and listened in on the conversation about the recent shopping trip to Ensenada.

"You help us decide," said one woman, holding up two pairs of flip flops. "Which do you like best?"

"They're for you! You should choose," I said, and Meira agreed.

"You'll be the one who wears them," she said.

Hannah pointed to the brighter of the two, with flowers on the straps. "I like those, I think. They're both nice, though."

The women shuffled the shoes around on the table. "Here, you take them then!"

Hannah backed away, hands waving. "No, no! I didn't mean for you to give them to me!"

The women grinned with pleasure. "But we want you to have them anyway. Here, put them on. See? They fit you perfectly!"

Hannah looked my way with concern, but I shook my head, smiling. "I don't think you're getting away without them. You might as well just say thank you."

Over by the sink, Bryan was trying to resist another onslaught of hospitality.

"Here, let me pour you a glass. It's sweet—not very strong."

"I'm good, thanks," Bryan said.

"Oh, you just need a little bit. Really, it's not very strong, not very strong."

Finally he gave in. "Okay, just a bit." He took a sip and laughed out loud. I glanced up to see him mouthing at me. "Not very strong? This is *port!*"

We sat for a little longer, ate the desserts brought out from the fridge, and said thank you more times than we could count. Finally, we pulled ourselves away.

"We have to sail on tonight, friends. We really must go. Many thanks. Many, many thanks!"

We walked back to Carlos's house in silence. We took turns receiving his benediction—handshake, hug, handshake. This was the hardest goodbye.

I held him close and then pulled away for one last look at his gentle face. I wanted to believe what the sailors say, "The world is round. We'll meet again."

He watched us load up and gave us a shove into the surf, waving as we rowed off. "¡Adios! ¡Adios!"

Chapter Thirty

ALL THE WATER IN THE SKY

Bahía San Quintín to Ensenada, Mexico
April 2014: Waning Crescent

*Waves are not measure in feet or inches,
they are measured in increments of fear.*
—*Buzzy Trent*

We pulled into Bahía San Quintín during a lull in the weather and I could almost see the restlessness filling up the boat, lapping at our ankles above the floorboards, threatening to rise. A storm was brewing and we didn't want to waste the calm. But without a fair wind, we didn't have enough fuel for the last thirty hours north to Ensenada.

The guide books said sailors could sometimes flag down fishermen for a ride up the estuary to town for fuel, but the fishing season was over and the few small boats around were oblivious to our calls. Every time we spotted a panga, Bryan blew the air horn while I waved a bright purple towel but they held to the western edge of the bay and headed on out to sea.

We'd also heard rumors that visiting sailors could get emergency help from the hotel to the east, the only structure visible on the wide, low shores of the bay so we hauled up our anchor and headed across.

I was skittish about the rising surf and nervous about leaving the kids aboard alone but we didn't have much of a choice. Bryan couldn't ask for help without my language skills. I couldn't carry the fuel without his strength. We tied everything into the dinghy—backpacks with money and water, shoes, gas cans, sunglasses, oars—and headed into shore.

The landing went pretty well—hardly any water in the boat. We dragged *Rover* high above the tideline and turned our back on the waves. We tucked our life jackets next to the seats and walked our gear to the backside of the hotel where, now out of the sea breeze, I stepped into a secluded stairway to strip off my long underwear. We stashed our gas cans by a bush in the parking lot and hoped we looked non-threatening as we walked our scruffy selves up to the check-in desk. I launched into my prepared speech.

"Necessitamos ayuda." *We need help.*

Right away the clerk started nodding along. Bryan stood listening, waiting for my translation: the dinner chef doesn't have anything else to do right now; he can probably take us into town. Within a few minutes we were in the back of his truck. My hair blew into my face as we passed greenhouse after greenhouse, the industry of agriculture in the middle of a desert.

We bought our gas, grabbed some cold drinks for the crew and our driver, and paid the bill. On the trip back I rode in the front and made halting conversation with the chef about his life on land, so very different from ours at sea.

Back at the hotel we thanked the driver and started leapfrogging the gas cans down to the shoreline. Bryan carried two at a time for a few yards, then came back for one to give his arms a break. He walked, sometimes straight, sometimes cockeyed, counterbalancing the weight of the fuel. I followed behind with our packs and drinks.

At the dinghy, we loaded everything in and shoved it all down to the water's edge. We retied all the cargo, packs and gas and shoes, threading a thin black line through the gunwales and through the straps of our sandals.

I stood and spotted *LiLo* through the breakers. All appeared to be well aboard. I set my fears firmly aside. *Rover* was heavier now, and this was the tough way, back through the waves. I took a deep breath. No point in panic.

I got in first, settling into the bow while Bryan shoved us off in the shallows. He rowed hard and fast, glancing over his shoulder to time the strokes with the swell. I stared at the safety of shore. I didn't want to tip the balance of the boat by craning my head around for a look. It wouldn't help anyway to know what was coming. Bryan was working hard; he'd started to really dig in with each pull and I knew we were headed through the biggest breakers. Motion caught my eye and I couldn't keep from looking up. Far above my head an impossibly high wave had just begun to break.

I didn't even have time for fear. Or maybe somehow I knew we'd be okay. So many things can go dreadfully wrong in a moment like this but miraculously none of them did. All the water in the sky came raining down but when we bobbed back up through the wave, everything we'd tied to the gunwales floated just within reach. We plopped the heavy jugs and sopping backpacks back into *Rover* and hopped out into knee-deep surf.

We tugged the overflowing dinghy back onto the sand and then realized our mistake. If we'd left *Rover* floating, we could have tipped her back and forth to slosh the water out but we weren't strong enough to turn her over here on land and the wood creaked in protest when we tried. I grabbed a sandal and started scooping. On each pass more water poured back into the boat than I could fling out. Bryan joined in with his hands, but our progress was imperceptible.

I stood up to push my hair back and saw a trio of fishermen backing their trailered panga down the beach. One in a wetsuit wrestled it off the trailer and stood in the surf, holding it close like a leashed puppy. Another drove the truck back up the beach to the parking lot. The third came loping our way.

"¿Necessitan ayuda?"

"Yes, please! We need help!"

He gestured to accentuate his rapid-fire Spanish.

"You," he pointed to me, "come with us. We will take the fuel and the bags and then he," a jab toward Bryan, "will be able to row himself."

A tiny bailing bucket appeared in his hands and he used it to scoop the water level down then dropped it in the sand and motioned for Bryan and me to help him tip out what remained in the dinghy.

While we bailed the driver had transferred the fuel cans and our bags to the panga and both fishermen were waiting now in the surf. Our helper set down his end of the dinghy and turned to sprint down the beach. I hurried to keep up and followed his friends into the boat, squelching my way to a seat.

With a graceful leap, he shoved the panga into deeper water, launching it and himself in one swift move. He landed next to me on the bench and we roared out to *LiLo*. Bryan stood down the beach, bewildered. He hadn't understood a word but caught on to the plan quickly and started pushing *Rover* back into the water.

Hannah and Meira had been waiting down below, but when they heard the motor revving close by, they came out into the cockpit to check it out. The fishermen tossed the fuel, the bags, and me over the combing and took off before I could say more than, "¡Gracias!"

I stood over the cockpit drain and watched as Bryan took another run at the surf, rowing backward with his head over his shoulder to gauge the waves. Without all the extra weight in the dinghy, he made it through easily. I stripped down to my underwear and was just toweling off when he pulled alongside.

"Well, that was exciting!" I said.

"Yes! You were talking to the guy and I didn't know what was happening and then all of a sudden you were leaving with three strange men in another boat. I figured everything would be okay, but still—I'm glad that worked out!"

"Me, too."

Still dripping, Bryan called a quick consultation.

"Here's the deal. If we leave right now, we should be able to pull into Ensenada before the weather turns impossible. It shouldn't get dangerous, but the last few hours are likely to be pretty uncomfortable. If we wait, we'll be stuck here another three days. Meira, are you up for taking the tough watches with me?"

"Absolutely."

"And Hannah, Bethany, are you up for tucking into a bunk and riding out the mess?"

I glanced Hannah's way.

"If that's all you need from us, I'd rather just get this over with."

"Me too," Hannah added.

"Okay!" Bryan was already on the move to the foredeck. "Just let me pull up *Rover* and we'll get on the way."

Meira hauled in the anchor and I took the tiller. Bryan changed into dry clothes and hung the wet gear in the sun. As we motored across the bay, he moved around the decks. He lashed the fuel cans in place and checked on *Rover*'s tie-downs.

"Hannah and I can take watch until midnight, no problem," I said to him. "You'd better get a break while you can."

By morning the seas had picked up enough that Hannah and I got queasy just trying to move around the boat. Meira sent us to bed.

"Dad and I can manage just fine. You lay down and stay out of the way."

Trying not to feel like the weakest link, I grabbed a couple of granola bars and a water bottle and took refuge with Hannah in the forward bunk. We lay facing each other, one on each side of the gap at the top of the V. Her legs twined with mine and every time she moved her feet in the point of the berth I pulled mine back, trying to find space away from her sweaty socks. I watched the exchange of sea and sky through the porthole past her head as we rolled and pitched in the unpredictable waves. I looked away.

I kept my head down under the low ceiling and flipped onto my stomach, leaned my torso to port to get a view of the cockpit. Meira was on watch at the moment and I hoped Bryan was resting. The boat lurched off a big crest and the jolt flipped me back against the wall. On the low side now, I watched the green water flow by outside my porthole, reached up to dog down the latches a little tighter, and wiped the drips off the wall. The hull shook as the boat dropped sideways off a wave and smacked into an arrhythmic swell. The surprisingly solid crash reverberated in the small space. Hannah reached for my hand and I held on.

"*LiLo*'s just doing the biggest belly flop ever," I said, hoping to reassure us both.

"She must like doing the cannonball."

"She's having way more fun than we are, that's for sure!"

We kept up our quiet chatter long after we'd run out of things to say. Finally, Hannah fell asleep. I pulled up our position on my phone's navigation app and promised myself to wait at least half an hour before peeking again. I made it ten minutes.

The motor droned on and I could hear the higher pitched whine of the auto pilot straining against the tiller. As we approached the cape on the southern edge of Bahía de Todos Santos, I wrestled myself out of the bunk. I stood in place for a moment to get my bearings and then timed my movements with the rolling hull. I caught Bryan's eye, stepped up onto the middle step, and turned for a look through the dodger.

"Once we round the point, we'll be on a broad reach," Bryan said. "With this onshore breeze, we should be able to sail across the bay the last few miles into Ensenada."

His mouth turned up, but his eyes stayed strained.

"How about you get the sails up and I take this last watch?" I asked.

"Sounds good."

I moved back to my berth for warmer clothes and shook myself fully awake. The swell rocked *LiLo* in new directions as we altered course. I tethered in and took the tiller while Bryan cut the throttle and went forward to raise the sails. Masses of towering gray clouds filled the sky to the east, directly over the Ensenada harbor. With every new swell from the west, I prepared to be swamped, thinking, *This is the one that will break into the cockpit.* I added another drop board to the companionway but *LiLo* took wave after wave in stride. Bryan stretched out on the cockpit seat. I was glad to have him close but determined not to wake him. I kept an eye on the storm straight ahead, trying to decide if it was getting bigger or if we were just getting closer.

As we neared the harbor entrance, I spotted the upper decks of a cruise ship above the sea wall. I eased the sheets and altered course a bit to give the larger ship the right-of-way. Bryan stirred and I nudged him awake.

"We should go ahead and get the sails down. We're just about there."

After so many slow-motion hours at sea, everything felt sped up to double time. The sails came down, the engine back on. The cruise ship cleared the channel and we turned to run north between the markers. As the swell diminished, the crew emerged; taking turns to pop their heads up under the dodger.

I sent them back below. "Go get presentable. We're almost there!"

Bryan took the tiller again while I called the marina for a slip assignment.

"They say to take any free slip on the north side of the first dock."

We prepped the dock lines for the first time in weeks and hauled out the fenders from the stern locker.

"Let's try for a port tie," Bryan said.

We slid smoothly into the slip and I stopped us with the midline.

"Welcome to Ensenada," I said as the crew piled out onto the dock. "You just finished the Baja Bash!"

Chapter Thirty-one

CAUGHT IN THE CURRENT

Ensenada, Mexico to San Diego, Santa Rosa,
and Morro Bay, California
April and May 2014: New Moon, First Quarter,
Full Moon, Third Quarter

For the sea one must sail
from one life to another
is treacherous and deadly
and no one makes it across unscarred

The weather that blew us into Ensenada kept us there for three or four days. We didn't mind the break and took advantage of the time at the dock to reprovision and clean our main water tank. Somewhere on the southern coast of Baja, our bilge pump had jammed, allowing bilge water to rise above the service port in our keel-installed water tank The grimy water seeped into the tank, through the water supply, and out our galley faucet.

We'd intentionally set up our plumbing system to isolate our three tanks in case of contamination or leaks, so we simply shut off the valves to the main tank and shifted to using water in bottles we filled from the auxiliary tanks beneath the quarter berths.

Now, with access to hoses and loads of fresh water, we poured dish soap into the main tank, added several inches of water and rocked the boat to slosh it around.

When we left St. Helens we only had a hand pump for the galley sink. Anyone who wanted to wash both hands at once had to ask for help to keep the water flowing. While in La Cruz de Huanacaxtle, Bryan had installed a foot pump and I hadn't stopped reveling in the relative luxury.

I stood at the sink on one foot, working the pump with my other to empty the soapy water out of the system. We ran gallons of water through the pipes until it stopped gushing bubbles, then Bryan gingerly tasted a glass.

"All clear!"

Despite all the horror stories we'd heard about heading north, I was finding it far less disorienting than our southbound trek. The good weather on the southern coast of Baja had helped our morale, for sure, but we were also flourishing as a team, scheduling our watches to take advantage of each crew member's strengths and working out kinks in *LiLo*'s systems. We'd left home on a quest for adventure and exploration. Now, about halfway back, our focus began to shift toward a safe return.

We watched the forecast for a break in the winds and savored our last few days in Mexico.

"Well, Babe," I said to Bryan one evening, "what do you say we head across the border tomorrow night?"

"Is the weather turning?" he asked.

"Yeah, it looks like an easy run to San Diego. If we leave right before sunset, we should get in about midmorning."

"One more day in Mexico, then."

You can't stop too often when climbing a mountain to see how far you've come or you'll look as well at how far is left. You'll just sit down and let the moss take over. We only allowed ourselves to examine our progress every couple hundred miles as we slipped into port for a breather but, still, reaching San Diego felt big. Like summiting a lesser Himalaya.

We sailed through a beautiful night back into US waters, took down our tattered Mexican courtesy flag, cleared customs, and motored over to the cruisers' moorage.

We dropped the anchor and rowed to shore like so many times before. Everyone sorted out their shoes from the jumble in the floor of the dinghy and slipped them on while Bryan tied *Rover* to the pier.

I slowed my steps and dropped behind my family a few paces. In the silence on the sidewalk, I found myself reflecting on our journey, curious what had changed in me since the last time I was here. I cast about for answers but I didn't even know yet what questions I was asking. *How do you know if you got what you came for if you don't know why you went?*

I had wanted to observe my own transformation. To watch myself get stronger. To watch myself get braver. I watched. But I just got hungry.

I walked my salty legs along the water's edge and wondered. *Had I let the sea be a place of change or just a change of scenery?*

This time, walking miles for a burger felt ordinary. Our bodies and minds had adjusted to the sailing life. My emotions strained to keep up. I was happy to be back in the land of NOAA weather radio, back where I could shop in English, happy to be heading back toward our friends and family, our little house at the edge of the woods, but never had the days slipped so quickly through my grasp. Every moment came surrounded by neon lights, arrows flashing, "Last Time."

I shook off my melancholy and stepped forward to lead the crew back to the downtown Smashburger for a victory celebration.

At the end of the meal, Bryan raised his beer and we clinked his bottle with our milkshake glasses.

"Welcome back to the United States!"

We spent a week in San Diego, taking care of business, grocery shopping, and visiting with friends. My focus shifted from sea to shore. With no plans to leave right away, I stopped checking the weather every few hours, limiting my obsession to once or twice a day.

I wondered how our adjustment to home would go. Some of the families we'd met were continuing on across the South Pacific, others were sailing to Hawaii. Many of the women and children we'd met had flown home from Mazatlán while the men made the long passages back with the help of hired crew.

Sometimes I imagined them, the women resuming their lives at home, the men sailing along under the idyllic trade winds. I knew these paths held their own dangers but on bad days it was hard not to wonder if we'd chosen the right course.

Other days, despite all my worry about what lay ahead, I felt confidence in my belly, unfurling from the trust we'd built as a crew and family and my own growing resourcefulness. But we still had miles to go, backward up the brutal western edge of the continent.

We reached out to Charlotte and Eric, our friends from *Rebel Heart*, and connected in person as soon as we could. We could only begin to imagine the devastation they'd suffered—losing their home and returning to the kind of national scrutiny no one should have to endure.

They'd been back in San Diego for a week or two but were still house-hopping from one place to another, staying with friends for a few days at a time while waiting for an apartment to open up. At one point, a friend offered them a few days in a house in Encinitas and they invited us to join them for the weekend.

We held ridiculously commonplace celebrations, hooting over the rush of water at the kitchen sink, marveling over bedrooms with doors and ice cream in the freezer. At night, the walk to the bathroom felt endless—out of bed, across the room, out the door, down the hall.

I fell asleep without the sound of my children breathing. I assume they did the same without me.

We woke to a simple breakfast with mugs that stayed where you put them. Bryan sat at the table amusing the baby from *Rebel Heart*. You'd never know to look at her how close she'd come to dying. The loss of their boat was still almost too bright to look at. The pain of it flared out from behind her blonde head, shattered when she laughed. I, too, would have let everything sink to save this child.

The media was still hyping the inaccurate, bestselling view of the story. Rescue in the Pacific: irresponsible parents take their children to sea.

I didn't write about our visit on my blog or even in my journal. Our friends weren't yet ready to say anything publicly and none of their story was mine to talk about. I don't know what I would have said anyway.

"We spent two nights on land." Who else would have understood the magnitude of this?

"I slept in a square bed, no one on watch."

"For forty-eight hours, I stopped being afraid my kids would drown."

Though we'd all borrowed cars to drive to Encinitas, once there we walked to the grocery store, still caught in the current—by sail if at sea; by foot if on shore. On our way up the coastline, through all the strange streets, I'd made Bryan take the wheel on our borrowed car, wondering if I would need to relearn how to drive. We weren't yet accustomed to asphalt and the house was too far from the ocean for any of the smells to be right.

Everything that should have felt familiar didn't. Now I was adrift on land.

I didn't feel ready to leave the friends we'd connected with in San Diego but when the sea state dropped we took advantage of the calm to head north. Mild Santa Ana winds gave us a perfect offshore flow for the reach back toward Point Conception. We whisked past Dana Point, Catalina Island, and Los Angeles overnight and landed on Santa Rosa Island to stretch our legs.

Bryan dropped the anchor in Bechers Bay and issued a general invitation. "I'm going to shore to hike the Cherry Canyon trail. Anyone want to come along?"

We'd made good time through the southern California waters and leaving Santa Rosa after a five or six hour hike would put us off Point Conception at midnight when we hoped the winds and seas would be calmest.

"I'm in," I said, and the crew agreed. We tossed water bottles and snacks into our backpacks and handed them down into the dinghy. Hannah and Meira piled their shoes on *Rover's* floor and I added mine to the heap.

Bryan rowed us in and we tied *Rover* off to the pier. We gathered our things and stepped onto the beach, which terminated only a few yards from the water in terracotta cliffs. Erosion had eaten them away in stripes, the harder stone protruding like a stack of pancakes. As I climbed the ladder up the pier, I reached out and ran my hand along the ridges where wind and waves had worn stone to sand. *How long had it taken this beauty to develop? What might it yet become?*

Once at the trailhead we filled our bottles at the water spigot and rubbed in sunscreen for each other.

Bryan drank a few big gulps and refilled his container. "There's supposedly water at the other end of the trail but with how bad the drought has been here, I'm not counting on it."

Now away from the sea breeze, I felt the full heat of the day. "Do you think we'll have enough for the whole hike?"

"I think we're okay. Let's just make sure we save some for the return trip."

He was right to be cautious; the gully at the end of the trail showed only old evidence of a river's flow. We found a shady spot and had lunch, sipping carefully what water we had left, then Bryan and Meira explored up the canyon while Hannah and I rested. They returned, telling stories and showing pictures of the beauty they'd encountered—red cliffs eroded into sculptured curves, caves with shadows below and skylights above—and soon we were all refreshed and ready for the hike back.

The trail wound across bare bluffs and over grassy slopes. The air shimmered over the green water of the bay. I wiped my face with my shirttail, trying to welcome the heat, to bank it for the chilly days ahead.

I paced myself, walking just fast enough to leave shame behind. I felt like the slowest, weakest member of the crew but no one minded but me. Up ahead, the kids walked together. Bryan stopped and waited for me to catch up.

"Want some water? I've got plenty."

I took a small sip but he urged me to take more.

"We're getting close, I think. Have all you need. We can refill at the pier again."

I glanced back at the path behind us, at how far we'd come, looked north across the water toward the challenge ahead.

"We need to leave right away to round the point before dawn," I said as we rowed back out to *LiLo*. "If you can get us going, I'll tuck away anything that might fly around down here just in case."

We settled back into our watch rhythms, rounded Point Conception uneventfully in the night, and by afternoon, still jubilant from the easy passage, we motored through the Morro Bay entrance and up the harbor to the guest dock.

"Want to get fish and chips at the pier again?" I asked as soon as we were tied up.

"Oh, yes. That was so good!" Meira said and the rest of the crew agreed.

We walked up the ramp to the commercial pier and found spots at a dock-side table. A couple of bites into his meal, Bryan put his hand to his mouth and pulled out a chunk of something white.

"Found a bone?" I asked.

"No, I think I just lost a piece of a tooth."

Bryan pulled out his phone, glanced at the clock, and stood abruptly.

"It's quarter to five on a Friday afternoon. If I'm going to get this checked, I'd better call a dentist right away."

Hannah and Meira looked at me with worried eyes.

"I'm sure we'll work it out somehow. We might as well eat while our food is hot."

A few minutes later, Bryan was back.

"I found a dentist in the area but they won't schedule an appointment to fix it until they've seen me to diagnose the problem so it will take at least two visits to get it taken care of. I explained that we're only here temporarily and that I'll be taking the bus or walking to get there but I don't think they understood. Every other place is closed now so I guess I'll just hope it doesn't start hurting over the weekend and we'll try to figure something out on Monday."

We finished our food and headed back to the boat, a little slower with the weight of this latest uncertainty. As we walked down the guest dock, a sailor called over from a boat moored nearby.

"Hey, is that your boat?"

"Yes, what's up?" Bryan answered.

"Oh, we were just looking for some crew for a race tomorrow and wondered if you might still be around. It's too windy out there to do much traveling. Are you heading north or south?"

"North, but not until the weather settles down a bit." Bryan looked at me and I shrugged.

"I'm not really up for a high-wind sailing day," I said softly, "but the kids might want to come."

"Yes, please!" said Meira just as Hannah added, "No, thank you."

Bryan called back across the water. "Looks like we've rounded up two crew for you. Good enough?"

"That sounds great. Unless it's canceled for too much wind, we'll head out about eleven, okay?"

"It's a plan."

The next morning, Bryan and Meira pulled on warm clothes and beanies and were waiting at the edge of the dock when their ride arrived. The race boat slowed just enough for them to step on board and then turned to head out to sea.

I hollered from the cockpit. "Have fun!" and they waved and smiled.

Hannah tucked into her bunk and I took advantage of the empty cabin to get some cleaning done. While I was washing dishes in the galley, I looked out the window to see a trio of young adults carrying a small sailing dinghy down to the guest dock. I finished the dishes, dried my hands, and ducked out into the cockpit just as the boat pulled away, leaving one of the three behind.

"Hi there," I said to the young woman on the dock. "Did they forget you?"

She laughed brightly. "No, we're a dinghy sailing team but it's a two-person boat so we take turns going out. Are you visiting Morro Bay?"

"Yes, we're heading back to Oregon from six months in Mexico. Not right now, obviously. It's too windy to be going north right now."

"You're heading *north*? All the way back to Oregon?"

"Yeah, I know. Not very many sailors go that way. But we've got a hardy crew and figured we'd at least try to get the boat back on our own. My husband and Meira, my youngest are out on another ship, crewing for the Saturday afternoon race but Hannah and I are just hanging out for the day."

"You have a Hannah? I'm Anna!" She stuck out her hand and we shook.

"I'm Bethany. So nice to meet you."

"Just the two kids? I have a sister, too. She still lives at home but I go back as often as I can. My parents live just up in the hills and I miss them if I don't get back every week or two."

"Just the two, yes. You must be at college nearby."

"Yes, I'm at Cal Poly, studying to be a vet. In my spare time, I sail and knit and play the violin."

"That's fabulous! Meira loves animals, I'm a musician, and I think Hannah is below knitting as we speak."

From the depths of the cabin, we heard Hannah holler. "I sure am!"

Anna smiled and bent over to wave through the window. She straightened up and glanced out toward her teammates.

"Looks like the boys are heading back. I'll have to go in a minute but, hey—it's been so great to meet you. I have a feeling my parents would love to meet you too. Any chance you might be free to come up to the house for dinner sometime in the next couple of days?"

"That's so generous! The weather's bad for three or four days so we're free. Our only plan for the week is finding a dentist. My husband just broke a tooth and we want to get it checked out."

Anna's smile broadened to engulf her whole face.

"No problem. My dad's a dentist! I'm sure he'd be willing to take a look and see if it can wait to be fixed." She laughed at my astonishment and stepped to the edge of the dock to pull in the dinghy sailer. "Give me your number before I leave. Once I talk to my parents, I'll call you with a plan!"

Tuesday afternoon found us climbing the ramp to the parking lot and into Anna's SUV. On our way into the foothills, she pointed out landmarks, favorite haunts from her childhood, and curious sights.

After twenty or thirty minutes on the winding mountain roads, she pulled into the circular drive in front of a large home. We stepped out into a stiff breeze.

"There's nothing to block the wind up here; sorry it's so frightful."

"It's just a good thing we're not fighting it out at sea."

Mrs. Kimball met us at the door with her husband just behind. "Come in! Come in! The meat is still on the grill but there's goat cheese and crackers here on the counter already." As she spoke she led us through the entryway into the kitchen. "Can I get you something to drink? Soda maybe?"

"Cold soda?" Meira asked, eyes wide.

Smiling at our hosts' confusion, I offered an explanation.

"We haven't had refrigeration for almost a year. Dairy, meat, and cold drinks are a huge luxury these days. You couldn't have chosen a better menu to make these sailors happy."

"Well, there's a fresh salad too, and ice cream for dessert."

"This all sounds amazing," I said as I moved to the sink to wash my hands. "How can I help?"

While I found a place in the kitchen, Anna nudged her father.

"Don't forget, Dad. I told Bryan you'd be glad to take a look at his tooth."

"Oh, that's right. I'll just get my mirror."

As Bryan stood sheepishly under the dining room light, Mr. Kimball peered into his mouth.

"Yeah, it looks like you lost a chip from that back molar. Nothing urgent, though. You can definitely wait to get seen until you get back home."

"That's good to hear," Bryan said. "It didn't hurt yet but I sure didn't want to end up out at sea when it started up."

After dinner, Anna and her sister pulled me over to the piano. "Would you play some music with us?" Anna said. "Elise and I don't often get a chance to play with a pianist."

Elise was already unpacking her violin and I sat down and glanced through the stack of sheet music.

"I've missed playing with friends so much. I'll play anything you want!" I said.

Both families shifted into the living room as the sisters tuned. I glanced behind me at the row of bright faces.

"Don't mind us," Mrs. Kimball said. "We're just so happy to have you here."

I turned back to the page, notes now blurring through grateful tears.

"How about 'Amazing Grace'?"

Chapter Thirty-two

WHEN THERE ISN'T A PATH TO FOLLOW

San Francisco, San Joaquin Delta, and Pittsburg, California
May and June 2014: Waning Crescent, New Moon, Waxing Crescent

*Where there is a way or path,
it is someone else's path.*
—*Joseph Campbell*

One day in late May we nosed under the Golden Gate for the second time. We anchored in Aquatic Bay again, just off Ghirardelli Square, and after a night's rest, made plans to head into Chinatown to celebrate Meira's birthday. On our first stop in San Francisco she'd fallen in love with green tea ice cream and all she wanted for her special day was to find the restaurant we'd visited before and have it again.

After watching Meira unwind a few gifts we'd wrapped in my scarf collection, we loaded our daypacks, piled into the dinghy, and rowed to shore. While Bryan cabled *Rover* to the pier, the crew and I stripped off life jackets, warm hats, and outerwear, dusted off our sandy feet, and sat on the curb to put on our socks and shoes.

We headed generally southeast, toward our memory of Chinatown. By the time we reached Dragon's Gate we were hungry. We ducked under paper lanterns and made our way past quiet tea shops, trying to recreate our previous path.

All along the voyage, fuel stations, grocery stores, and propane outposts had registered in my mind, little location flags of memory in case we came back the same route. But the last time we came to Chinatown, we'd arrived on the cable cars, never thinking we needed to remember how to find our way back. We'd left knowing our orientation but not our destination. This time, we knew our destination but not our orientation.

We stopped at every corner, stared down every street. Occasionally one or another of us would venture a guess.

"Um, I think I remember walking by that red wall."

"Didn't we pass that fruit stand last time?"

And off we'd go, down another road, through another alley. Tired and hungry, we harnessed all of our hard-learned kindness to wind our way together. At one point I stopped our progress to comment.

"Have you noticed how astonishing it is that we haven't yelled at each other yet?" Our laughter buoyed us as we spiraled closer and closer to our goal. At last we turned a corner and spotted it. The familiar columned entrance, the balcony where we'd sat more than six months earlier, amazed we'd come this far.

Hannah and Meira picked up speed, walking with a bit of sailor's swagger. It was hard to tell how much came from the roll of the sea, how much from the life lived on it.

"Don't you ever get out of bed on that boat?"

I cleared my throat and tried to respond sensibly to the unexpected phone call as the voice continued.

"I've been anchored off your starboard bow for half an hour and have seen no signs of life. Get up and come on over!"

I poked my head out into the morning sunlight. *Jubilee* swung at anchor to the north. I caught a glimpse of Alcatraz beyond. Cold-water swimmers from the nearby Dolphin Club stroked by, black swim caps glistening in the morning sun.

"Get up, kids. Al's here!" Their sleepy confusion gave way to delight. We'd exchanged emails with Al since we left Half Moon Bay on the southbound journey but had thought we might miss him altogether on our trip back north. We tossed on clothes and life jackets and rowed over to his boat.

"Just tie up off the stern here. Come aboard! Come aboard!" We piled over the sugar scoop stern into his gleaming cockpit.

He pulled out a gift bag and handed it to me. "Here's some local wine I thought you'd enjoy. And I threw in some more of that home-canned tuna too. And here, I think you'll need this."

Ever the navigator, I perked up at the sight of a map.

"Those storms off the cape have you pretty locked in here, huh?" Al said.

"Yes, it looks like we're going to be in the bay for a while. We hear even the commercial fishermen haven't been able to get around the cape in weeks. We don't have plans but our anchorage permit here is up in a couple of days so we'll have to find someplace else to go."

Al nodded along. He'd already thought ahead of us. "You should go up into the Delta," he declared. "It's beautiful and warm and quiet."

I laughed. "You had me at warm."

Since returning to San Francisco, the weather hadn't been miserable. But we spent much of each day walking through the breezy streets and returned each night in our damp dinghy to a frigid boat. Our engine-driven heater was no help in port.

Every afternoon ashore, we stuffed our extra layers into backpacks but evening found us on the beach, putting them all on again—sweaters, jackets, stocking caps—and then stripping off our socks and shoes to launch *Rover* through the tide.

Al said that just a few miles up the Sacramento-San Joaquin River Delta we'd find a vast waterway with small towns, remote anchorages, and best of all, warm weather. We chatted until he had to leave, trading our stories for his welcome advice.

Back on *LiLo* we started to make a plan, the promise of forward motion giving us more energy than we'd had in days. The morning felt fresh, clean-scrubbed, full of possibility.

"We'll have to make a trip for provisions," Bryan said.

"If I remember right, there's a Trader Joes not too far away."

"How are we doing for fuel and water?"

"Pretty good. I think we can be ready to leave tomorrow."

We spent most of the day getting the boat ready for travel and rowed in that evening for a grocery run. Only a block or so up the street we stopped short. We'd passed the Dolphin Club every time we walked to town, but this evening, the upper half of the elevated Dutch door was open. Light and chatter spilled out into the street. We took turns jumping to see inside and pulled ourselves up onto the skinny step to get a better look. A team of dusty workers bowed and straightened like dipping birds, sanding rhythmically inside the hull of a long wooden skiff. Someone noticed our faces peeking over the sill.

"Come on in!" they hollered over the commotion. "It's Boat Night!"

"Yes," another echoed, opening the door. "Come see what we're doing. We'll put you to work!"

We got a brief tour of the facility and an introduction to the traditions of boat night.

"Every Tuesday we get together to do maintenance on our fleet of rowing vessels. If you're up for helping, we could use a few more sanders and I think the kitchen needs another set of hands for dinner. You'll stay for dinner, of course."

"Well, we were on our way to get groceries so we can leave tomorrow," I said, continuing quickly as the kids' faces fell, "but we can leave the next day instead. Show me to the kitchen."

The evening was magical. We gathered in the main boathouse under gleaming rowboats hanging from warm, wooden beams. Someone pulled a few more chairs up to the expansive table and ushered us to places near the middle. Stories for supper—a fair exchange—though we listened as much as we talked. We were not the only ones with tales to share and each one sparked another memory. Laughter rolled in waves up and down the smiling faces. Late into the evening we sat together, our hunger for food and companionship both fully satisfied.

As small as the sailing world can be I shouldn't have been surprised when, a few days later in a marina up the delta, we ran into one of our new boat-night friends. She invited us aboard her classic sailing scow and gave us a little more history about the fleet of flat-bottomed cargo schooners that used to ply the local waters.

As we left she passed along several helpful tips about the area, ending with, "Oh, and you'll probably sink into the mud here at low tide. Don't worry too much; you'll float free just fine. Just don't try to get out of the marina on the ebb or you'll get stuck in front of everyone for hours!"

Thanks to her good advice and Al's, we made it out of the marina and spent several enjoyable days exploring the winding delta waterways. We kept an eye on the weather, watching for a chance to slip north of Cape Mendocino before the summer high settled in, bringing steady north winds to the whole west coast. This far up the river, we would need several days to get back to the bay and up to the cape and I struggled to figure out the best timing.

I checked the forecast morning and night, wondering every time it changed if I'd made the wrong call to stay put. The crew noticed my tension, made some signs, and hung them prominently on both bulkheads. No matter where I was standing in the cabin, I couldn't help but see them. "NO!" read the bold lettering, "You may NOT second guess yourself!"

When it seemed like there might be a break in the winds, a twenty-four hour opportunity to round the cape, we started the long beat back toward San Francisco Bay.

LiLo slid to a stop, mired in the muck at the edge of the channel. The sudden stillness stunned me for a moment and then we all sprang into action.

Meira stuck her head out of the cabin. "Did we just run aground?"

"Yes. Come on out. We might need your help," I said as I checked the chart for deeper water. Bryan revved the engine in reverse, trying to back out of the mud.

"Sally ship," he hollered, "and quick! The tide's falling. If we don't get out right away we'll be stuck for the night."

The crew and I scurried to the cabin top.

"Port," he called, and we ran to the left, holding onto the shrouds and leaning hard over the toe rail.

"Now starboard!" Three sets of bare feet dashed in unison across the deck. Three heads levered out over the shallow water. The keel shifted slightly in the mud, then stuck again.

"I think you're steering the wrong way," I hollered as I ran by. "Want me to try?"

"Sure, let's switch," Bryan said, hurrying out of the cockpit as I hopped down. "I'm heavier anyway." He leaned in rhythm with the crew, swung his free leg over the lifeline.

"It's helping," I called up. "Try again!" Back to port, another heave, another run to starboard.

"Keep the RPMs up," Bryan hollered on one pass. "The prop wash might help clear the mud around the rudder."

I revved the engine high as the crew's combined weight set the ship rocking.

"I think we moved a few inches but we're stuck again. Keep going. I think we're almost there...Yes! That did it!"

Bryan and the kids stood at the mast as I pulled us carefully back into the channel.

"Whew! There must have been some silt built up there," I said, "We should be good now."

A few minutes after our grounding we approached Three Mile Slough Bridge.

"There's supposed to be a bridgetender here day and night to raise the bridge for us," I said, looking up from our cruising guide. "I'll see if this phone number is still accurate."

Before I could call we heard the warning bells from the bridge above as the gates on the road began to lower, halting traffic on the span.

"Oh, I think they must have seen us circling," I said. "Yes, look—it's going up!"

Once through the bridge and out into wider water, Bryan took the tiller and I sat down straddling the companionway opening. I'd been reading to the crew and this quiet stretch of river offered the perfect opportunity to enjoy a few more chapters. Hannah and Meira sat below, out of the sun, but Bryan stopped me periodically to point out the unusual sights along the way—fields just feet above the surrounding canals, lonely cattle grazing beneath colossal wind turbines. After a few more hours, we pulled into Pittsburg Marina, planning to stop for a night before heading on.

Things didn't go according to plan.

We needed to catch a falling tide to make our way back to the Golden Gate. All week long, the ebbs ran out in the afternoon, when the wind picks up against the river, or in the middle of the night, neither time ideal for travel. But if there was any hope of getting around Cape Mendocino during the upcoming weather window we had to get out of the bay right away. So we spent a night in the Pittsburg Marina and took off on the next day's ebb.

Only a few miles out, our engine coughed and died. Bryan tore into the engine compartment and squeezed the priming bulb. Empty. Somewhere in the fuel line, we were sucking in air. The channel was too narrow to tack into the wind and it wasn't safe to drift with the tide so I sailed back upriver while Bryan replaced the priming bulb. This time, the pressure held and we turned the engine on and swung back downriver, relieved it was such an easy fix.

A few minutes later, the engine started coughing again. Again, I sailed with the wind upriver while Bryan upended himself in the engine compartment. He fiddled with something or replaced something else—I don't know; I was sailing!—and we started the motor up and turned downriver.

Soon, it was clear that we hadn't found the problem and we sailed back upriver again. This pattern repeated itself all afternoon—Plugs? Nope. Coil? Nope. Points? Nope. Distributor cap? Nope—until he'd exhausted the on-river fix possibilities and I grew bewildered by the repeated change in direction. The channel was constricted by shallows on one side and a military zone on the other, complete with forbidding signage. "Restricted: Explosives"

Every time we turned around, we were in a slightly different place in the river, and I kept the chart handy to remind myself of the hazards, leaning down to check on it while working to stay centered in the channel.

Eventually, the ebb tide slacked and the flood began. We wouldn't be going anywhere else tonight. So we turned upriver for good and sailed the few miles back to Pittsburg. Bryan flipped on the ailing engine at the breakwater, but we didn't trust it to get us in. We sailed back through the narrow entrance and took a couple of short tacks into the slip. The crew worked the sheets and lines briskly in the tight quarters and we all cheered when we completed the tricky maneuver.

Bryan and I walked several miles up the road to the auto parts store for carb cleaner and he spent the evening in the cockpit cleaning and rebuilding the carburetor in a dishpan so none of the important parts would fall overboard. When he got everything back together again, the engine wouldn't start at all.

A neighbor noticed us working late and came by to see what was up. We filled him in and he hurried back to his boat for ice cream for the crew, chocolate for me, wine for Bryan, and a cruising guide to the Bay.

Spirits lifted, Bryan went back to work and got the engine running. I checked the tide charts and we left Friday afternoon, hoping to make it a few miles downriver before the flood tide began, hoping to catch the midnight tide across the bar and out to sea. The wind was high and we weren't making very good progress. And then, only a few miles out, the engine died again. So we turned around again. This time Bryan coaxed the motor into helping us back to our slip at the guest dock.

We'd been hoping to make the jump up to the cape and sneak around during the tiny weather window we saw approaching on the forecast. With every engine issue, this possibility grew less and less likely. My parents had plans to meet us in Crescent City if it didn't take us too long to get there, and I texted daily with updates, mostly just saying, "I don't know."

The constant uncertainty was starting to wear heavily. One hour we were readying the boat and ourselves for an ocean passage, the next we were living with our house transformed into an engine repair shop—galley and bunks inaccessible, and the plans for our return on hold again.

One evening we had a hard conversation.

"I checked the long-term slip prices and they're not too bad," I said. "If we can't get out and around the cape this week, I think we might need to leave *LiLo* here and come back in the fall to finish the trip."

Bryan sat for a minute before replying, "I've been thinking about that, too. I sure hate to get this close and have to quit but my boss is asking when I'll be back to work."

"It needs to be pretty soon. Our renters are moving out this month."

"Well, I think I got the engine fixed but I thought that before. We won't know for sure until we head out again."

"I hope it works. I can't wrap my brain around ending the trip like this," I said. "We've been pushing for so long, how could we just be done? But every time we walk to town, we cross the railroad tracks and I think about packing a bag and taking Amtrak home."

"I don't think we're quite out of options yet, Beth. Let's see what the next tide brings."

I curled up in bed and tried to rest. But the whistle on the northbound train echoed across the marina.

Chapter Thirty-three

This Is How it Ends

Pittsburg to Noyo River, California
June 2014: Waxing Crescent, First Quarter

The sea finds out everything you did wrong.
— Francis Stokes

It felt just barely safe enough. I never liked navigating out at night, but if we didn't get out of the bay on this ebb we'd almost certainly miss the weather window around the cape. We'd spent so much time on this piece of the river, breaking down and turning around and breaking down again, it was starting to feel familiar. So we took the chance and cast off on the midnight tide.

The brisk afternoon winds had freshened into the night and whipped up a serious chop in the channel. Bryan was getting regularly and thoroughly drenched. Only one of us needed to be wet at a time, so I climbed into bed and attempted to get some sleep before my watch. The seas were launching me up off my bunk and I turned onto my stomach and wrapped my arms around the cushion to add its weight to my gravity. I tossed around on salty sheets, still in my sweaty sundress from the day.

I'd long ago learned to rest even if I couldn't sleep, but I couldn't tune out the clank of the halyard on the mast, the crash of the bow on the waves. I leaned over to the opening of the V-berth and squinted up at Bryan as he steered by hand in the bucking sea. Through the open companionway door I watched him glance down at the chart, neatly dodging the spray from a wave, and then lean out to starboard, back to port, spotting the buoys that kept us on course. He found a three-part rhythm—a dance between swell and light—find the red, find the green, duck and check the chart while the wave rolls over. Flash. Flash. Duck. Flash. Flash. Duck. Each buoy has its own light pattern, sometimes blinking every second, sometimes every two-and-a-half or four. In a tight channel, in a bouncy boat, four seconds is a long time.

I might have dozed off. I can't really remember. I might not have even known the truth at the time, caught in the trembling sway and the constant hum of near-panic. But I know I came suddenly and completely awake when the anchor started to fall.

Usually the rattle of the chain through the vent, up onto deck, and over the bow roller means safety, the end of a passage, a good night's sleep. I couldn't think of any reason why Bryan would be dropping anchor here, in the middle of the shipping channel, shoals on one side, explosives on the other.

I somersaulted out of my bunk and up the companionway.

"We just lost our anchor!" I saw my confusion reflected on Bryan's face.

"What? No. That can't be right."

"No, really. I just heard the chain go over."

He moved his tether from the anchor point in the cockpit to the jack lines on the side deck and started to make his way up to the bow. I'd tossed on a life jacket already and I tethered in and shifted automatically to the tiller, shivering in the midnight chill. It was no use trying to tell what he was doing and dangerous to think of anything but blinking buoys and the winding channel. Then, over the rumble of the engine, I heard Bryan shout, "Shut it down!" and I cut the engine and slammed the throttle home.

I waited in the spray and the silence while he made his careful way back to the cockpit, his face revealing the bad news before his voice could.

"The anchor's still attached, but we're stuck hard in the mud. And when it went over, it took the bow line with it, and it's completely fouled around the prop. I don't know how we're going anywhere soon, much less around the cape and home."

We'd already talked through our escape plan if we couldn't make it out, picked out a marina where we could leave the boat, discussed the logistics of coming back in the fall for the final leg. *That's it then,* I thought. *There's just no way we can dive on the prop in these seas, in this dark. So this is how it ends.*

I took a deep shaky breath and gave up. My soul started slipping north.

I looked up at Bryan expecting to see the same blend of resignation and disappointment on his face, but his mouth was fierce and fixed.

"I haven't sailed my ass 4,500 miles to quit now. And we've got an extra propeller if this one's shot."

He flipped the engine to neutral and fired it up again.

"When I holler, give it just a little reverse," he said, and climbed the rolling deck to the bow. "Okay, now!"

I eased the throttle back until the engine started to shudder, kicked the gear shift back to neutral.

"Try forward!" he called, and I did.

"Now a little more reverse."

Every underwater vibration shrieked through the tiller into my listening hand. I pushed my instincts to their edge and beyond, holding the throttle just a little higher, a little longer than felt safe.

Forward. Back.

I didn't even know what to hope for.

Forward. Back.

The shudder seemed to be shifting and Bryan called encouragement.

"I got a bit of slack! Whatever you're doing, keep it up!"

Forward. Back.

With a growl from the engine and a roar from the bow, we broke away. Bryan gathered up the frayed dock line and carried it back to the cockpit, no hunter ever more proud of his prey. "I got it! We did it! We're free."

Then the mad scramble to haul up the anchor and get reoriented before a barge came through. We were both still keyed up from the near disaster and my thoughts felt as dim and winding as the channel.

I can't believe we did it! We can sail on. But now we have *to sail on.*

I dredged up the energy to offer to take a watch.

And we still have the hardest stretch ahead. I don't know if I can do this.

Bryan must have seen my reluctance. "I'm feeling pretty good," he said, grinning. "You get a little more sleep."

We knew at some point the ebb tide would turn against us and we planned to find a spot to drop anchor and wait out the flood. But when the sun woke me the next morning we were already through Carquinez Strait and headed out into the wide open bay.

"Do you need a break?" I said, still a little sleepy.

And the welcome reply, "Nope! We're making great time! I think we might make it all the way out the gate before the tide turns."

I dozed a little more and then got up for tea. Angel Island rose to the right, Alcatraz down on our left. I pulled on waterproof gear over a base layer and prepped my pockets with snacks for a sea watch.

Just as Bryan predicted, we slipped under the Golden Gate a few minutes after slack tide, made a wide right turn and headed north. The marine layer rolled in as we inched out and we flipped on the automatic fog horn—an upgrade we'd purchased in San Diego—to alert other traffic to our presence.

Still weary from the night before and dulled by the gloom, I slept in the two-minute increments between blasts, letting the horn serve as my watch alarm. Meira started to stir and soon poked her head up to say, "Good morning." We chatted for a few minutes and planned the day's watch schedule, though I was reluctant to turn the helm over until we made it past the busy entrance. Soon beyond the dangers of Potato Patch Shoal, we rounded Point Reyes in the fog. Drakes Bay was still socked in, invisible.

The cloudy day gave way to a mild afternoon. Bryan came back on deck to relieve the crew and we motored on through the night, passing the seals and fishermen of Bodega Bay, ever closer to the cape.

The next day brought big, rolling swell and sunny skies. We managed to keep up speed through the seas and started the turn in toward Noyo River about mid-afternoon, plenty of time to be in before dark.

I was concerned about the entrance though. The guide book told a tale of close, looming sea walls only a couple of boat lengths apart and described an unusual system of range markers—red, green, and white. If coming in directly on the safe course, the lights would appear white. A degree or so off to the south and you'd see red; the same to the north and green would appear.

We'd been riding the westerly swell pretty well all day, rocking toward land as the waves passed under. But turning east put the swell at our stern and the shallowing sea floor intensified its power. It took all Bryan's concentration and strength to keep *LiLo* straight in the seas, surfing down the fronts of the waves without broaching. I came up on deck and tucked myself in front of his frame, copied his wide, braced stance. I lifted the salty dodger window, locked my vision on the range lights, and chanted above the engine.

"White, white, green, green, white, white, red, red, RED, white, white, white." My voice a steady rhythm to guide his ever shifting helm. Occasionally, an outsized swell obscured the lights for a moment and I held my breath and scanned until they came back in sight.

Even before we entered the outer harbor, the swell had diminished, cut by the stone jetties we were trying to avoid. A few more moments and we were in, the high walls now friendly shelter at the tiny river mouth.

On the short motor up to the marina I was surprised by my visceral reaction to this terrain, so very like that of our home port. The knot of vigilance at my center unwound at the sight of all the green. Tall firs stood watch on sloping hills. Leafing alders stepped down to the water's edge. Ferns everywhere.

Somewhere along the journey finding our way into strange harbors had become routine. I'd called ahead and gotten a slip assignment from the harbormaster, written down his perplexing directions—past the sea wall, beyond the white sign, port tie across from the fuel dock. I'd learned to hold these in mind like puzzle pieces, fit them into place when the way became clear. Because the way always became clear.

Chapter Thirty-four

Homesick Ever After

Noyo River to Crescent City, California
June 2014: Waxing Gibbous, Full Moon, Waning Gibbous,
Waning Crescent

*Over and over, you will get lost and return home
until one day you begin to make a home in being lost
You will no longer know any other way to live*

The weather window we'd been watching crept closer on the forecast charts. The seas wouldn't have time to settle, but it looked more and more likely that the winds would take a twelve-hour break. If we were ready to run when the wind died down, we might just make it around Cape Mendocino, the last of the big hurdles. I texted the news to my parents and they took off right away.

We refueled and rested, checked and rechecked the weather reports. I called the Coast Guard for advice about timing our departure across the Noyo River Bar and then, because we could, we walked to the other side of the harbor to their local station to thank them in person.

The small crew was friendly with a camaraderie that extended to all who seek the sea. "We're running a drill in the morning out at the bar. Call before you leave and we'll give you up-to-the-minute information about the conditions."

The next morning I flipped on the radio to hear the bar report. It was a stale recording, four or five hours old already. I heard the engine from the Coast Guard cutter fire up and slip into gear. I stepped out on deck just in time to see it head out, all orange paint and crisp uniforms. A seaman spotted me and waved.

I headed back down to rouse the crew and get some breakfast. It was only about thirty-five miles to Shelter Cove, a small cut on the south side of the cape where we planned to stage our attempt at a rounding. We didn't have to leave until midmorning so we settled our nerves with some boat chores. I flipped the radio back on again to hear the new bar report. Conditions sounded ideal and the swell outside wasn't too turbulent.

We backed out of our slip and turned toward the breakwater just as the Coast Guard ship returned. I took courage from their casual stances and relaxed faces. Surely they'd stop us if this was a bad idea.

"Where are you headed today?" one called over, suddenly attentive. It was more than just friendly conversation. If we got into trouble out there he would be on the rescue team. When we hollered back that we were just heading up to Shelter Cove, not trying to round the cape yet, he visibly relaxed before wishing us well.

We motored past the flashing rough-bar warning lights and even though I knew the conditions weren't dangerous, they still gave me a moment's pause. As I had for our entrance, I kept an eye on the range lights, looking backward this time, while Bryan stood at the tiller, facing the steep oncoming waves and guiding us back across the bar to the sea.

The run up to Shelter Cove was uneventful. The little bay offered only minimal protection from the swell and *LiLo* swung like a pendulum in the rollers. Bryan set our ground tackle to minimize the motion and went to bed. I stayed up with Hannah and Meira for a while, watching a movie while braced across the cabin, knees locked and feet planted on the galley cupboard doors. The moon rose over the coastline and a pelican dropped in for a visit. He landed precisely on our lifelines and balanced beak with tail on his precarious perch. We pointed and whispered from below and watched him stretch and preen before taking off again.

Between the rolling bunk, the anticipation and worry, and the 4 a.m. wake-up call, we didn't get very much sleep. I checked the weather before I got up. Calm winds off the cape still looked likely. We'd done all our prep the night before so it only took a few minutes to get underway. We let the crew sleep while they could.

By midmorning, we'd reached the southern edge of the cape. I scoured the weather conditions, trying to find the calmest route to sneak north. We opted to stay close to shore, as the cape-effect seas seemed to extend for miles and miles. Bryan stayed on watch beyond our typical schedule. Neither of us could relax so we settled into our most comfortable roles—helmsman and navigator.

I kept refreshing the current conditions, wincing at our decreasing speed as we edged toward the lighter seas that lay just north of the cape's westernmost bulge. I resisted voicing the ever-present question—*Do you think we'll make it?*—but we conferred every hour or so about the sea state and the wisdom of continuing. We knew that any decision to turn back would mean traveling through these waters again. Every crash of the bow felt doubled. Speed and fuel calculations stuck on repeat in my mind.

When we reached the midpoint of the rounding I started looking for the promised easing conditions. My hopes rose when the swell diminished, crashed back down when the large waves resumed. I questioned my senses and stared past the bow.

Another hour or so brought tentative optimism, even to the cautious captain. "I think it's really calming down out here. Good thing, too. I sure don't want to turn around and do that again."

Within another few hours the seas had died down completely and we were shooting along on the smoothest surface since southern California. As the sun set, spirits rose and we settled in for the night.

We'd hoped to arrive in Crescent City by 9 or 10 a.m., but the easy last few hours had us there before sunrise. We slowed to a crawl and waited in the predawn silver until the entrance rocks shone and sea birds broke the morning silence.

My parents had asked us to call no matter what time we got in. I knew my dad would be up at 5 a.m. and, for once, my mom would welcome an early morning awakening. Still, we waited until we'd tied up and had a cup of coffee to pick up the phone.

"We made it in. We can't wait to see you!"

Though it was almost summer, Mom had brought Christmas gifts for each of us. We gathered around their hotel bed and pulled packages from our stockings, eating the candy, and handing back most of the gifts.

"Can you keep these a few more weeks for us? The boat is overloaded already but we'll get them from you soon. We have to get that Crescent City picture from you anyway," I said.

Mom grinned, "I was hoping you'd forget about that. You said we could hang it on the wall so we did. We've gotten so used to having it above the fireplace. We're going to have to find something else to go there when it's gone."

I didn't have to look to know Bryan was smiling at me. All throughout the year, we'd been looking for gifts to bring our parents and just the week before, I had observed aloud that we hadn't found anything for my mom and dad. Bryan had a suggestion.

"Assuming we can make it to Crescent City, what about letting them choose one of the glass photos we bought in that gallery?"

"Oh, I think they'd really like that!"

So later that day, we returned to the art gallery. I wondered if the proprietor would be there again, if I'd even know it was her. I shouldn't have worried. Even if I hadn't recognized her—and I did—she certainly remembered us.

"You're back!" Sally greeted us at the door. "And you're safe! I've been thinking of you all year. Sometimes I check on your blog to see how you're doing. I was hoping you'd come back this way."

"Yes, we're so glad to be here, to see you again." I gestured to my parents and they stepped forward and shook hands. "My parents are visiting while we wait out some weather. We were hoping to buy them one of the glass photos as well."

"So nice to meet you. The Bryant Anderson collection is right over here. If you don't see what you like in the size you want, we might be able to special order a print for you." As we wandered over to the wall of paintings and photographs, Sally stepped back into her office, saying, "Why don't I just call him right now to make sure?"

A few minutes later I heard the jingle of the bell on the door and looked up to see a man approaching.

"I hear you're interested in getting some of my work." He stuck out his hand. "Hi, I'm Bryant."

The art on the walls took on new meaning as we listened to the stories behind its creation. Bryant was just as interested in our stories, too. Once again we treasured the power of the sea to sweep away divisions and connect us to new friends.

We spent the next few days hiking in the Redwoods, marveling at the massive trunks and dense canopy far overhead. I hadn't yet grown tired of the wide-open ocean views but I missed the feel of the forest shade, the smell of the dark, loamy soil underfoot.

We drove down to Arcata and surprised Jason and Bethany at their church's evening service. Though we weren't home yet we were starting to get a taste of homecoming as, one after another, friends welcomed us back and peppered us with questions. The last legs—up the coast of Oregon, up the Columbia River—seemed small compared to the enormity of the entire northbound journey. The transition back to land life loomed as the next real challenge.

We sent my parents back home with hugs and promises of "See you soon!" The forecast predicted the winds would die down in another day or two and we hoped to make it all the way to Newport on our next passage.

Our last night in Crescent City, my last walk down the dock, I stopped to watch a night heron fishing from a cleat. Glints of green shone from his glossy black head and his stillness rippled across the water to envelop me in a moment of pure attention. *Soon this won't be your everyday rhythm anymore.*

I was already missing the sea birds, the life that surrounded me here at the salty edge and yet I felt called back to my forest home and the family and friends nearby. There was no way to live in both simultaneously. The heron flew away. I resigned myself to being a little bit homesick ever after.

"What's the point of waiting for a good forecast? The wind's just going to be on the nose anyway." I kept my voice low in the red light of the darkened cabin but my frustration came through loud and clear. "I finally just covered the GPS screen with a towel. I couldn't handle watching the speed go up and down. Mostly down. We're not even averaging one knot. We could *walk* home faster than this."

I usually tempered my report to ease Bryan into his watch but tonight I couldn't hold back. "I'm hoping it's just the cape effect around Cape Blanco but we're quite a ways north of the point already. At this rate we're going to have to turn around and run back to Charleston to pick up enough fuel to make it to Newport. I knew we shouldn't have told people we might come in there tomorrow."

"We made sure they knew it was only a possibility. If we don't make it, at least anyone who drives down will have a nice day at the beach." As I stripped off my outer layers, Bryan donned his and slipped into his life jacket with a practiced shrug. "Get some sleep, sweetie. One way or another, we should know by morning."

Daybreak brought no more certainty. The currents and winds had lessened a bit in the night but we still couldn't be sure our fuel would last all the way to the harbor at Yaquina Bay. I texted my brother and Bryan's cousin-in-law, Jenny. "We don't know if we'll make it in today, sorry. If we have to turn around, the nearest gas is twenty-four hours south."

I could feel the yearning behind the understated responses.

"Stay safe and keep us updated."

"Do what you need to do. We'll see you when we can."

Every fifteen minutes I allowed myself to check the math and by 10 a.m. the trend was clear. I raised my voice so the whole crew could hear. "We're going to make it to Newport today!" I waited for the cheering to subside before adding, "We're not that far out, so you'd better find your least stinky clothes and brush your teeth."

I called ahead for a slip assignment and sent the good news to our family. Jenny texted back, "The kids think we're just here for a beach weekend. Message us when you get in and we'll walk down the dock to surprise them."

We pulled under the bridge and into our slip. We tied up quickly, texted our family, and hid back below. *LiLo*'s cabin buzzed with suppressed excitement as we peered out the windows for beloved faces.

I heard a familiar voice from the dock, " ... and this is the marina where the cousins will stop on their way home." I peeked through the curtains as footsteps approached. "They'll be in a slip just like this one." Jenny held her camera in one hand and pointed to *LiLo* with the other.

"Okay, now!" I whispered, and the crew erupted onto the deck, hollering like pirates.

"Arrrrrrrrrr, Matey!"

"Ahoy there!"

"Who dares to approach my ship!"

I followed behind, tears pricking at my eyes as I stepped onto the dock and into a hug. "I can't believe we made it. We're almost home."

We spent one glorious day reuniting with family, drinking in all the love and encouragement we needed to make one last big push home. And then we waited.

We wanted our last night in the ocean to be an easy one. After the miserable trip to Newport and the long, long beat back from Mexico we were just so weary. The visits from family had taken the edge off the homesickness and we decided to stay put until we could be absolutely sure of good weather. Finally, the radio robots predicted fair seas, even hinted at the possibility of following winds. Anything but wind on the nose and we'd gladly brave it.

I calculated the timing, checked the bar report and the Columbia River tides. No other bar crossing required such precision. If we missed the calm of the flood, we'd be stuck outside, pacing the entrance for hours, maybe even overnight.

The next morning, just before our scheduled departure, we eased away from the marina on the north side of the bay and wound down the channel a few hundred yards to the more commercial marina to the south. We pulled up to the fuel dock for one last fill, but signs on the shack warned us off. "Fuel dock closed for construction, Monday and Tuesday."

"Is today Tuesday?"

"I think so."

The wind and the tides had governed our lives for so long but days of the week were going to matter again soon. Bryan did some quick math on the minimum fuel needed for the jump to Astoria and I double-checked his numbers. "I don't think we need to fill the tank, just the jerry cans. I'll walk them up to the parking lot and try to hitch a ride to town with one of the fishermen."

I carried an empty jerry can up with him, recalculating hours along the way. "If we can get out by 1 p.m. I think we'll still make it across the bar tomorrow."

Back on the fuel dock, I waited in the sun. *LiLo* was already battened down for sea and any cleaning I should be doing could just wait until home.

Home. Days away now, not weeks or months. One leg, not thirteen. No more laundry stops or grocery runs. Less than one shower cycle away. And only one more night at sea.

A tall, broad man came down the ramp and headed my way. I glanced up, then looked again. His smile of recognition prompted my own.

"Mike, I can't believe we ran into you again."

"Me either. You're just about home, right? Looks like you've had some adventures."

Almost a year ago, we'd come in wet behind the ears and everywhere else, our only accomplishments keeping the mast up through that first awful night and not giving up when the head flooded the floor.

All these months later and here we were again, back on the same dock. What did he see in us this time? Did the storms show on my face? Could he read the hours of fear and boredom, smell the weary days? Or did he only sense the triumph of a journey almost done?

"Remember how you told me I should keep my systems simple and just get going?" Mike beamed. "Well, I'm on track to leave a little later this summer."

We spoke for a few minutes about his preparations and our journey and as we did Bryan returned, hefting fuel aboard with ease. I stepped below and dug through the books for our copy of *Spanish for Cruisers*. It was beat up, dog-eared, and a little bit damp but still totally serviceable. My throat tightened at the thought that we wouldn't be needing it again.

I rushed back above board just as Bryan lashed the last of the jugs on the foredeck.

"Mike, we have to catch the tide. But please, take this. It served us so well and we hope it serves you too."

The kindness of strangers had carried us through so many times. It felt like the smallest token of thanks to become, just for a moment, the generous strangers ourselves.

Chapter Thirty-five

What We Could Not Do Alone

Newport, Astoria, Rainier, and St. Helens, Oregon
June 2014: Waning Crescent, New Moon, Waxing Crescent

Coming back to where you started is not the same as never leaving.
—Terry Pratchett

"Only twenty-four hours to the bar," I said to the crew. "Let's make one last watch schedule and knock this out."

I reached into the navigation station for the weather notebook and a dull pencil, flipped to a blank page, and started to write.

"Hannah, what do you want? Evening? Sunset? There's hardly any moon, so it's going to be a dark night."

The kids sat in the cockpit with Bryan and I took advantage of the space to put a few things away in the galley. My sister-in-law had brought flowers to greet us in Newport and they were starting to wilt in the wall vase hanging on our bulkhead. I pulled them out and dumped the water down the drain. I buckled into my life jacket and stepped up on deck.

"I think we should say thank you to the ocean." I pressed a few blossoms into each hand. "What are you thankful for?"

We tore the petals free and tossed them into our wake.

"For holding us up."

"For carrying us through."

"For the fish and for not swallowing us."

My thanks felt as insubstantial as the roses, already sinking into the deep. "I can see why sailors worshipped the sea gods. An uncaring ocean, with no Neptune at the bottom? That's just too big to know what to do with." I turned to the wide, gray expanse. "Thank you for being our home for a while."

The mark we made in the water was already closing behind us as the sea rolled on, unchanged.

I flipped on the radio for the bar report. The voices glibly ran through current conditions and I listened for the nearest location.

"Cape Disappointment, west wind at five knots."

"What?" Bryan stuck his head below to protest. "I can see the cape just a few miles away but it's blowing twenty-five on the nose out here. What are they talking about with this 'west wind' nonsense?"

"I don't know. Maybe it will shift as we get closer to the channel?"

Our last day at sea was not the easy one we'd hoped for. A north wind had picked up around midnight and we'd slowed to a crawl against the current. Now in the daylight, the prospects looked dim.

"It better shift in a hurry or we're going to miss the tide. We're already five hours behind schedule and if we don't get across the bar before the change we'll have to stay out through another cycle."

"I can see why sailors sometimes make foolish decisions at the end of a long passage. We've only been out one night and already I can't stand the thought of getting stuck for one more. I'm so ready to be done with this coastline. But if it comes to it, we'll just hang out off the entrance until morning. No sense coming this far to take chances now."

I pulled up the tide charts for the north jetty, Astoria, and Tongue Point and tried to calculate how soon the tidal seas would build.

"We've crossed on a rough ride before. I just don't want to end the trip needing to be pulled off a sinking boat, you know?"

"There's no way to tell how much longer we'll be fighting this wind and current. We might break free any minute or it might become really obvious we can't cross tonight. Let's just wait and see."

Maybe the sea cares after all, I thought. *It sure doesn't seem to want to let us go.*

I hadn't ever unwrapped the farewell packet from *Gratitouille,* the one Jodi had said to open when everything was falling apart. Every time I considered it, on sad days and in scary conditions, I chose to save it in case harder days were yet to come. And in the worst moments there was no space for anything but safety.

But now, in what I hoped were our very last hours at sea, I decided it was time. I pulled the packet out of my locker, where I'd slept over it for months.

"Hey, kids. Want to see what *Gratitouille* gave us?"

"Yes, yes!"

"What is it?"

I peeled open the envelope and pulled out a card. As I opened it up, a packet of strawberry pop rocks fell into my hand.

"Pop rocks!" I said, holding them up. "What a great idea!"

Everyone held out their hands and I divided the packet among the crew. I licked the last of the sparkling candy from my palm and grinned as it fizzed and popped behind my teeth. It tasted like courage.

The last few hours seemed interminable. We crept along the coastline, racing the tide to the river's mouth. At three p.m. I flipped on the radio and listened for the latest forecast and bar report.

"They're still saying we should be free of this headwind so I'm not sure whether to trust the bar conditions either, but so far it still sounds safe in the channel."

"Well, we're coming up on the turn into the river now. I guess all we can do is trust it's okay in there."

Fourteen miles from buoy number one to the Astoria harbor breakwater. We hugged the edge of the channel to stay out of the way of the big ships but close enough to scoot into deeper water if the tide kicked up breakers over the shoals. I watched the rip tides curl around each point we passed and counted down the miles. Here on the last minutes of the last sea passage, in the swirl of saltwater and fresh, my heart swirled too with joy and grief.

Bryan hollered down to the crew, "We're less than an hour out now! Anyone who's dressed and on the dock five minutes after we tie up gets taken to the Wet Dog Cafe for dinner."

The crew dove into their bunks for the cleanest of their clothes and I reached into the head for a hairbrush. Ponytail time again.

I called into the marina for a slip assignment and then peeked at the chart on my phone. "Maybe just ten more minutes." I pulled on a sweater and my life jacket and joined Bryan in the cockpit. His gaze flickered my way and returned to the river ahead.

"We're almost there, Beth. We're in off the ocean for good."

Just a few feet shy of the Astoria bridge we turned to the south and cut back toward the break in the seawall. I blasted the air horn as we made the tight corner and felt the wind die behind the harbor walls.

"Head a little more east, to the C dock. We should be toward the sea end, port tie."

Bryan steered us in and the crew leaped onto the dock to take the lines. I had barely slipped into my shoes when Bryan killed the engine and jumped down.

"Lines look good. Everybody good to go?"

"I just have to toss the drop boards in. You have your wallet? Need a jacket?"

"I've been ready for hours," he said.

One more walk along the water's edge. One *last* walk along the water's edge. By the time we reached the restaurant we were almost too hungry for sentimentality. In a rare fit of extravagance, we ordered entrees, drinks, and desserts all around. "Get anything you want," Bryan said. "Friday we'll celebrate with our friends and family, but tonight is just for us."

When dessert was delivered and all the drinks refilled, Bryan raised his beer to each of us in turn.

"Well, we did it. You'll never again have to sail the ocean with me unless you choose to." Tears pricked at my eyes as I savored my family's faces.

Hannah spoke first. "I'd go to sea with you anytime, Dad."

Then Meira. "Me too, Dad. Anytime, anywhere."

I clinked my glass to his and looked deep into his tired eyes. "I wouldn't want to go to sea with anyone else. Thanks for bringing us home."

Two days on the Columbia blurred together into one. The autopilot seemed to have forgotten how to handle river currents so we split up the first day into easy shifts and hand steered the winding channel. We caught the upriver tides and rode them as long as we could all the way into Rainier for the night, only twenty miles away from our home port.

While in Newport, we'd made reservations for a celebration dinner in St Helens and hoped we wouldn't have to reschedule. It looked like we were going to make it just fine. Friends and family texted, asking about our timing. The calendars and schedules of land-based life were beginning to tether us again. I'd missed the easy connection with our wide community, but I savored the last morning of our floating routine, talking weather and passage planning over coffee and tea.

"We told them we'd be to the city dock about three but the current is going to be against us until noon or so. What do you say we leave about eleven?"

"Sounds good. We can always slow down if we are going to come in too early."

Meira stuck her head up over the steps. "Or we could hide behind Sand Island and surprise them by coming in from the other direction."

Every moment felt like liturgy, every move now a ritual as Bryan got us going this final time. The sound of the engine a church bell, calling me to attention.

I tried to hold my mind steady, like clutching a tiller through a rip tide's eddies. This dream of a day, once impossibly far off, had finally revolved into the present. It felt like a moment since we'd cast off; it felt like lifetimes. I couldn't wait to be done living in this awkward, cramped space and I wondered if anything in my life would ever compare.

There are no pictures of the rainy days. Wet doesn't show up well on film. A rough day at sea takes both hands to be safe, leaves no one free to work the camera. There are no pictures of the way tepid, filthy dishwater feels when there are only six dishes left but the water tanks are empty and heating up more means walking to the spigot, lugging bottles back, and boiling it in the kettle.

There are no pictures of the not-enough-room, one-at-a-time getting dressed, the days we are all trying to go somewhere at once, but as soon as anyone is ready, they sit down to wait and next thing we know, everyone is sitting down and no one goes anywhere.

There are definitely no pictures of the way damp, week-old laundry smells in the sail bag at the head of my bed.

There are no pictures of the constant shuffle of too many things, of not quite enough room for everything-in-its-place. No pictures of the digging, when what you want is always at the bottom, in the back, behind the cushions, at the foot of the bed. No picture of "What if the Coast Guard closes the bar?" or "What if we run out of fuel?" or "What if the engine dies *right here*?"

But there are also no pictures of the laughter when someone says something truly funny in the middle of a hard moment. No picture of the feeling of accomplishment from sailing into anchor without using the engine. No pictures of the way it tastes when we share our last bit of chocolate.

We can never photograph the joy of family game night, all of us tucked in tight around the table, or the relief of crawling into a warm, dry, still bed after a night at sea.

There is simply no way to capture the gift of spending these days side by side or the power of facing a challenge together and, together, accomplishing what we could not do alone.

I could feel my grasp slipping already on these, my dearest ones. For a year, we were a team; the Lees and *LiLo* sailing the sea. Who would we be now with no common struggle?

I could see, not very far into my future, a glimpse of the day we no longer even lived in the same house. Once lines and halyards no longer held us together, what would serve to bind us close?

"Let me take a little turn, Bryan. I need to be out in the fresh air."

"Sounds good. I could use another cup of coffee anyway. Better put on a jacket. It looks like we might actually get some rain."

For the first few months of the trip I hadn't really paid attention to the unusual dry spell. I knew California and Baja California had been experiencing an extended drought but from our home in soggy Oregon it had been a news item, not my daily reality.

About six months into the trip I noticed we hadn't once experienced rain at sea. Sure, we'd run to port to escape some storms and had been rained on in countless towns along the way. But during an actual voyage, we'd only been drenched with sea spray.

I came out on deck and looked past Bryan over the stern to the gathering western clouds.

"Yeah, I don't think there's any way we stay dry today."

Bryan shook his head and chuckled. "Our first rain out on the water here on the very last day."

"You go get some coffee. I'll see how long I can stay ahead of the clouds."

The current didn't ease up as soon as I'd expected and we were making poor time up the river. Hannah came out on deck to join me and soon had taken over steering in her favorite position—sitting back on the port side, both feet up on the tiller. We'd switched back to our beat-up paper charts for the river journey and I flipped pages in our spiral bound book as we slipped through the quadrants in the grid. We didn't really need to track our position, just stay out of the way of any other boats. Still, I couldn't resist pulling out the dividers and measuring miles.

"Ten miles left, and we're speeding up a bit. I think we might actually make it by three like we said."

Meira put on our family playlist—all the songs that had become the soundtrack to our lives this year. "Play that Funky Music," "Kokomo," and "Who Let the Dogs Out"—all favorites from the blaring poolside speakers in Mazatlán. "Ice, Ice, Baby"—which we sang every time we filled the icebox. Latin bands we heard in Mexico. Upbeat a capella cover songs. Everyone found places in the cockpit and we sang together the *LiLo* versions one last time.

Behind my smile, my voice cracked. "Want a turn to steer before we get in, Meira?" So much was too big to say out loud so we shared the tiller around like a chalice, each one taking a sip.

I went below for one last look around and tucked a few things out of sight in case we had visitors later. Bryan took the helm and called down.

"I can see the island up ahead. We're probably only ten minutes out."

The rain had begun in earnest now. Hannah tucked the charts under the dodger and pulled her hood on tight. I stood on the steps and squinted through the salty windows at the shoreline, the flag pole, the work dock, the marina. Up ahead, I could see huddled figures on the dock, under a black umbrella and bright, drooping balloons.

"Time to get the lines ready, crew."

We stepped to our typical places—Hannah with the bowline, Meira at the stern. I held the shrouds and the midline.

So many rough nights at sea I'd comforted myself with the image of arriving safely at the next port. I'd rehearsed the feel of a line held in my palm, danced my hand through the twists and turns of a cleat hitch at a dock—once around, loop across, loop, flip, snug. I'd wondered how it would feel on the very last day.

I was about to find out.

The dock came close. Through the rain, my dad's face came clear; I spotted my mom's eyes under her hood. Michele and Trina and my nephew, Josiah, stood near, dripping wet. And under the umbrella behind them all was Wil, a local sailing friend and part of our strong home community.

The engine shifted into neutral and then ground into reverse. I lifted both feet over the lifeline and stepped onto the dock, turned to whip the line into place and pull the boat to a stop. Bryan cut the engine and the crew stepped down too. Our greeters stood back until we coiled our lines and then reached in for sodden hugs.

Hannah and Meira grabbed their cousin and headed in out of the rain. As they stepped into the cabin, we heard Josiah say, "Welcome back to the heart of the Pacific Northwest!"

The whole year, behind my other worries stood the biggest one of all, the one I could hardly even glance at. *What if we don't all make it home?* I watched Bryan in his mother's arms and took a moment to finally look this fear straight in the eyes. No one fell in the sea; no one died. I laid a hand on *LiLo's* hull and sent a silent thanks for carrying us through.

Wil took us and our families back to his house on the hill to dry off and get warm before dinner. We told meaningless stories of the last few days; the big ones would have to wait.

Then the happy chaos of a long table filled with friends and family. Only those seated closest to us could hear what we were saying so I spent the meal turning around to greet a steady stream of well-wishers behind my chair.

Before long our people peeled off, heading away into their ordinary lives. I was trying to figure out how we were going to do the same.

The rain had blown over by the time we stepped outside and started walking to the boat.

Herb and An Der, who had seen us off that first day so many months ago, had joined the party at the restaurant and now Herb caught my attention before we got too far down the ramp. "Do you mind if An Der and I come down for a few minutes? I have something I want to share with you."

We dried off the cockpit cushions and pushed the tiller out of the way. And as the sun went down over my shoulder, Herb pulled out his ukulele and played a song he'd written to tell our story, "Out to the ocean, yes out to the sea. I'm gonna stop dreaming my life and start living my dreams."

I reached across the seat and took Bryan's calloused hand in mine.

Epilogue

You need only claim the events of your life to make yourself yours. When you truly possess all you have been and done, which may take some time, you are fierce with reality.

—*Florida Scott-Maxwell*

For weeks after we returned my skin peeled off in tiny flakes from my feet, my legs, my arms, my face. It hadn't seemed dry or sunburned at sea so I couldn't stop feeling like I was shedding, molting, growing a new layer.

The next few months were strange as we readjusted to life on land, resumed some of our old routines, and navigated new schedules. Sometimes we were mini-celebrities, sharing our story with friends in our community. Sometimes I woke panicked from dreams where the anchor was dragging. Running water remains a miracle.

We called on our journeying skills often.

After freshman orientation at her new school, Hannah emerged smiling. When I asked her if there was anything hard in her day, she shrugged, "Well, I was lost and confused a lot. But that's how it goes on the first day in a new place. I'll figure it out."

Her first time riding the school bus, I sent her with the middle schoolers by mistake. She came home unfazed.

"You'd think six months in Mexico would have taught me to always ask where the bus is going."

Meira joined the high school robotics team and Bryan jumped in as mentor and coach. She regularly pulled spare parts from her pockets to jury-rig solutions and fixed the robot on the go, running alongside the transport cart as it rolled down the halls to the playing field. During her senior year, she led the team to the world championships with skills she'd learned from our time on the ocean.

When competitions got intense, she stayed surprisingly calm. "At least here," she said, "if something goes wrong, no one is going to fall overboard."

Though our days looked different and our adventures a little more tame, our family bond held. After trusting each other with our lives at sea, we knew we could trust each other on the shifting ground here as well. We could always navigate to safe harbor together.

When differences of opinion arose we talked things over and altered course if conditions changed. Hard-won habits of kindness served us well on stressful days. And no one ever complained about the bathroom being too small.

Occasionally, I pulled out the sign the kids had made in the Delta and set it where I could see it, the message just as powerful despite the crumpled paper. "NO! You are NOT allowed to second guess yourself." I needed that reminder more often than I liked.

I felt like the trip had torn something open in me. A few months after our return, my depression returned too, bringing trauma to the surface I hadn't faced since childhood. I worked to recalibrate my nervous system which, after months of being on high alert at sea, didn't seem to have a low setting anymore.

Our family's close connection and common goals expanded as the kids stretched beyond us to make their own way into the world. Each of us worked to find our footing in this unpredictable season. Despite a shared language and culture, our feelings of displacement and uncertainty lingered.

I compensated by over-explaining, telling anyone who would listen of our recent return from the sea. Hannah and Meira hardly spoke of it at all. They quickly learned that any mention of their year aboard brought every conversation to a halt and all eyes to them, an unwelcome effect in the halls of high school. Bryan went back to work and his tanned skin faded under the fluorescent lights.

Our memories too, started to fade, so before they were lost altogether, I began to write about them. Some days I couldn't believe I was the same person who had gone to sea, treasured every glorious day, survived every fearful moment. But as I move further from that time on the water, the soul of the year grows more brilliant in me.

Now from the torn places, music and poetry pour out. Stormy days are no longer just metaphors for hard times. The tides, the seasons, the moon, and I—we all ebb and flow. And I don't need to imagine the power of love as wide as an ocean. I know.

Once, our adventure was a tale to tell, places we had been, things we had done. In the telling, I learned: our lives are never just the story of what we have accomplished but of how we have unfurled.

I no longer wonder if I can make it home.

I am becoming home.

* * *

Acknowledgments

I sit writing these words in Wil and Nancy's lovely home, so thankful for all the places that sheltered me while writing especially the Kulla cabin, the Edgefield porches, and the nook by the window in the house near the forest.

I'm grateful, too, for the boats that have carried me. For *Nissa*, so patient with us as beginner sailors. For *LiLo*, who took us so many amazing places and now carries a new family into adventures of their own. For *Splitpea*, who ran away with the wind. I hope you found a happy ending.

For *Rover*, who came into being because we needed her and has carried us cheerfully ever since. And now *Sanctuary*, whose story intersected with ours long before we knew. Let's make some new stories together, okay?

Many thanks to all who encouraged me to make this book, especially Eric Lee and Di Murphy and, if you're reading this, you. I hope it was worth the wait.

To Peggy, Polly, Paula, Katie, and Erika and everyone who read pieces of this story along the way. To Jenn, for all the moments you were my second mind and my backup courage. To Hannah for listening anytime I needed to read something aloud. To Tamarah, who dissolves my self-doubt with laughter. To Laureen, whose faith in this story buoys mine daily.

Thanks to Kim for the gifts of words and friendship.

Thanks to Brett, who heard my words and my heart and made my illustration dreams come true.

Neither this book nor I would be complete without Kate.

And thanks to Eric and all the folks at Fernwood Press, especially Mareesa, Emma, Elyse, Kati and Jo, who reminded me to let go of making it perfect and then helped me make it so much better.

Deep thanks to our home sailing community, especially Herb and An Der and Wil and Nancy.

And to all the friends we met on our voyage: everyone named in this book, and all who weren't, like Jen and Steve and Tamiko and so many others. You're in the extended cut version, friends, and in the stories we tell around the campfire while everyone laughs. You're in our hearts. Fair winds and following seas.

This book is a love song to my family. For Hannah and Meira, who pumped the faucet when I needed to wash my hands, who stayed polite when we were in each other's way, who stopped at every bookstore and library and bakery and braved every storm. You pulled stores out of the howling wilderness, walked through every new place with curiosity, and filled all our passages with wordplay and kindness and dancing and laughter. Thank you for all of it. (But I'm calling dibs on the head.)

And for Bryan, thank you for choosing me to navigate through life with you and for following up "I've been thinking…" with the very best ideas. For every kiss at the end of every passage and every brilliant, on-the-fly repair job. For telling me it was going to be okay and then always making it okay. I wouldn't want to go to sea with anyone else.

And finally, deep thanks to my own bravest self, who met me again and again at the surface of the water and keeps showing up for each new day.

Glossary

Here are some brief definitions for many of the sailing words used in this book, mostly as they pertain to *LiLo*.

Beam: the widest part of the boat from port to starboard, also refers generally to the side of the boat.

Bitter end: the end of the anchor line without the anchor. It should stay tied to the boat. If it comes untied from the boat and slithers overboard with the anchor, you will understand why it's called *bitter*.

Block: a set of pulleys.

Broach: a sudden, uncontrolled shift in a boat's direction caused by wind or waves, possibly ending in capsize. Similar to a car skidding on ice, you can't control it, only work to prevent it.

Chainplates: metal bars used to attach shrouds to the hull.

Chop: many small waves, usually caused by wind. These can rise on the surface of larger swells and make the day at sea very uncomfortable.

Clew: the lower aft corner of a sail.

Coaming: a vertical surface on the deck of a ship designed to deflect water, typically around a hatch or opening. On *LiLo*, the raised rim around the edge of the cockpit.

Companionway: the doorway from cockpit to cabin.
Dinghy: a small boat used to get to and from a larger vessel when not at a dock.
Dodger: a spray hood over the companionway, usually made of canvas or fiberglass with vinyl or acrylic windows to shelter the sailor from sun, wind, and waves. As in dodgeball, the point is to avoid being hit.
Drifter: a nylon headsail good for light winds.
Drop boards: wooden slats that drop into the tracks at the edges of the companionway to close off the cabin from the cockpit.
Ebb: an outgoing tide.
Fetch: distance across the open water. Wind builds higher swells over longer fetch.
Flood: an incoming tide.
Following seas: waves traveling the same direction as the vessel. If these are too high, there is a risk they can break into the cockpit and swamp the boat. But "Fair winds and following seas" is also used as a toast or to wish sailors well since a reasonably sized following sea can be a very comfortable course.
Gimbal: a swinging bracket that allows what it supports (e.g. a lamp, stove, or compass) to stay level while the boat revolves beneath it.
Ground tackle: all equipment used in anchoring such as rode, shackles, and anchor.
Gunwale: the upper edge of the hull, often with a reinforced strip to strengthen the boat. Pronounced "gunnull." Don't ask me why.
Halyard: the line used to haul up the sails. It runs from a shackle at the head of the sail up to the top of the mast, over a rolling sheave and down again.
Head: a marine toilet—see chapter two.
Heave to: (also "be hove to") to set the sails and rudder in a way that stalls the boat's progress through the water.
Jacklines: lines running from bow to stern (one on each side deck). This allows a harnessed crew member to attach a tether and walk freely and securely along the deck especially in heavy weather or

reduced visibility, when the risk of falling overboard is greatest. Picture a cable dog run on the deck.

Jib: a medium-sized headsail.

Knot: a measurement of speed. One knot equals one nautical mile per hour (or 1.1508 statute miles per hour) and is a little faster than one statute mile per hour. Not to be confused with knots, which show up (intentionally or otherwise) in every bit of line or hair on board.

Lifeline: A cable run through posts above the gunwale from bow to stern. On *LiLo* we installed safety netting from this cable to help prevent gear or crew from falling overboard.

Line: If you bring a rope aboard a boat, you stop calling it a rope and start calling it a line. Some lines also get fancy names like "rode" or "sheet."

Lee: downwind, also the protected side of an island or slope. If plural (i.e. The Lees): the best crew ever.

Midline: a dock line attached about halfway between bow and stern. This can be used to help pivot the boat while docking or embarking.

Nautical mile: A measurement of distance equal to one minute of latitude or 1.1508 land miles, called "statue miles."

Painter: a line, usually made from floating rope, used to tie the dinghy to the boat or a dock or piling.

Panga: an open, outboard-powered, planing-hull fishing boat.

Reef: On a sailboat, this means reducing the amount of sail area to keep the boat under control in higher-wind conditions. You want to reef as soon as you begin to wonder if you should.

In the water, a reef is a strip of rock or coral you don't want to run into. Example sentence: "Reef your sails and stay clear of the reef."

Rode: The rope and/or chain used as an anchor line.

Rub rail: protective edging along the gunwale where a boat might rub when it comes alongside a dock or another boat.

Sally ship: A maneuver used to float a grounded boat. The crew runs in sync back and forth across the deck amidships to try to shift the keel enough to float free. It helps to holler things like, "Yo Ho Ho!" and "Avast, ye mateys!" while running.

Seacock: a valve fitting in a through-hull.

Sheave: a pulley wheel. On *LiLo*, they guide the halyards at the top of the mast.

Sheets: lines used to control the sails. These attach at the clew and usually run through a block to a winch for trimming the sails.

Shroud: cables supporting the mast from side to side. These often run over the spreaders and attach to the chainplates at the deck.

Skeg: The sternward projection of the keel or (in *Rover*'s case) a stabilizing fin toward the rear of a small vessel or surfboard.

Sloop: a sailboat with one mast, capable of flying a mainsail and any of a variety of headsails.

Spreaders: structures projecting perpendicular to the mast to provide support for the shrouds and keep them attached at the proper angle for mast stability.

Stays: cables supporting the mast from front to back. *LiLo* has a backstay and a forestay. Headsails are also connected to the forestay at the front of the sail (called the luff).

Swell: rolling waves, usually in a relatively even pattern, caused by wind in another part of the ocean. Local winds can add choppy waves to the top of swells and make for an uncomfortable ride.

Tender: a small boat used to tend a larger vessel. Another word for *dinghy*. Can also describe a boat more prone to tipping on a spectrum from tender to stable.

Through hull: fitting in the hull for water input or drainage. These are often sealed with a valve called a *sea cock* to allow for closure.

Thwart: strut or plank that extends across an open boat from one side to the other, often used as a seat.

Toe rail: supportive trim at the top of the gunwale, often used for jib sheet tracks or to catch your toes when stepping on and off the deck.

Traveler: on *LiLo*, a track on the stern along which runs the main sheet block.
Whisker pole: spar used to hold a nylon headsail open in light wind.
Windward: upwind, toward the wind, or the unprotected side of a mountain or island.

Printed in the USA
CPSIA information can be obtained
at www.ICGtesting.com
LVHW031540210524
PP18203600001B/2